From Shakespeare to Autofiction

COMPARATIVE LITERATURE AND CULTURE

Series Editors
TIMOTHY MATHEWS AND FLORIAN MUSSGNUG

Comparative Literature and Culture explores new creative and critical perspectives on literature, art and culture. Contributions offer a comparative, cross-cultural and interdisciplinary focus, showcasing exploratory research in literary and cultural theory and history, material and visual cultures, and reception studies. The series is also interested in language-based research, particularly the changing role of national and minority languages and cultures, and includes within its publications the annual proceedings of the 'Hermes Consortium for Literary and Cultural Studies'.

Timothy Mathews is Emeritus Professor of French and Comparative Criticism, UCL.

Florian Mussgnug is Reader in Italian and Comparative Literature, UCL.

From Shakespeare to Autofiction

Approaches to authorship after Barthes and Foucault

Edited by

Martin Procházka

Murray,

with many thanks and admiration

Martin

Prague, 20 May 2024

UCLPRESS

First published in 2024 by
UCL Press
University College London
Gower Street
London WC1E 6BT

Available to download free: www.uclpress.co.uk

Collection © Editor, 2024
Text © Contributors, 2024
Images © Contributors and copyright holders named in captions, 2024

The authors have asserted their rights under the Copyright, Designs and Patents Act 1988 to be identified as the authors of this work.

A CIP catalogue record for this book is available from The British Library.

Any third-party material in this book is not covered by the book's Creative Commons licence. Details of the copyright ownership and permitted use of third-party material is given in the image (or extract) credit lines. If you would like to reuse any third-party material not covered by the book's Creative Commons licence, you will need to obtain permission directly from the copyright owner.

This book is published under a Creative Commons Attribution-Non-Commercial 4.0 International licence (CC BY-NC 4.0), https://creativecommons.org/licenses/by-nc/4.0/. This licence allows you to share and adapt the work for non-commercial use providing attribution is made to the author and publisher (but not in any way that suggests that they endorse you or your use of the work) and any changes are indicated. Attribution should include the following information:

Procházka, M. (ed.) 2024. *From Shakespeare to Autofiction: Approaches to authorship after Barthes and Foucault*. London: UCL Press. https://doi.org/10.14324/111. 9781800086548

Further details about Creative Commons licences are available at https://creativecommons.org/licenses/

ISBN: 978-1-80008-656-2 (Hbk)
ISBN: 978-1-80008-655-5 (Pbk)
ISBN: 978-1-80008-654-8 (PDF)
ISBN: 978-1-80008-657-9 (epub)
DOI: https://doi.org/10.14324/111. 9781800086548

Contents

List of figures vii
Notes on contributors ix
Acknowledgements xiii

    Introduction: authors that matter 1
    Martin Procházka

1 The rise of Shakespearean cultural capital: early 21
configurations and appropriations of Shakespeare
Jean-Christophe Mayer

2 Religious conflict and the return of the author in early 41
modern dramatic paratexts
Jeanne Mathieu

3 'Many more remains of ancient genius': approaches to 55
authorship in the Ossian Controversy
Petra Johana Poncarová

4 Translation of indigenous oral narratives and the concept of 73
collaborative authorship
Johanna Fernández Castro

5 In the name of the father: Darwin, scientific authority 91
and literary assimilation
Niall Sreenan

6 Dead Shelley 109
Mathelinda Nabugodi

7 The author as agent in the field: (post-)Bourdieusian 123
approaches to the author
Josef Šebek

8 Autofiction as (self-)criticism: suggestions from recent   141
   Brazilian literature
   Sonia Miceli

9 Latin American autofiction authors as *trans*formers: 159
   beyond textuality in Aira and Bellatin
   Gerardo Cruz-Grunerth

10 The scene of invention: author at work in J. M. Coetzee's   173
   The Master of Petersburg
   Laura Cernat

Index   201

List of figures

1.1	Title page of Shakespeare's First Folio displaying Martin Droeshout's engraving of the author, Fo. 1 no. 71.	23
1.2	A collage portrait of Shakespeare in the box containing the Broadhead First Folio.	26
1.3	First flyleaf recto of a Second Folio, which once belonged to John Sherwen. In its centre is an inserted portrait of Shakespeare. The portrait is framed by five pasted slips of paper containing manuscript extracts in praise of Shakespeare, Fo. 2 no. 53.	28
1.4	Preliminary epistles in honour of Shakespeare copied out by readers, Fo. 1 no. 28.	32
1.5	John Lister signatures in Fo. 1 no. 70.	33
1.6	Leaf facing the title page of *The Winter's Tale* in Fo. 3 no. 8.	34
1.7	Third flyleaf of Fo. 1 no. 45.	35
1.8	Close-up of third flyleaf of Fo. 1 no. 45.	36
1.9	Close-up of a page of *Macbeth* (Shakespeare 1664, sig. Ooo4v) in Fo. 3 no. 8.	37

Notes on contributors

Johanna Fernández Castro works on Translation Studies and Latin American Cultural Studies. She received her PhD from the Justus Liebig University of Giessen, with a fellowship from the International Graduate Centre for the Study of Culture (GCSC). She is co-editor of *W(h)ither Identity. Positioning the self and transforming the social* (2015). Her book *Kulturübersetzung als interaktive Praxis. Die frühe deutsche Ethnologie im Amazonasgebiet (1884–1914)* (2020) addresses the concept of cultural translation and its role in the production of knowledge about indigenous cultures. She is currently a Director of the Welcome Center for International Researchers at the University of Mannheim.

Laura Cernat is an FWO (Flemish Research Foundation) postdoctoral researcher at KU Leuven, Belgium, working on the project 'Biofictions of Border-Crossing: A world literature for outsiders'. She has contributed to the edited volumes *Virginia Woolf and Heritage* (Clemson UP/Liverpool UP, 2017), *Theory in the 'Post' Era: A vocabulary for the 21st-century conceptual commons* (Bloomsbury, 2021) and *Imagining Gender in Biographical Fiction* (Palgrave Macmillan, 2022). She has also guest-edited a special issue of *American Book Review* on autofiction and autotheory. Her articles have been published in the journals *Biography: An interdisciplinary quarterly* and *Partial Answers*. Together with Lucia Boldrini, Alexandre Gefen and Michael Lackey, she is currently editing the *Routledge Companion to Biofiction*. In September 2021 she organised the hybrid bilingual conference 'Biofiction as World Literature', https://www.arts.kuleuven.be/biofiction-as-world-literature.

Gerardo Cruz-Grunerth is Visiting Assistant Professor of Hispanic Studies at Boston College and is the author of *Mundos casi imposibles. Narrativa postmoderna mexicana* (2018), *Eugenia 2218. La visión posthumana de Eudardo Urzaiz* (2022) and a number of chapters of books and journal articles. As a fiction writer, he has published *El fuego camina* *conmigo* (2014) and *Tela de araña* (2010), among others. He taught Hispanic literature and culture at Boston University and the University of Guadalajara, Mexico.

Jeanne Mathieu is Senior Lecturer in Early Modern Studies at the University of Toulouse – Jean Jaurès (France). Her research interests focus on the representation of the religious conflict on the early modern stage through scenes of dispute. She has worked extensively on plays by Thomas Dekker, Christopher Marlowe and Thomas Middleton. Her latest article, 'Interconfessional negotiations in Thomas Dekker and Philip Massinger's *The Virgin Martyr* (1622): Truce as disputation', was published in 2022 in *Early Modern Literary Studies*. She has also edited an issue of *Caliban: French Journal of English Studies* on 'Religious dispute and toleration in early modern literature and history', published in December 2023.

Jean-Christophe Mayer is a Research Professor employed by the French National Centre for Scientific Research (CNRS). He is also a member and the deputy head of the Institute for Research on the Renaissance, the Neoclassical Age and the Enlightenment (IRCL) at Université Paul Valéry, Montpellier. He is the author of *Shakespeare's Hybrid Faith* (2006), *Shakespeare et la postmodernité: Essais sur l'auteur, le religieux, l'histoire et le lecteur* (2012) and *Shakespeare's Early Readers: A cultural history from 1590 to 1800* (2018). He is co-general editor of the journal *Cahiers Élisabéthain: A journal of English Renaissance studies*. Professor Mayer is currently working on a new project provisionally entitled 'Handwriting and the English imagination from 1500 to 1700'. https://cnrs.academia.edu/JeanChristopheMayer.

Sonia Miceli holds a PhD in Comparative Studies (University of Lisbon, 2017) and is an independent researcher based in Lisbon, Portugal. Her research fields include contemporary Brazilian literature, landscape studies and relationships between anthropology and literature. She has recently joined the cluster 'Lit&Tour – Literature and Tourism' (CIAC – University of Algarve) as an external collaborator. Some of her latest publications are 'Os triângulos de Ruy Duarte de Carvalho' (in *Diálogos com Ruy Duarte de Carvalho*, Buala and Centro de Estudos Comparatistas, 2019) and 'Autoria, identidade e alteridade: Entrevista com Bernardo Carvalho' (Revista Navegações, 2019).

Mathelinda Nabugodi was a Leverhulme Trust Early Career Fellow in the Faculty of English at the University of Cambridge. She was the first to be awarded a PhD in Creative Critical Writing from UCL for a thesis entitled 'Life after Life: Reading Percy Bysshe Shelley and Walter Benjamin'. She has edited Shelley's translations from Aeschylus, Calderón and Goethe for *The Poems of Shelley: 1821–1822*, as well as the essay collection *Thinking Through Relation: Encounters in creative critical writing*. She has secured postdoctoral fellowships at Newcastle University, the Bodleian Library and the Huntington Library (https://profiles.ucl.ac.uk/35053-mathelinda-nabugodi). She is now Lecturer in Comparative Literature at University College London.

Petra Johana Poncarová is a Marie Curie Fellow at the University of Glasgow, working on a project which explores Gaelic magazines founded by Ruaraidh Erskine of Mar and their impact on Gaelic literature and Scottish nationalism (erskine.glasgow.ac.uk). She serves as secretary of the International Association for the Study of Scottish Literatures (iassl.org) and as one of the co-directors of Ionad Eòghainn MhicLachlainn | National Centre for Gaelic Translation (gaelictranslation.org). She was the manager of the 3rd World Congress of Scottish Literatures (Prague, 2022). Her monograph *Derick Thomson and the Gaelic Revival* was published by Edinburgh University Press in January 2024. https://www.gla.ac.uk/schools/critical/staff/petrajohanaponcarova.

Martin Procházka is Professor of English, American and Comparative Literature at Charles University, Prague. He is the author of *Romanticism and Personality* (1996, in Czech), *Transversals* (2008) and *Ruins in the New World* (2012) and is also a co-author of *Romanticism and Romanticisms* (2005, in Czech). He is a Fellow of the English Association (EA), an Advisory Board member of the International Association of Byron Societies (IABS), a member of the Steering Committee of the International Association for the Study of Scottish Literatures (IASSL), the founding editor of the international academic journal *Litteraria Pragensia*, the visiting professor at the University Porto and the Honorary Professor at the University of Kent. https://ualk.ff.cuni.cz/staff/academic-staff/martin-prochazka/.

Josef Šebek is Assistant Professor of Czech and Comparative Literature at Charles University, Prague. His publications include the books *Texts in Circulation: Anthology of cultural materialist approaches to literature* (in Czech, 2014, with Richard Müller), *Literature and the Social: Bourdieu, Williams and their successors* (in Czech, 2019) and *The Emerging*

Contours of the Medium: Literature and mediality (2024, co-author), as well as chapters in collaborative volumes and translations. He is a managing editor of the journal *Slovo a smysl / Word and Sense* (Scopus). https://uclk.ff.cuni.cz/ustav/lide/zamestnanci/josef-sebek/.

Niall Sreenan holds a PhD in Comparative Literature from University College London (2016) which forms the basis of his first research monograph, *Rethinking the Human in the Darwinian Novel: Zola, Hardy, and Utopian fiction,* forthcoming 2024. He is the author of several peer-reviewed publications, on the work of Michel Houellebecq, Utopianism in Irish literature and the representation of islands in literature and philosophy, and is also a member of both the British Comparative Literature Association and the British Society for Literature and Science. He was a Visiting Research Fellow at King's College London's Centre for Modern Literature and Culture and a Research Associate at King's College London's Policy Institute. He is now a Lecturer in Comparative Literature in the School of Modern Languages at the University of St Andrews. https://www.st-andrews.ac.uk/modernlanguages/people/french/ns259.

Acknowledgements

The research for this book was supported by the European Regional Development Fund Project 'Creativity and Adaptability as Conditions of the Success of Europe in an Interrelated World' (No. CZ.02.1.01/0.0/0.0/ 16_019/ 0000734).

Chapter 4, 'Translation of indigenous oral narratives and the concept of collaborative authorship', was written in the framework of Johanna Fernández Castro's doctoral thesis, published as: *Kulturübersetzung als interaktive Praxis. Die frühe deutsche Ethnologie im Amazonasgebiet (1884– 1914)* (Bielefeld: transcript, 2020). Johanna Fernández Castro would like to thank Professor Martin Procházka for his insightful comments and remarks and Madeleine LaRue for her excellent support in the editing of this chapter.

The research for Chapter 9 formed a part of the activities of the research project 'PERFORMA2. Metamorfosis del espectador en el teatro español actual (PID2019-104402RB-I00) (2020-2023)', financially supported by the Spanish Ministry of Science and Innovation in the framework of the State Plan of Scientific and Technical Research and Innovation 2017–20 [*Este trabajo forma parte de las actividades del proyecto de investigación 'PERFORMA2. Metamorfosis del espectador en el teatro español actual (PID2019-104402RB-I00)' (2020–2023), financiado con una ayuda del Ministerio de Ciencia e Innovación en el marco del Plan Estatal de Investigación Científica y Técnica y de Innovación 2017–2020*].

The research for Chapter 10, 'The scene of invention: author at work in J. M. Coetzee's *The Master of Petersburg*', was generously supported by the FWO (Research Foundation – Flanders, project 1240823N). The author expresses her thanks to Martin Procházka, Ortwin de Graef, Michael Lackey, Ioannis Tsitsovits, Ella Mingazova and Kahn Faassen for their careful readings and suggestions.

Introduction: authors that matter
Martin Procházka

Beckett as a springboard

'What matter who's speaking, someone said what matter who's speaking,' wrote Samuel Beckett in the English version of his *Texts for Nothing* (2006, 302). In 1969 Michel Foucault borrowed the original French version of this passage, 'Qu'importe qui parle, quelq'un a dit qu'importe qui parle' (Beckett 1958, 143), as a point of departure for his lecture 'Qu'est-ce qu'un auteur?' (Foucault 1969, 73–104). Disregarding the often desperate, self-destructive irony of Beckett's *Texts*, Foucault interpreted the ambiguous passage as a statement of 'indifference' to the author's 'deepest self [...] authenticity or originality' (Foucault 1998, 205, 222). He called this 'indifference' to 'one of the fundamental ethical principles of contemporary writing' and elevated it to an 'immanent rule [...] dominating writing as a practice' (1998, 205–6).

Contrary to Foucault's high-flown statements, the ethical *relevance* of his use of the Beckett quotation is difficult to deny. Foucault used Beckett as a springboard to make sweeping generalisations about the 'unfolded exteriority' of writing and its 'interplay of signs' functioning 'like a game [*jeu*] that inevitably goes beyond its rules and transgresses its limits' (1998, 206). He chose to ignore the crisis of authorship and individual identity in *Texts for Nothing* in order to establish Beckett as the 'founding authority' (Hird 2010, 291) for the critique of the main tenets of Roland Barthes' essay 'The Death of the Author' (1967; Barthes 1977).

Barthes' substitution of the author by 'the modern scriptor' who is 'born simultaneously with the text' in order to prove that 'every text is eternally written *here* and *now*' (1977, 145) might have provoked Foucault to rephrase the statement of the author's death in terms of his discourse theory formulated in *The Archaeology of Knowledge* (1969;

Foucault 1972). His suggestion was 'to locate the space left empty by the author's disappearance' (Foucault 1998, 209) and study it as a historically changeable 'discursive field' (Foucault 1972, 28), showing the ways in which 'the author's name manifests the appearance of a certain discursive set and indicates the status of this discourse within a society and a culture' (1998, 211).

To accomplish this rather demanding theoretical goal, Foucault had to reduce the author, ceremoniously buried by Barthes, to the 'author function' characterising 'the mode of existence, circulation, and functioning of certain discourses in society' (Foucault 1998, 211). As Foucault explained, the 'author function […] does not refer purely and simply to a real individual, since it can give rise simultaneously to several selves, several subject-positions that can be occupied by different classes of individuals' (1998, 216).

However, the transformation of the author into a 'function' was not the most important objective of Foucault's argument. Its principal purpose was the invention of 'another, more uncommon, kind of author', exemplified by Marx and Freud, who were called the 'founders of discursivity' (1998, 217). Their exceptionality was given by their paradoxical 'transdiscursive' position: creating 'a possibility for something other than their discourse, yet something belonging to what they founded' (1998, 217–18).

Surprisingly, these super-authors do not include any writers of literature. In Foucault's words, they 'make possible something altogether different from what a novelist makes possible' (1998, 217). In contrast to 'a certain number of analogies' produced by literary authors, the 'founders of discursivity' are entrusted with making 'a certain number of differences' (Foucault 1998, 218) to 'open' the discourse 'up to a certain number of possible applications' or re-examinations modifying specific discursive fields: 'reexamining Freud's texts modifies psychoanalysis itself' (1998, 219).

It is hard to accept the implications of this statement, even at the time it was made. Did Foucault indicate, for instance, that a recent radical 'reexamining' of Marcel Proust's *In Search of Lost Time* by his friend Gilles Deleuze (1964)[1] had not produced significant changes in literary studies, as well as in semiotics and philosophy? Moreover, Foucault used to claim that 'a single work of literature can give rise, simultaneously, to several distinct types of discourse' (1972, 221). It is rather difficult to see how this statement differs from his previous postulation of 'transdiscursivity'.

Some light on these quandaries may be shed by the *The Discourse on Language* (1971), where Foucault revisits the concept of the 'author function':

> Of course, it would be ridiculous to deny the existence of individuals who write, and invent. But I think that, for some time, at least, the individual who sits down to write a text, at the edge of which lurks a possible œuvre, resumes the functions of the author. What he writes and does not write, what he sketches out, even preliminary sketches for the work, and what he drops as simple mundane remarks, all this interplay of differences is prescribed by the author-function.
> (Foucault 1972, 222)

Later on in Foucault's text, the prescriptive 'author function' is substituted by the restrictive 'author principle' that 'limits this same chance element through the action of an *identity* whose form is that of *individuality* and the *I*' (Foucault 1972, 222). Foucault's problem with the existence of the author thus seems to consist in the incompatibility of the 'author function' as a phenomenon related to 'discursive formation' (1972, 38, 107) and the author as a human being with an 'individuality' and 'identity'.

A partial explanation of this disjunction can be found in Foucault's 'enunciative analysis' dealing with 'the statement' as the basic component of discourse (1972, 105–17). According to Foucault, 'language, in its appearance and mode of being, is the statement' (1972, 113). It 'belongs to a description which is neither anthropological nor transcendental [...] nor a way that has been reopened in the direction of inaccessible origins, nor a creation by a human being of its own meanings' (1972, 113). It appears that Foucault's exclusion of literature, its authors and authorship is an effect of his strenuous effort to postulate an impersonal, immanent and non-anthropological 'order of discourse' (1972, 113, 144, 209).

One may wonder why this theoretically demanding exclusion of the author from Foucault's account of 'discursivity' and its 'founders' did not discourage scholars in literary and cultural studies from using Foucault's approach as an important methodological source. Yet the opposite is true.

'What matters...?' Materiality of bodies and multiplicities of authors

This volume, whose origins can be traced to a conference of the HERMES Consortium for Literary and Cultural Studies on 'Authors,

Authorship and Authority', is in fact no exception, since more than half of its chapters refer to Foucault's discussion of the author and some even allude to Barthes' essay. Yet none of the contributors shares Foucault's 'indifference' to authors' individuality, authenticity or originality. All of them agree that authors *matter*, whether as cultural, political or social agents, 'creative employers', collaborators and translators, products of biographical or autobiographical fictions, or even as dead bodies.

This is reflected in the present Introduction's title, whose first part echoes Judith Butler's famous phrase *Bodies That Matter* (Butler 1993). While Butler focuses on the 'materiality' of bodies resulting from the repetition ('citationality') of regulative heterosexual norms, whose repressive power of 'abjection' must be countered by 'a radical resignification of the symbolic domain' (1993, 12–15, 21–2), the approaches to authors in this volume reveal a heterogeneity of their 'empirical', historical, paratextual, performative, fictional, charismatic or fetishistic forms of existence. The focus on the heterogeneity of authors and forms of authorship is the key feature of this book. Nonetheless, heterogeneity, as shown below, does not mean simply a chaotic form of existence. The present approach features a methodology that helps us to grasp the structure of dynamic open systems.

Whereas Butler's bodies matter due to the necessity of overcoming repressive strategies of their *unification*, the authors discussed in this volume matter because of their *multiplicities* (Deleuze and Guattari 1987, 3–10) – their often plural forms of existence manifested on diverse levels. These levels cannot be hierarchised, but they can be seen as an open dynamic system similar to the 'rhizome' which is 'composed not of units, but of dimensions, or rather directions in motion' (Deleuze and Guattari 1987, 21). The rhizome can be imagined as 'plateaus' or regions of intensities and 'multiplicities connected to other multiplicities' (Deleuze and Guattari 1987, 22).

Similar to some modern literary works, which multiply 'narratives like so many plateaus with variable numbers of dimensions' (Deleuze and Guattari 1987, 23),[2] this book describes diverse forms of modern authorship as an assemblage of theoretical, historical and fictional narratives. These in turn recast a number of key concepts of cultural and literary studies, such as *discourse, translation, paratext, literary field, the performative* and *the symbolic*, into specific historical, sociological, linguistic, semiotic or psychoanalytical contexts, and thus enhance their more nuanced understanding.

The rhizome of modern authorship: 'assemblages of enunciation'

Undertaking 'enunciative analysis', Foucault identified the statement with 'language' (1972, 113). No wonder he needed to replace the author with the 'author function' (1998, 209) as a potent means of discursive unification. In contrast to Foucault's approach, Deleuze and Guattari have shown that the book can be seen as a 'collective assemblage of enunciation', which is 'plugged into an immense outside, that is multiplicity in any case' (1987, 23–4). The 'agents' of this 'collective assemblage' are not 'peoples or societies, but multiplicities' (Deleuze and Guattari 1987, 37). In discussing authors as multiplicities, this book reveals their links to a number of outside multiplicities that form their cultural and social contexts.

The narratives of authorship included in this book are 'plugged into' a number of multiplicities, such as the 'autobiographical, fictional and historical components' of J. M. Coetzee's *The Master of Petersburg*, blending the historical details of Dostoevsky's times, writings and biography with the fictional accounts of his life and literary creation, as well as the author's autobiographical reminiscences. The focus on multiplicities may also allow us to see the 'collaborative authorship' as 'a product of cultural networks and their acts of authorization'. Or to discover that 'the image of the author', in this case the dead Romantic poet Percy Bysshe Shelley, was assembled from a multiplicity of textual details identified 'alongside the editing of his text'. Even the 'charismatic economy' of modern authorship, inaugurated by the series of the folio editions of Shakespeare's works, suppresses 'the question of what authorizes the author, what creates the authority with which authors authorize' (Bourdieu 1993, 76) and re-situates the work of art within a set of multiplicities – 'the contexts, cultural territories and textual rites that make that work possible and which that work makes possible' (Viala 1993, 143; quoted by Meizoz 2007, 14).

Deleuze and Guattari have described books as '[c]*ollective assemblages of enunciation* [...] connected to very diverse modes of coding (biological, political, economic, etc.)', linking 'a language [...] to a whole micropolitics of the social field' (1987, 4, 7). In their understanding, '[a] rhizome ceaselessly establishes connections between semiotic acts, organizations of power, and circumstances relative to the arts, sciences, and social struggles' (1987, 7). If, in their view, '[a] semiotic chain' can 'agglomerat[e] very diverse acts, not only linguistic, but also perceptive, mimetic, gestural, and cognitive' (1987, 7), authors and forms of authorship can also be seen as parts of 'collective assemblages of enunciation'. Devoid of their traditional 'paternal' position and freed of reductive schematisation in Foucault's theory of discourse, authors and authorship become meaningful and specific only when connected to an open field of multiplicities of diverse orders. This rhizomatic perspective characterises the individual chapters of this volume.

These chapters cover a wide historical span of modernity, starting with the authorship of early modern drama in the sixteenth and early seventeenth centuries and ending with Ibero-American 'autofictions' of the twenty-first century. The chronological ordering of the chapters is a mere formal choice which does not interfere with the rhizomatic structure of the volume. What, then, are the 'plateaus' of which this book consists?

'Plateaus of intensity' and 'the plane of consistency'

This volume, in its versatile engagement with the issues of author, authority and authorship, includes diverse 'plateaus of intensity' communicating on the 'plane of consistency' (Deleuze and Guattari 1987, 69–70, 157–8, 251–2, 254, 506–8).[3] Therefore the discussion of particular immanent plateaus (1987, 158) will be followed by a description of their consistent communication. While these 'plateaus' can be understood as manifestations of individual forms of authorship, their 'plane of consistency [...] creates continuity for intensities that it extracts from distinct forms and substances' (Deleuze and Guattari 1987, 70), that is, from the distinct 'plateaus' of modern authorship.

Disappearance of the 'empirical author': the rise of Shakespeare as 'cultural capital'

The plateau to be discussed first comprises diverse dynamics of the transformations of authors as empirical and historical entities. While the early modern authors are often seen as persons legally responsible (and punishable) for their published works, their actual, empirical and historical existence is no longer directly accessible to anyone except the agents of law and economic or political power.

Jean-Christophe Mayer's chapter 'The rise of Shakespearean cultural capital' uses the example of the famous Droeshout portrait of the dramatist and of the first four folio editions of Shakespeare's works to show how the author as an empirical individual in the early seventeenth century was transmuted by means of iconic strategies and diverse readers' inscriptions and glosses into a cultural and fetishised figure. For instance,

Martin Droeshout's engraving in the folio editions 'stimulated a whole array of author-centred solutions and practices that [...] inevitably fostered the charisma surrounding Shakespeare'. The emerging 'cultural realm of literary authorship' had transformed the author into a figure whose work 'presents itself as a metonymic fetish of a person' (Meizoz 2007, 42). As a result, the figure of Shakespeare emerging in the seventeenth century as 'cultural capital' (Bourdieu 1986, 241–58) is chiefly a product of the 'charismatic economy' (Bourdieu 1993, 76) obscuring the actual historical and literary aspects of his authorship.

The function of paratexts: 'empirical author' and the rise of the modern publishing industry

As Jeanne Mathieu's chapter 'Religious conflict and the return of the author in early modern dramatic paratexts' demonstrates, the representation of empirical authors – often followed by their transformation into literary figures – is frequently accomplished by means of paratexts, especially by authors' prefaces to their published dramatic works. Although these paratexts can be interpreted as means of returning 'empirical authors' to the literary scene in order to sustain 'a more pertinent reading' of their works (Genette 1997, 2), their influence should be seen, more importantly, as 'operating through the reader's experience of the text' and continuously informing 'the process of reading, offering multiple points of entry, interpretations, and contestations' (Smith and Wilson 2011, 6). As a result, the actual and presumed responses of the readers start to influence significantly the self-representations of early modern dramatists. Moreover, the importance of their paratexts consists in the formation of specific relationships of empirical authors to other agents involved in the process of publication, such as visual artists or publishers. From this perspective, the 'return of the author' mediated by paratexts may appear as 'a mere part of the birth' of the modern publishing industry.

Transforming the oral tradition: the Ossian Controversy and 'cultural translation'

The dynamic of collaborative authorship forms another plateau of this book. In Petra Johana Poncarová's discussion of the 'Approaches to authorship in the Ossian Controversy', the clash between the collective authorship typical of oral literature and the modern legal concept of authorship as the individual form of intellectual ownership is seen to determine the controversy about the authenticity of the ancient Celtic Ossian poems, popularised by means of their widely influential English adaptations by James Macpherson. Whereas during the last 250 years most scholarly approaches emphasised the problem of Macpherson's 'forgery' of old Celtic oral culture, many recent critics, including some representatives of Comparative Celtic studies, have focused on different dimensions of Macpherson's activities instead – as a collector, compiler and transformer of oral tradition, or even as its 'creative employer' (Meek 1991, 19). Moreover, Macpherson's authorship is now mainly seen as a product of a massive reader response widely ranging across cultures in the late eighteenth and a considerable part of the nineteenth century.

This reassessment also consists of rethinking the role of translation during the creation and reception of modern Ossian poems. Rather than an indirect evidence of Macpherson's 'forgery', the view of the poems as 'translation[s] without an original' (Kristmannsson 1997, 449–62) testifies to the importance of 'cultural translation' (Asad 2009, 223–47) – a multi-level communication process that translates 'not only between Gaelic and English, but also between the oral culture of the depressed rural communities of the Scottish Highlands, and the prosperous urban centres of Lowland Britain, where the printed word was increasingly dominant' (Stafford 1996, viii). As a result, the Ossian Controversy can be reinterpreted as the history of activation of a multiplicity of 'cultural translations' which have refashioned old Celtic oral tradition and deeply influenced modern popular culture – including, for instance, even its most recent forms, such as 'fan fiction'.

The author as a multiplicity? Collaborative authorship and 'cultural networks'

A different process of collaborative authorship is studied in Johanna Fernández Castro's chapter 'Translation of indigenous oral narratives and the concept of collaborative authorship'. Whereas the case of Macpherson's adaptations is fairly straightforward, the situation of the indigenous narratives, collected between 1911 and 1913 by the German anthropologist Theodor Koch-Grünberg during his expedition to the Roraima region in north-western Brazil, is more complex, since it also includes their use in the major literary work of Brazilian modernism, Mário de Andrade's *Macunaíma* (1928), inspired by Koch-Grünberg's collection of oral tales.

The chapter focuses on the influence of 'intercultural relations opened by the intertextual dialogue' (Sá 2004, 39) and on the emergence of collaborative authorship 'as a product of cultural networks and their acts of authorization' (Berensmeyer, Buelens and Demoor 2012, 8).

The anthropologist downplays his authorial role and acknowledges the importance of indigenous narrators and translators for his recording of oral narratives. Moreover, the modernist writer Andrade describes his literary creation inspired by indigenous narratives as 'copying'. This is a complex case of collaborative authorship as a performative act, including an instance of 'precursory authorship' which entails 'a significant contribution from an earlier writer incorporated into the work' (Love 2002, 40).

On the plateau of collaborative authorship, the individual author is replaced by a multiplicity of *'authemes'*, including an 'author, collector, translator and editor' (Love 2002, 39). Nonetheless, this substitution re-opens the legal problem of authorship and demonstrates the necessity of its revision, which should legalise the restitution of indigenous oral narratives to their actual collective authors.

'Transcendental anonymity'? Darwin's name as a symbol of the authority of science

The absence of the empirical or historical author in the modern discourse of authorship increases the importance of the author's name as an abstraction, indicating the author's disappearance but also signifying a certain status of the author's œuvre. The author's name and its diverse uses establish yet another plateau of intensity in the rhizome of modern authorship. The analysis of the use of Charles Darwin's name in Niall Sreenan's chapter 'Darwin, scientific authority and literary assimilation' demonstrates that the name as 'the empirical characteristics of the author' is transposed 'into transcendental anonymity' (Foucault 1998, 208), which amounts to creating 'an individual without individuality'.

Although the chapter uses Foucault's 'author function' as a point of departure, it shows different effects of the substitution of the empirical author from those described by Foucault. Darwin's name becomes a symbol of the death of divine, religious authority and its replacement by the signifier of 'a transcendent scientific method' – still seen by some Darwin scholars as the universal approach to evolution, which can explain all its forms including the processes of literary history (Carroll 2004, Carroll 2011). This is also the way in which Émile Zola's *Germinal* (1885) uses Darwin's name: as 'a literary abstraction devoid of empiricity' but tenuously connected 'to the works associated with that author', which in the late nineteenth century appear in a grossly reductive ideological discourse.

In contrast to Zola's fiction, Thomas Hardy's novels (exemplified by *The Return of the Native*, 1878) refrain from using Darwin's name but make 'silent allusions' to Darwin's work. These in turn open 'the possibility of undermining normative models of thought in biology'. As a result, the use of Darwin's name in nineteenth-century literature and recent scholarship not only demonstrates some aspects of Foucault's 'author function', but also offers an 'implicit critique of our desire to put Darwin into interdiscursive circulation without attempting first to apprehend the complexity or breadth of his work'.

Pitfalls of deconstruction: the author's dead body as a 'historical accident'

In contrast to the disappearance of empirical authors beyond the 'transcendental anonymity' of their names, Mathelinda Nabugodi's chapter 'Dead Shelley' deals with the fiction of the presence of the author's dead body. The fact that the body of the Romantic poet Percy Bysshe Shelley had been cremated, after his death in a shipwreck, on the beach of Viareggio on 16 August 1822 did not dissuade Paul de Man from constructing the poet's disfigured body as an 'emblem of a certain conception of literary writing [...] inherently mutilated by historical accident'. As a result, the way in which Shelley's death 'fragments' his unfinished poem 'The Triumph of Life' (de Man 1979, 39–73) 'is representative of how history fragments literary writings'.

De Man inscribes his construct of Shelley's dead body in the margins of his final work, in order to transform the dead poet's corpse into a symbol of 'something that always happens: all texts are shaped by events, accidental or otherwise, that lie beyond the bounds of the text and yet serve as their decisive articulations'. Although 'unrelated to the rhetorical structures operative in the work', Shelley's defaced corpse transforms the poem into a general allegory of reading as 'the endless prosopopeia by which the dead are made to have a face and a voice which tells the allegory of their demise and allows us to apostrophize them in our turn' (de Man 1979, 68). Performing this transformation, de Man forgets that the text of the poem is based on a rather chaotic manuscript defragmented by the first editor of Shelley's *Poetical Works*, the poet's wife Mary.

De Man's reading of Shelley thus lacks an important historical dimension, the awareness of 'Mary Shelley's editorial effort which turned Shelley's chaotic manuscripts into his *Posthumous Poems*'. As a result, 'Shelley Disfigured' (de Man 1979, 39–73) tells us more about the pitfalls of de Man's deconstructive criticism than about the fragmentation of

Shelley's manuscript which allows him to read the poem as an assemblage, 'an increase in the dimensions of a multiplicity' (Deleuze and Guattari 1987, 8), of significations and textual gestures, whose sense can 'only be deciphered and joined by guesses, which might seem rather intuitive than founded on reasoning' (Shelley 1839, 4:226).

Importantly, Nabugodi's intertextual reading of 'The Triumph of Life' is not limited to de Man's 'Shelley Disfigured'. It demonstrates more productive aspects of deconstructive reading by tracing, instead of the marginal occurence of the dead poet's body, the paths of the poem's afterlife. Focusing on other essays in *Deconstruction and Criticism* (Bloom et al., 1979), namely Derrida's 'Living On: Border Lines' (Derrida 1979, 75–176) and Miller's 'The Critic as Host' (Miller 1979, 217–53), as well as Blanchot's novella *Death Sentence* (Blanchot 1976, 379–403), the chapter demonstrates that '[t]he relations between texts mean that no authorial signatory is a boundary that cordons off a text from other writings' and that 'each individual text itself participates in the afterlife of prior works'.

Yet even this is not a conclusive statement: the chapter's Coda (written in 2022) reminds us of the historical framework neglected in all other chapters of this book: 'Like too many canonical texts of its time, Shelley's "The Triumph of Life" has nothing to say about the systematic destruction of Black life that took place across the Atlantic'. Thus the Coda points out our 'ethical responsibilities in engaging with the literature produced during the long centuries of racial slavery'.

Authorship as agency: French theories of the 'literary field'

Although Deleuze and Guattari assume that 'it is not impossible to make a radical break between regimes of signs and their objects' (1987, 7), the bridging of this gap by 'the author as the focus of the mediation between the social and the textual' is crucial for the 'sociology of authors' (Baethge 2005, 118) pioneered by Pierre Bourdieu. The dynamic of this approach, especially the moments of the author's *agency*, forms another plateau of this volume.

Setting out to discuss recent sociological trends in literary and cultural studies, Josef Šebek's chapter 'The author as agent in the field' focuses on the work of Bourdieu's followers in the first decades of the twenty-first century. Bourdieu's analysis of the literary field as 'a microworld with its internal rules', 'historicity' and 'autonomy' (manifesting itself in its relation to power, the aesthetic functions of literature and critical relationships to other social fields) is seminal for the understanding of the author as 'agency' constituted 'only in relation to the literary field'. This agency is engendered by the interplay of the author's *habitus* (the social and aesthetic determination of their work) and the possibilities opened by the historical and aesthetic dynamic of the field.

Bourdieu's approach to 'agency' has been refined by Gisèle Sapiro, who made a distinction between conscious and even intentional 'social strategies of the author' (2013, 180) and 'strategies of writing' (2013, 163–81) which 'are less accessible to research'. Jérôme Meizoz has further developed the theory of the author's agency; he uses the term 'literary posture', which refers to the self-presentation of the author as an agent in the literary field by means of 'textual effects and social behaviour' (2007, 21). Although this 'posture' can be seen as the author's deliberate construction of their own literary identity (choosing from a repertory of postures), it is not based on any 'internal' (psychologically or philosophically determined) stance. Rather, it is a mask or a media-image. These can be freely multiplied, allowing authors to disconnect their agency from problems of personal identity. This is demonstrated in Šebek's 'case study', which analyses a rather problematic posture of the major Czech fiction writer Ladislav Fuks (1923–1994) in the literary field under communist dictatorship, and especially in the period of 'normalisation' after the Soviet invasion of Czechoslovakia in 1968.

In Deleuze and Guattari's terms the arborescent structure of identity, grown from the inner self of an individual, is replaced by a rhizome of agency deriving from three interconnected processes of mediation (the field mediates between the author and the work, the work mediates between the field and the author, and the author mediates between the work and the field). The rhizomatic nature of this interrelationship is caused by the multiplicity of postures and their performative character. As a result, the position of the author as an interface between the literary and social fields seems even more problematised than Sapiro or Meizoz have supposed. To see the author as the agent in the literary field actually means understanding the literary field no longer in its 'autonomy', but rather as a part of the plateau of agency in the rhizome of collective enunciation.

Autofiction as a 'performance of authorship'

This rhizome of collective enunciation is even more evident in some recent forms of 'autofiction' and critical responses to this phenomenon in Latin American literatures of the last decade of the twentieth and the first two decades of the twenty-first centuries. As Sonia Miceli's chapter 'Autofiction as (self-)criticism' points out, autofiction cannot be understood as a literary genre derived from autobiography, as indicated in Philippe Lejeune's theory of 'the autobiographical pact' (1975; 1989, 3–30) and subsequent speculations of Serge Doubrovsky, who coined the term 'autofiction' in 1977. Rather, it is 'a performance of authorship', distinct from a mere representation, having 'an existence of its own' (Iser 1993, 281) and lacking a clear discursive identity.

Autofiction takes place 'at the intersection of several discourses: of the writer, the media, readers, academic critics, etc.', and involves readers in its game. The public life of authors, their images in media and on social networks are also part of this performance of authorship. As *Divorce*, a novel by Brazilian author Ricardo Lísias (Lísias 2013) implies, only 'the physicality' of the body seems to exclude the author from the autofictional game. Yet even in this case the skin of the body cannot function as a clear divide separating empirical and fictional identities of the author, since Lísias's experience is not available in any other but fictionalised form. This fact allows us to read Lísias's novel as a collective assemblage of enunciation, where 'semiotic chains of every nature are connected to very diverse modes of coding' (Deleuze and Guattari 1987, 7) and the performativity of autofiction is the source of the dynamic of this plateau.

'Authors as *trans*formers': the deferral of identity and the emergence of alterity

Nonetheless, there are some autofictions which cannot be explained as performatives. The chapter 'Latin American autofiction authors as *trans*formers' by Gerardo Cruz-Grunerth focuses on the works of the Argentinian César Aira and the Mexican Mario Bellatin, which contain 'mechanisms of authorial identification, as well as moments of denial, concealment and crisis of autofiction caused by autofiction itself'. This ambiguity, first noticed by the Spanish critic Manuel Alberca Serrano (Alberca Serrano 2007, following Lejeune 1989), manifests itself in a number of binaries, including those of empirical and fictional existence, presence and absence, speech and silence, male and female gender, life and death, and many others. These binaries no longer constitute oppositions but mark the spatial or temporal deferral of meaning as well as the dissolution of identities. This process determines '[t]he economic character of differance' (Derrida 1973, 151) and makes an opening for the emergence of alterity seminal for the autofictions discussed in this chapter.

The chapter shows how the deferral of presence, identity and meaning and the emergence of alterity complicate the performative reading of autofictions. In view of this, authors of autofictions can be better described as *'trans*formers' rather than 'performers'. The former term was used by Jean-François Lyotard (1990, 31) to interpret Marcel Duchamp's *Large Glass* (*Le Grand Verre*, 1915–23), a complex work of Dadaism that combines painting, sculpture, drawing and verbal text. The chapter suggests that Lyotard's use of *'trans*former' and the neclogism *'trans*formance' (1990, 31) implies 'a metamorphosis of the self which is difficult to revert, like, for example, in trans-sexual gender change'.

To interpret this 'metamorphosis' as an important feature of autofiction, the chapter draws a parallel between the modernist assemblage of Duchamp's *Large Glass* and Mario Bellatin's eponymous experimental set of three texts (2007, 2015). Similar to the former work, which develops 'a system that allows Duchamp to expand his gender identity beyond the limits of the masculine', Bellatin allows his characters to migrate from one world to another, but he also disrupts their attempts at identification. This process culminates in the third text of *The Large Glass*, where the narrator turns into a composite figure moving between different identities (the author / a marionette-like girl / a young man). In doing so, the narrator creates a rhizomatic compound of fictional worlds. This enhances the autoreflexivity of autofiction, linking its fictional and metafictional features. It can be said that both the deferral and the transgression of identities, as well as a constant oscillation between the text and the paratext, fiction and metafiction, are the major sources of the dynamic of this plateau.

Agency and desire: Coetzee's Dostoevsky

The closing chapter of this volume, 'The scene of invention' by Laura Cernat, takes a different view on the author as a source of agency from recent approaches of literary sociology. Focusing on J. M. Coetzee's biofiction on Dostoevsky, *The Master of Petersburg* (Coetzee 2004), the chapter demonstrates the impact of the stereotyped Platonic approach to authors as 'privileged recipients of inspiration' on recent biographical novels and films about artists and scientists. Almost all of the works examined in the introductory part of the chapter exemplify recent 'mythologies of writers at work', which represent the creative process as a linear development of an accidentally revealed idea. In spite of the Platonic origins of this mythology, the linearity of this process owes much to the conventions of 'the age of print – the book as the unalterable form of a literary work, the reader's linear progression through it and the concrete author's withdrawal from it'. As a result, the dynamic of the creative process is explained in analogy with the traditional (pre-Barthesian) understanding of the process of reading, or as the 'reduction of the author in the interests of establishing a science of literature' (Burke 1998, 10).

This view obscures the complex relationships between fiction, history, biography and autobiography in Coetzee's novel on Dostoevsky. The chapter compares Coetzee's biofiction with a relevant selection of Dostoevsky's novels – chiefly *Demons* (1873), but also *Crime and Punishment* (1866) and *The Brothers Karamazov* (1880) – and his notebooks and letters documenting the genesis of *Demons* as well as Dostoevsky's views on the creative process.

Apart from distinctive analogies and differences between the works of both authors and their historic contexts, Cernat points out the importance of the autobiographical moments of Coetzee's novel. Her complex view of Coetzee's biofiction reveals that the author 'is using the fictional Dostoevsky not just as a self-projection, but also to address the historical writer' in a specific way: the autobiographical, fictional and historical components of Coetzee's narrative are similarly interrelated as Lacan's notions of the Symbolic, the Imaginary and the Real. This structure, resembling a Borromean knot (Lacan 2016, 11), distorts the parallels between individual events in Coetzee's and Dostoevsky's novels and baffles the efforts of some critics to draw analogies between Coetzee's work and Dostoevsky's life.

As a result, the relationship between the autofiction and biofiction in Coetzee's novel lacks symmetry. This absence of symmetry establishes the dynamic and intensity of a plateau integrating multiplicities from the author's real and fictional life as well as those from Dostoevsky's biography and novels. The notion of the 'implied author' (Booth 1983, 73) may be helpful in describing this dynamic – but only when Coetzee's novel is understood as a specific 'use' of Dostoevsky, exemplified in what the chapter calls 'the impersonal "he"', namely the use of the third person pronoun 'with no explicit reference' (Lejeune 1977, 34).

However, if Coetzee's major theme, the creative process, is understood as a dynamic interrelationship of multiplicities and as an assemblage of collective enunciation, it is clear that it cannot be systematised, not even in the Lacanian way. As Deleuze and Guattari have shown, 'in Lacan, the symbolic organization of the structure, with its exclusions that come from the function of the signifier, has as its reverse side the real inorganization of desire' (Deleuze and Guattari 1983, 328). It can be said, then, that the last plateau of this volume emphasises the orientation of the author's, as well as the reader's, desire to 'a signifier of lack' (Deleuze and Guattari 1983, 310), and that the intensity forming this plateau is based on the tension between collective enunciation, the desire oriented to a 'signifier of lack' and 'the real' as 'an inassimilable externality' (Stanizai 2018, 5).[4]

'The plane of consistency'

As Deleuze and Guattari have pointed out, '[t]he plane of consistency […] is opposed to the plane of organization and development. Organization and development concern form or substance […]' (1987, 507), while 'the plane of consistency […] *constructs continuums of intensity*: it creates continuity for intensities that it extracts from distinct forms and substances' (1987, 70).

Creating 'continuums of intensity', the plane of consistency does not consolidate by means of unification, stratification or hierarchisation. It never schematises to reduce multiplicities by means of a common principle or purpose. Unlike 'the plane of organization and development', it 'ties together heterogeneous, disparate elements as such: it assures the consolidation of fuzzy aggregates, in other words, multiplicities of the rhizome type' (Deleuze and Guattari 1987, 508). As mentioned above, it is precisely such rhizomatic multiplicities that form the various 'plateaus of intensity' discussed in this volume.

The process of consolidation of these plateaus produces a continuum of intensity based on their mutual tensions. These tensions are not seen as sources of dialectical opposition or antagonism, but rather as differences establishing the concrete 'posture' and agency of each discussed form of authorship, thus producing the immanent intensity and dynamic of individual plateaus.

For instance, while the subjective attitudes of early modern authors may be expressed in their paratexts, the power and impact of these texts is determined by the multiple agents in the literary field, such as the readers, visual artists or publishers. This tension is increased, on the one hand, by the rise of the symbolic role of modern authors as representatives of 'cultural capital', the authority of science (as in the case of Charles Darwin) or even as dead bodies (here in the case of P. B. Shelley). On the other hand, further tensions producing a continuum of intensity are engendered by the increasing importance of collective authorship and cultural translation. Another set of tensions emerges with the shift from authorial identity to agency, and further still to the performance or transformation of this identity (including its deferral and emergence of alterity) in autofiction. Finally, the fictionalisation of authorship also includes the problem of the unconscious and the dynamics of desire and lack which surfaces in individual works of biofiction such as J. M. Coetzee's *The Master of Petersburg*.

The plane of consistency of modern authorship, then, can be seen as a continuum of intensity determined by several vectors: some conveying authors (and their names or even bodies) from empirical existence to symbolic meaning and value, some transposing collective authorship typical of oral cultures to the power of intercultural communication, others driving the author's agency to the performance, transformation and ultimate dissolution of individual identity, others still combining this agency with operations of unconscious desire. It is within this continuum of intensity that our interpretations of modern forms of authorship are situated.

Notes

1 The second edition of Deleuze (1964) appeared in 1970.
2 Deleuze and Guattari (1987, 3) refer to Marcel Schwob's *Children's Crusade* (1896).
3 'A plateau is a piece of immanence'. Plateaus communicate 'with other plateaus on the plane of consistency' (Deleuze and Guattari 1987, 158). Deleuze and Guattari refer to Gregory Bateson (1972, 113).
4 Stanizai refers to Jacques Lacan's RSI seminar of 11 March 1975 (Lacan 1975).

References

Alberca Serrano, Manuel. 2007. *El pacto ambiguo. De la novella autobiográfica a la autoficción.* Madrid: Biblioteca Nueva.
Asad, Talal. 2009. 'The concept of cultural translation in British social anthropology' (1986). In *Critical Readings in Translation Studies*, edited by Mona Baker, 223–47. London and New York: Routledge.
Baethge, Constanze. 2005. 'Une littérature sans littérarité: Pour une autonomie de l'œuvre d'art.' In *Le symbolique et le social: La réception internationale de la pensé de Pierre Bourdieu*, edited by Jacques Dubois, Pascal Durand and Yves Winkin, 117–25. Liège: Université de Liège.
Barthes, Roland. 1977. 'The Death of the Author' (1967). In *Image Music Text*, selected and translated by Stephen Heath, 142–8. London: Fontana Press.
Bateson, Gregory. 1972. *Steps to an Ecology of Mind*. New York: Ballantine.
Beckett, Samuel. 1958. *Nouvelles et textes pour rien*. Paris: Minuit.
Beckett, Samuel. 2006. 'Texts for nothing' (1950). In *The Grove Centenary Edition*, edited by Paul Auster. Vol. 4. *Poems Short Stories Criticism*, 295–340. New York: Grove Press.
Bellatin, Mario. 2007. *El Gran Vidrio. Tres autobiografías*. Barcelona: Anagrama.
Bellatin, Mario. 2015. *The Large Glass: Three autobiographies*. Translated by David Shook. London: Eyewear Publishing.
Bellatin, Mario. 2014. 'Los cien mil libros de Bellatin'. In *Obra reunida 2*, 653–64. Madrid: Alfaguara.
Berensmeyer, Ingo, Gert Buelens and Marysa Demoor. 2012. 'Authorship as cultural performance: New perspectives in authorship studies', *Zeitschrift für Anglistik und Amerikanistik* 60.1: 5–29.
Blanchot, Maurice. 1976. *Death Sentence* (1948). Translated by Lydia Davies. *The Georgia Review* 30.2: 379–403.

Bloom, Harold, Paul de Man, Jacques Derrida, Geoffrey H. Hartman and J. Hillis Miller. 1979. *Deconstruction and Criticism*. New York: Seabury Press.
Booth, Wayne C. 1983. *The Rhetoric of Fiction*. 2nd edition. Chicago, IL: University of Chicago Press.
Bourdieu, Pierre. 1986. 'The forms of capital'. Translated by Richard Nice. In *Handbook of Theory and Research for the Sociology of Education*, edited by John G. Richardson, 241–58. Westport, CT: Greenwood Press.
Bourdieu, Pierre. 1993. 'The production of belief: Contribution to an economy of symbolic goods'. In *The Field of Cultural Production: Essays on art and literature*, edited by Randal Johnson, 74–111. Cambridge: Polity Press.
Burke, Seán. 1998. *The Death and Return of the Author: Criticism and subjectivity in Barthes, Foucault and Derrida*. 2nd edition. Edinburgh: Edinburgh University Press.
Butler, Judith. 1993. *Bodies That Matter: On the discursive limits of sex*. London and New York: Routledge.
Carroll, Joseph. 2004. *Literary Darwinism: Evolution, human nature, and literature*. London and New York: Routledge.
Carroll, Joseph. 2011. *Reading Human Nature: Literary Darwinism in theory and practice*. Albany: SUNY Press.
Coetzee, J. M. 2004. *The Master of Petersburg* (1994). London: Vintage.
de Man, Paul. 1979. 'Shelley Disfigured'. In Harold Bloom et al. *Deconstruction and Criticism*, 39–73. New York: Seabury Press.
Deleuze, Gilles. 1964. *Marcel Proust et les signes*. Paris: PUF.
Deleuze, Gilles and Félix Guattari. 1983. *Anti-Oedipus: Capitalism and schizophrenia* (1972). Translated by Robert Hurley, Mark Seem and Helen Lane. Minneapolis: University of Minnesota Press.
Deleuze, Gilles and Félix Guattari. 1987. *A Thousand Plateaus: Capitalism and schizophrenia* (1980). Translated by Brian Massumi. Minneapolis and London: University of Minnesota Press.
Derrida, Jacques. 1973. 'Differance' (1968). In *Speech and Phenomena and Other Essays on Husserl's Theory of Signs*, translated by David B. Allison, 129–60. Evanston, IL: Northwestern University Press.
Derrida, Jacques. 1979. 'Living On: Border Lines'. Translated by James Hulbert. In Harold Bloom et al. *Deconstruction and Criticism*, 75–176. New York: Seabury Press.
Foucault, Michel. 1969. 'Qu'est-ce qu'un auteur?' *Bulletin de la Société française de philosophie* 63.3: 73–104.
Foucault, Michel. 1972. *The Archaeology of Knowledge and The Discourse of Language* (1969, 1971). Translated by A. M. Sheridan Smith. New York: Pantheon.
Foucault, Michel. 1998. 'What is an author?'. Translated by Josué V. Harari. In *Aesthetics, Method, and Epistemology, Essential Works of Michel Foucault 1954–1984*, vol. 2, edited by James D. Faubion, translated by Robert Hurley and others, 205–22. New York: The New Press.
Genette, Gérard. 1997. *Paratexts: Thresholds of interpretation*. Translated by Jane E. Lewin. Cambridge: Cambridge University Press.
Hird, Alastair. 2010. '"What does it matter who is speaking," someone said, "What does it matter who is speaking": Beckett, Foucault, Barthes'. *Samuel Beckett Today / Aujourd'hui* 22: 289–99.
Iser, Wolfgang. 1993. *The Fictive and the Imaginary: Charting literary anthropology* (1991). Baltimore, MD and London: The Johns Hopkins University Press.
Kristmannsson, Gauti. 1997. 'Ossian: A case of Celtic tribalism or a translation without an original'. *Transfer: Übersetzen – Dolmetschen – Interkulturalität*, edited by Horst Drescher, 449–62. Frankfurt/M., Berlin, Bern, New York, Paris, Vienna: Peter Lang.
Lacan, Jacques. 1975. 'Seminar XXII. R.S.I., 11 March 1975'. Translated by Jack W. Stone. Lacanian Works Exchange. https://www.lacanianworksexchange.net/lacan. Accessed 9 January 2022.
Lacan, Jacques. 2016. *The Sinthome: The seminar of Jacques Lacan, Book XXIII*. Translated by A. R. Price, edited by Jacques-Alain Miller. Cambridge and Malden, MA: Polity Press.
Lejeune, Philippe. 1977. 'Autobiography in the third person'. Translated by Annette and Edward Tomarken. *New Literary History* 9.1: 27–50.
Lejeune, Philippe. 1989. 'The autobiographical pact' (1975). In *On Autobiography*, edited by Paul John Eakin, translated by Katherine Leary, 3–30. Minneapolis: University of Minnesota Press.
Lísias, Ricardo. 2013. *Divórcio*. Carnaxide: Objectiva.
Love, Harold. 2002. *Attributing Authorship: An introduction*. Cambridge: Cambridge University Press.

Lyotard, Jean-François. 1990. *Duchamp's TRANS/formers* (1977). Translated by Ian McLeod. Venice, CA: The Lapis Press.
Meek, Donald E. 1991. 'The Gaelic ballads of Scotland: Creativity and adaptation'. In *Ossian Revisited*, edited by Howard Gaskill, 19–48. Edinburgh: Edinburgh University Press.
Meizoz, Jérôme. 2007. *Postures Littéraires. Mises en scène modernes de l'auteur*. Geneva: Slatkine Érudition.
Miller, J. Hillis. 1979. 'The Critic as Host'. In Harold Bloom et al. *Deconstruction and Criticism*, 217–53. New York: Seabury Press.
Sá, Lúcia. 2004. *Rain Forest Literatures: Amazonian texts and Latin American culture*. Minneapolis: University of Minnesota Press.
Sapiro, Gisèle. 2013. 'Stratégies de l'écriture et responsabilité auctoriale.' In *On ne peut pas tout réduire à des strategies*, edited by Dinah Ribard and Nicolas Schapira, 163–81. Paris: PUF.
Shelley, Mary. 1839. 'Note on the poems written in 1822, by the editor'. In *The Poetical Works of Percy Bysshe Shelley*, edited by Mrs. Shelley, vol. 4, 225–36. London: Edward Moxon.
Smith, Helen and Louise Wilson. 2011. 'Introduction'. In *Renaissance Paratexts*, edited by Helen Smith and Louise Wilson, 1–14. Cambridge: Cambridge University Press.
Stafford, Fiona. 1996. 'Introduction'. In *The Poems of Ossian and Related Works*, edited by Howard Gaskill, v–xxi. Edinburgh: Edinburgh University Press.
Stanizai, Ehsan Azari. 2018. 'Lacan's three concepts: The imaginary, the Borromean knot, and the gaze', 1–8. Nida Lacan Study and Reading Group. Sydney: National Institute of Dramatic Arts. https://www.nida.edu.au/__data/assets/pdf_file/0011/47396/Three-Concepts-The-Imaginary,-the-Borromean-Knot,-and-the-Gaze.pdf. Accessed on 9 January 2022.
Viala, Alain. 1993. 'Éléments de sociopoétique'. In *Approches de la reception: Sémiostylistique et sociopoétique de Le Clézio*, edited by Georges Molinié and Alain Viala, 139–222. Paris: PUF.

1
The rise of Shakespearean cultural capital: early configurations and appropriations of Shakespeare
Jean-Christophe Mayer

This chapter will first discuss Shakespeare's presence in part of the culture around us and then turn to the past in order to understand the journey that has led the Stratford-born dramatist and poet to become the quintessential figure of the author that he is now. After examining some postmodern theoretical views of Shakespeare, as well as the current circulation and merchandising of Shakespeare's representations on the internet and in mainstream culture, the chapter will demonstrate how such trends find their roots partly in the early configuration of his works in print (especially in the seventeenth century) and in their reception by early readers. Some of the preliminaries of Shakespeare's works will be examined (particularly the now-iconic Droeshout portrait of Shakespeare), as well as the traces and inscriptions left by readers in those books. The end of the chapter will focus on actual or 'empirical' readers and their intensive work of appropriation to explain how Shakespeare first began to gain such cultural capital as a literary author. His paradoxical position in postmodern culture as an author both revered and parodied can be enlightened by analysis of the complex early modern construction of Shakespeare as a literary figure and the material configuration of his early works.

The postmodern circulation of Shakespeare

Shakespeare's impact on – and transformation by – postmodern culture is a well-known phenomenon. His works are the most performed globally in a myriad of adaptations and his reach extends beyond elite circles to encompass popular culture, in particular through various forms of neo-capitalist merchandising. Thus Shakespeare's name is used to sell merchandise with only remote connections to the Elizabethan playwright or to his works themselves. Shakespeare mints, mobile phone covers, ties or uncanny tissue box covers and costumed dolls appear perhaps less related to the Shakespeare studied at school or university than to the Shakespeare of wedding cakes or Valentine's cards, which relies vaguely on an old trope: Shakespeare the love poet. Needless to say, the postmodern transmedia Shakespeare has also his own Facebook page. This both personalises the author and yet depersonalises him as soon as we access the page, which displays a string of generally disconnected posts (Facebook 2018).

Recent scholars now see his texts as 'always in transit'. Shakespeare is construed as 'ever-other-than-itself' and is considered as 'an aggregate forever in flux' (Lanier 2014, 29, 31, 32). Some postmodernist features throw further light on these phenomena. As Brian McHale writes,

> The rewriting or recycling of canonical texts is a typical postmodern practice. Sometimes parodic, sometimes not, it occurs throughout the postmodern decades.
>
> (McHale 2015, 51)

Roland Barthes had already paved the way by noting that the meaning of classical texts nearly always remains in a state of 'suspension' (Barthes 1975, 216–17). In the field of media history, he is currently regarded as a 'paradigmatic author' (Donaldson 2011, 225), one who is 'media-intensive' and a source 'of narratives that move across media as well as space' (226). Moreover, film studies are characteristically 'marked by narrative excess and by an approach to Shakespeare that combines reverence and burlesque' (230). All of these views explain in part why Shakespeare occupies a powerful but paradoxical position in contemporary culture. The First Folio itself (1623), a source of intense scrutiny by textual scholars and theatre practitioners alike, appears in this light as 'a link in a metonymic chain of legacy media' (Donaldson 2011, 233). Some critics would go further, seeing the First Folio as a crucial element of an overall Shakespeare allegory marked by 'self-conscious and sacralizing nostalgia in response to authoritative but in some sense faded origins', or as a book offering a somewhat equivocal 'journey back to a foreclosed origin' (Fineman 1981, 29, 42).

Many of the aforementioned comments are useful in helping us to understand how Shakespeare still shapes the world around us. Nonetheless, they remain for the most scholarly narratives which

Figure 1.1 Title page of Shakespeare's First Folio displaying Martin Droeshout's engraving of the author, Fo. 1 no. 71. By permission of the Folger Library.

obfuscate an incredibly large part of the rise of Shakespearean cultural capital. While I agree that one cannot possibly pinpoint the origins of that rise, I would not describe all journeys into the past as 'foreclosed' or leading necessarily to 'faded origins'.

On the contrary: a material approach, combined with reception and appropriation studies, as well as the history of the book and the history of reading, can illuminate the long and uncertain rise of Shakespeare as a figure larger than himself. It only requires us to take a more empirical look at these so-called 'faded origins' to gain awareness of the many agents involved in Shakespeare's rise: publishers, engravers, booksellers and, last but not least, his readers and their traces in that crucial but foundational period, which spans roughly from the sixteenth to the eighteenth century. The story which I am about to tell was not ineluctable, as Shakespeare, like other authors, disappeared from view at certain moments. There are in fact enough material traces to be able not to produce a teleological tale, but rather to point to the particular ways he was configured in print, how he was marketed well before the postmodern era and how those who received the least attention for a long time – his readers – appropriated him through their numerous marks and annotations.

The rise of iconic Shakespeare: the visual impact of the Droeshout portrait and the collective quest for the author's image

Among Shakespeare's early material configurations in print is the notorious Droeshout portrait of Shakespeare. The portrait – or engraving, to be precise – originally appeared in the first collected edition of Shakespeare's plays published in London in 1623, the First Folio, opposite Ben Jonson's epistle 'To the reader' (sig. π 2r) – which speaks directly of 'This Figure, that thou here seest put', but then appears to try to lead the reader into the plays, as no picture seemingly can live up to them: 'Reader, looke/ Not on his Picture, but his Booke' (Fig. 1.1).

Whether Jonson was demeaning the picture, or simply praising the works, it is true that the engraving has been a repeated source of speculation and criticism. Among the harshest and most famous critiques of the portrait is Samuel Schoenbaum's:

> a huge head, placed against a starched ruff, surmounts an absurdly small tunic with oversized shoulder-wings. [. . .] The mouth is too far to the right, the left eye lower and larger than the right, the hair on the two sides fails to balance. Light comes from several directions simultaneously: it falls on the bulbous protuberance of forehead [. . .].
>
> (Schoenbaum 1970, 11)

Since then, other distinguished Shakespeareans, such as Paul Edmondson and Stanley Wells, have likewise cast serious doubts about the authenticity of the portrait. They have argued instead in favour of a picture discovered in 2006, an early Jacobean panel painting, the Cobbe portrait displayed at Hatchlands Park in Surrey. The portrait is so-called because it was formerly owned by Charles Cobbe, Church of Ireland (Anglican) Archbishop of Dublin (1686–1765) (Edmondson and Wells 2012, 1–14).

Yet new archival research by June Schlueter has confirmed that the First Folio portrait is by Martin Droeshout the younger (1601–c.1640). He was a third-generation member of a family of artists and engravers, established in London for 40 years at the time of the publication of the First Folio (Schlueter 2017, 18, 23). Backed by concordant documentary evidence, Schlueter further argues that the engraving was probably done before 1622, when Martin Droeshout was still a novice and trying out his skills as an engraver. As he was just 16 when Shakespeare died, it is possible that he sketched his engraving from another composition. This would explain the relatively simple but poor quality of the portrait, which was not meant for publication. Supported by a number of facts, Schlueter concludes that the Folio syndicate, which no doubt had earlier professional links with the Droeshout family, chose to buy the already existing engraving by Martin Droeshout. The portrait was therefore never 'commissioned, but acquired' (Schlueter 2017, 25–8).

There is good reason to believe this version of events. Indeed, engravings were far more prestigious than woodcut portraits, but producing a book such as the First Folio was a risky financial enterprise. Thus it naturally made more sense to buy an already existing engraving (however imperfect it might be) at a cheaper price than one created especially for the Folio by an experienced engraver.

It seems that the potential impact of an engraving (rather than a woodcut) on readers superseded considerations of exactitude. Judging not only by the portrait's future renown (no portrait of Shakespeare has been more reproduced or is more immediately recognisable than the Droeshout portrait), but also by the noticeable attention given to it by Shakespeare's early readers, the Folio syndicate had, with hindsight, taken the right decision.[1] However imperfect the portrait, what Roger Chartier calls 'the assignation of the text to a single "I" immediately visible' is there to 'reinforce the notion that the writing is the expression of an individuality that gives authenticity to the work' (1994, 52).

What is more, the portrait continued to be printed (with some minor alterations) repeatedly in the seventeenth-century Second, Third and Fourth Folios. It obviously left an imprint in the minds of thousands of readers, who purchased or borrowed the volumes well into the eighteenth century and beyond.

For instance, special attention appears to have been given to the portrait by an eighteenth-century reader who ruled in red ink the frame of the portrait in Folger Shakespeare Library (henceforward, FSL) Fo. 3 no. 13. The Droeshout engraving also stimulated the search for other portraits of Shakespeare. Thus FSL Fo. 1 no. 54, which contains a facsimile of the original engraving, is still supplemented, probably by Captain Charles Hutchinson of the Royal Navy (fl.1870), by a reproduction of the Janssen portrait of Shakespeare and another copy of the Droeshout portrait, with

Figure 1.2 A collage portrait of Shakespeare in the box containing the Broadhead First Folio. By permission of the Library of Congress.

handwritten notes under the images. These read respectively for each portrait: 'This is from the Portrait by Jansen, 1610, supposed to be the best & most authentic, portrait of the great Bard' and 'This from old Droeshout's engraving of Shakespeare's portrait; but the original is but a course performance' (front flyleaves, three verso and four recto).

Not all readers were as dismissive of Droeshout's work. Some were just interested in comparing the portraits, as the search for the 'real' author's image was well underway. The Library of Congress Broadhead First Folio has six engraved portraits of Shakespeare with an engraving of 'The House at Stratford in which Shakespeare lived'. They are currently placed in the same box as the Broadhead First Folio. One of the portraits (Fig. 1.2) is a rather weirdsome collage indicative of the lengths some readers would go to in their quest for Shakespeare's image.

It is a well-known fact that the first few pages of early books often go missing. It is no different for the folios. Not having the Droeshout engraving could thus be frustrating to some readers who lacked that precious iconic link between the author and his works. In such cases a number of readers sought to fill the void, either by purchasing facsimiles of the portrait or by adding other images of Shakespeare. Such is the case of FSL Fo. 3 no. 8, which lacks the title leaf and the accompanying portrait. To remedy this, the owner of the folio in question inserted a facsimile of William Marshall's (fl.1617–49) engraving of Shakespeare in his *Poems* (1640), most likely in the late nineteenth century (the facsimile corresponds to the frontispiece in Alfred Russell Smith's facsimile edition of the *Poems* from 1885).

While the iconic strategies put in place by the readers described above are relatively limited and their logic is fairly apparent, there are also more extreme examples, both in terms of length and breadth. The case study we are about to offer can be linked to what became a nationwide passion for extra-illustrated books (also called grangerised works) that began in the late eighteenth century and reached great heights in the nineteenth century (Ferrell 2013, online). The fashion is not so far from our contemporary practice of compiling scrapbooks but also differs from it in a number of ways, as we shall see.

Before closing this section, let us examine the work carried out by surgeon and apothecary John Sherwen (1748–1826) on what is now known as FSL Fo. 2 no. 53.

Sherwen's Second Folio did have a number of pages missing, as well as a few misbound leaves; it lacked the Droeshout engraving as well.[2] Yet the preliminaries designed by Sherwen go well beyond the intention of merely filling gaps.

The printed texts, manuscript annotations and illustrations he assembled are not just attempts at reconstructing the folio's opening pages; they form a largely idiosyncratic, miscellaneous and exploratory collection. In fact Sherwen turned the folio's preliminary pages into something that resembles a miscellany, which he has at times illustrated.

As we have noted, the folio is devoid of its Shakespeare portrait and – characteristically – a small oval representation in profile of Shakespeare

Figure 1.3 First flyleaf recto of a Second Folio, which once belonged to John Sherwen. In its centre is an inserted portrait of Shakespeare. The portrait is framed by five pasted slips of paper containing manuscript extracts in praise of Shakespeare. Fo. 2 no. 53. By permission of the Folger Library.

bearded was cut out and glued onto its inside cover. Moreover, the first flyleaf recto has in its centre an inserted portrait of Shakespeare, clearly inspired by the Chandos painting (Fig. 1.3). The portrait is framed by five pasted slips of paper containing manuscript extracts in praise of Shakespeare. Then, on the verso of the second flyleaf, is a reproduction of Shakespeare's monumental bust erected in Holy Trinity Church, Stratford-upon-Avon, between his death in 1616 and 1623.

The miscellaneous manuscript notes begin on the recto of the third flyleaf and continue for seven pages (more than four leaves). These pages were in fact composed over several years, perhaps decades, as the references on the first flyleaves tend to be taken from books printed before 1800, but from the fifth flyleaf recto onwards extracts are solely from nineteenth-century sources.

Whereas, as we know, in all four folios Ben Jonson's epistle 'To the Reader' directs the gaze away from the facing Droeshout engraving of Shakespeare ('Reader, looke / Not on his Picture, but his Booke'), Sherwen built a genuine paper shrine to Shakespeare around the inserted portrait. He used cut and pasted manuscript fragments of quotations to create an intertextual and transmedia collage of homage and worship. The assembled extracts go beyond the Folios' transformation of Shakespeare into a literary figure; they raise the author as creator to superhuman heights. In this way, the portrait is of course of paramount importance as it personifies and authenticates the works. Many of the extracts are there to illustrate Sherwen's belief that portraits reveal the truth of a person.

In this Second Folio an ink transcription of a poem by Mark Akenside (1721–1770) is pasted onto the top of the page. Interestingly for our purposes, its lines draw a direct link between the dramatist's features and his literary legacy:

> [...] Approach: behold this portrait. Know ye not
> The Features? [...]
>   This was Shakespeares Form:
> Who walk'd in every path of human Life.
> Felt every Passion; and to all Mankind
> Doth now, will ever, that experience yield [...].
>   (Akenside 1795, 256)

On the right-hand side of the page Sherwen recounts how 'Sir Godfrey Kneller painted a Picture of Shakespeare, which he presented to Dryden' and how the latter repaid Kneller by writing lines which are driven by a visual cult of the dramatist. Furthermore, they not only place Shakespeare in a literary genealogy, but also give him a 'godlike' standing among all other writers:

> Shakspeare, thy Gift, I place before my Sight,
> With Awe I ask his Blessing as I write;
> With Reverence look on his majestic Face,
> Proud to be less, but of his godlike Race.[3]

It should be clear by now that the Droeshout portrait acted as a cue for many readers to firm up the links between author and work. It also stimulated a whole array of author-centred solutions and practices that engaged readers in an intense search for the 'real' Shakespeare and inevitably fostered the charisma surrounding Shakespeare as well as, indirectly and implicitly, increasing the value of what was considered to be his sole creations – his works, which readers annotated fervently too. Indeed Jonson's epistle, as well as the list of actors present in the folios, redirected the gaze towards the plays and the more collective and collaborative world of theatre. In this sense, the First Folio and its ensuing editions adopted an ambivalent stance: not only encouraging the praise of Shakespeare, but also recalling a past and illustrious world, that of Shakespeare's company of actors, thus completing the Shakespeare legend.

From a postmodern perspective, the charisma surrounding Shakespeare could be dismissed, as Pierre Bourdieu and others have observed, because the essentialist belief in the charisma of a work is an illusion: a creation of what Bourdieu calls the 'charismatic economy' which suppresses 'the question of what authorizes the author, what creates the authority with which authors authorize' (1993, 76). Nevertheless more recent critics, such as Jérôme Meizoz, do see authorship as plural, but are careful to resituate the work of art within the contexts, cultural territories and textual rites that make that work possible in the first place (2007, 14). This is precisely the kind of critical work which we have been trying to do in this section.

The origins of Shakespearean appropriation: gaining cultural capital through the work of early readers

The last section of this chapter focuses on the work of actual readers of Shakespeare. Before we examine the traces they left in Shakespeare's books, it might be worth remarking that the First Folio does in fact partly require the active assistance and engagement of its readers. In other words, the fate of the volume relied closely not just on its buyers, but also on its readers. This is made particularly clear in the lines of Heminges and Condell addressed 'To the great Variety of Readers', referring to the book's succession of prefaces and commendatory epistles. The preface seeks explicitly to expand the network of readers *and interpreters* of the text:

> And so we leaue you to other of his Friends, whom if you need, can bee your guides: if you neede them not, you can leade your selues, and others. And such Readers we wish him.
> (Shakespeare 1623, sig. A3r)

The idea, as far as we can tell, is that First Folio readers will encounter other readers in the book's paratext; they in turn will encourage new people to join this prestigious and yet open community of commentators.

Consequently what follows will attempt to show not only what the book brought to readers, but also what they brought to the book, as they took it on numerous personal journeys. The marks that readers left inside their copies can be construed as forms of consumption of the book and as traces of material, intellectual and emotional involvement. In many cases these types of engagement could lead to the construction of yet another author figure. Indeed, as much as readers ventriloquised Shakespeare's writings, they themselves could be ventriloquised by them.

Traditionally looked upon as marks of desecration, graffiti in most instances intriguingly celebrate the work and, at the same time, their own authors. It is common to find parts of the preliminary epistles in honour of Shakespeare copied out by readers in the opening pages of the folios (as, for instance, in FSL Fo. 1 no. 28; Fig. 1.4).

What can be regarded as penmanship exercises or pen trials may be seen either as attempts at self-expression sparked by Shakespeare's work or as confident assertions by extremely literate individuals of their mastery of the written medium in a rare book (Scott-Warren 2010, 368). In FSL Fo. 1 no. 32, on the page bearing Hugh Holland's epitaph 'Vpon the Lines and Life of the Famous Scenicke Poet, Master William Shakespeare', one late seventeenth-century reader has made an incomplete (and possibly half-humorous) attempt at self-expression:

> margarit by is my name and
> with my peen I wright this same
> and if my peen hade ben better
> i sholld

To the memory of my beloued,
The AVTHOR
Mr. WILLIAM SHAKESPEARE:
AND
what he hath left vs.

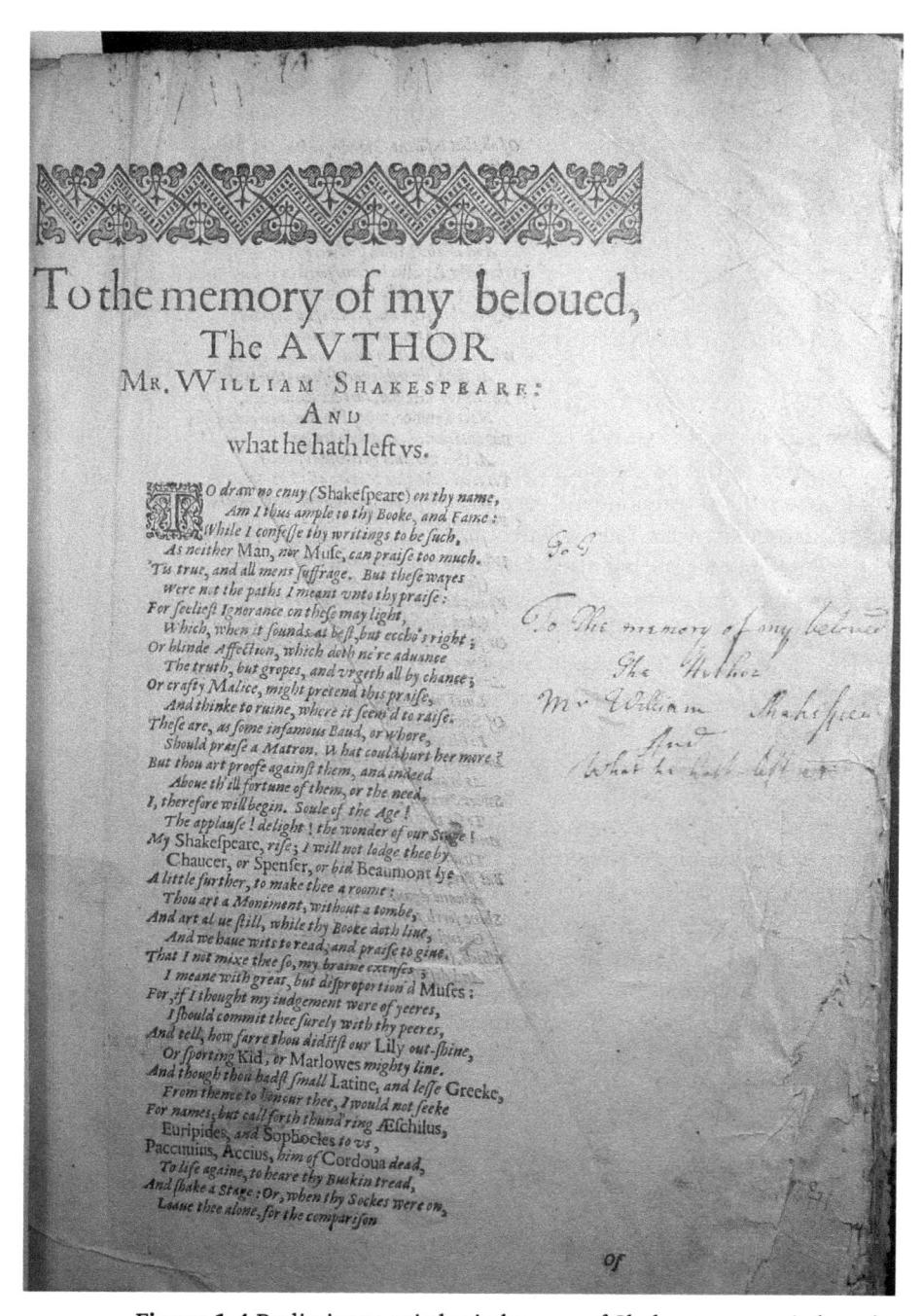

To draw no enuy (Shakespeare) on thy name,
Am I thus ample to thy Booke, and Fame:
While I confesse thy writings to be such,
As neither Man, nor Muse, can praise too much.
'Tis true, and all mens suffrage. But these wayes
Were not the paths I meant vnto thy praise:
For seeliest Ignorance on these may light,
Which, when it sounds at best, but eccho's right;
Or blinde Affection, which doth ne're aduance
The truth, but gropes, and vrgeth all by chance;
Or crafty Malice, might pretend this praise,
And thinke to ruine, where it seem'd to raise.
These are, as some infamous Baud, or whore,
Should praise a Matron. What could hurt her more?
But thou art proofe against them, and indeed
Aboue th'ill fortune of them, or the need.
I, therefore will begin. Soule of the Age!
The applause! delight! the wonder of our Stage!
My Shakespeare, rise; I will not lodge thee by
Chaucer, or Spenser, or bid Beaumont lye
A little further, to make thee a roome:
Thou art a Moniment, without a tombe,
And art aliue still, while thy Booke doth liue,
And we haue wits to read, and praise to giue.
That I not mixe thee so, my braine excuses;
I meane with great, but disproportion'd Muses:
For, if I thought my iudgement were of yeeres,
I should commit thee surely with thy peeres,
And tell, how farre thou didst our Lily out-shine,
Or sporting Kid, or Marlowes mighty line.
And though thou hadst small Latine, and lesse Greeke,
From thence to honour thee, I would not seeke
For names; but call forth thund'ring Æschilus,
Euripides, and Sophocles to vs,
Paccuuius, Accius, him of Cordoua dead,
To life againe, to heare thy Buskin tread,
And shake a Stage: Or, when thy Sockes were on,
Leaue thee alone, for the comparison

Of

Figure 1.4 Preliminary epistles in honour of Shakespeare copied out by readers, Fo. 1 no. 28. By permission of the Folger Library.

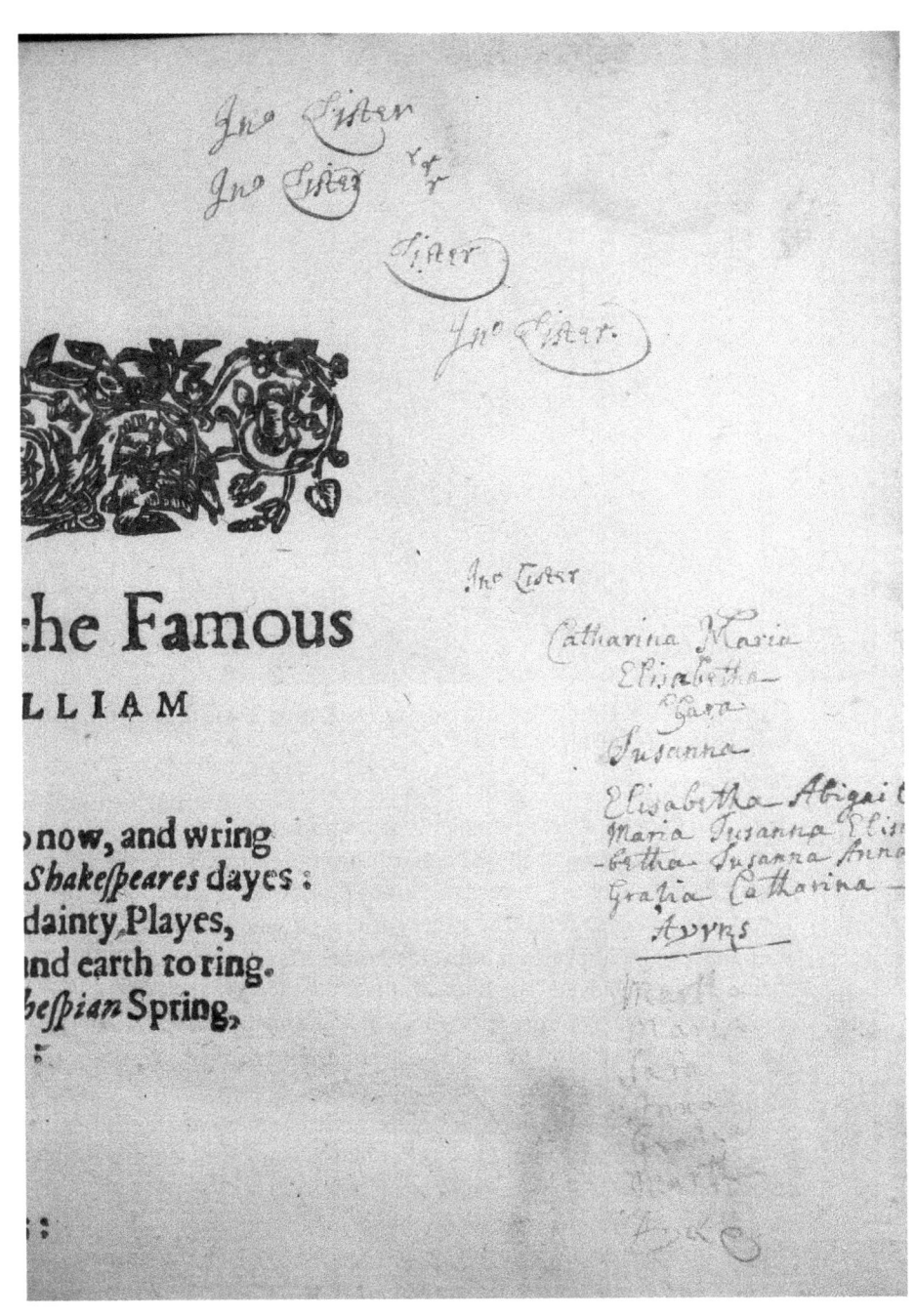

Figure 1.5 John Lister signatures in Fo. 1 no. 70. By permission of the Folger Library.

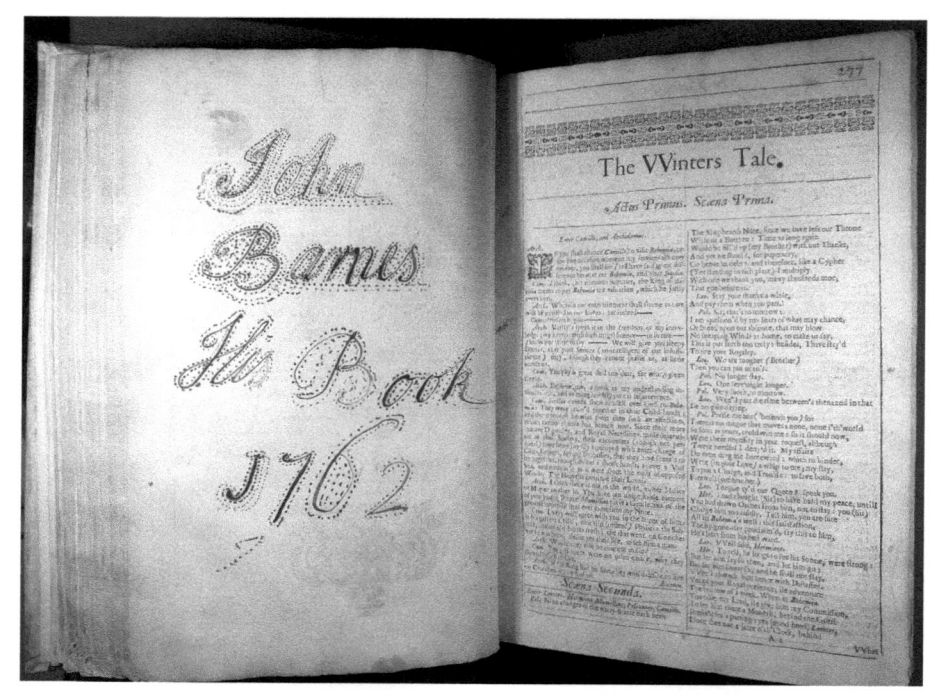

Figure 1.6 Leaf facing the title page of *The Winter's Tale* in Fo. 3 no. 8. By permission of the Folger Library.

In FSL Fo. 1 no. 54, a late seventeenth-century reader by the name of Olivea Cotton signed her name above Leonard Digges's epitaph to Shakespeare: 'To the Memorie of the Deceased Author Maister W. Shakespeare'. John Lister – another reader of the same period – signed his name in a large italic hand just above Ben Jonson's homage to Shakespeare ('To the memory of my beloved, The Author') in FSL Fo. 1 no. 70 (Fig. 1.5). Lister also inscribed his signature in elegantly calligraphed letters no fewer than five times near the Hugh Holland epitaph ('Upon the lines and life of the famous scenicke Poet, Master William Shakespeare').[4]

No less obsessive and no less determined to leave an imprint in his own edition, Joseph Batailhey, another late seventeenth-century reader, signed his name on almost every play of FSL Fo. 1 no. 76.

Many of these inscriptions can be seen as traces of the way in which culture operates as a cycle. As I have suggested, the Shakespeare folios in particular create their own sense of prestige through their format and the manner in which their prefatory material has been configured. To write in such a book was for many early modern individuals a source

Figure 1.7 Third flyleaf of Fo. 1 no. 45. By permission of the Folger Library.

of prestige and is in some regards empowering ('what one is depends on what one owns', De Grazia 1996, 34). But such writing – often self-consciously ostentatious – inevitably adds further prestige to the book. It is a conscious or subconscious message to other potential readers and is a way to authorise Shakespeare's works.

In a number of folios, individuals celebrate Shakespeare and simultaneously make a show of their own intellectual confidence gained by their ownership of the book. Some of the graffiti in early Shakespeare editions could in fact be considered to be forms of life-writing. In the case of the Shakespeare folios, the books' physical size combined with their prestige as cultural objects and as expensive commercial items could lead at times to extravagant expressions of the self. For instance, in a later Folio (Shakespeare 1664; FSL Fo. 3 no. 8), the blank page that occurs after *Twelfth Night* and opposite the opening page of *The Winter's Tale* is entirely covered with the inscription 'John Barnes His Book 1762', drawn in ink and with decorative dots (Shakespeare 1664, sig. Z6r) (Fig. 1.6).

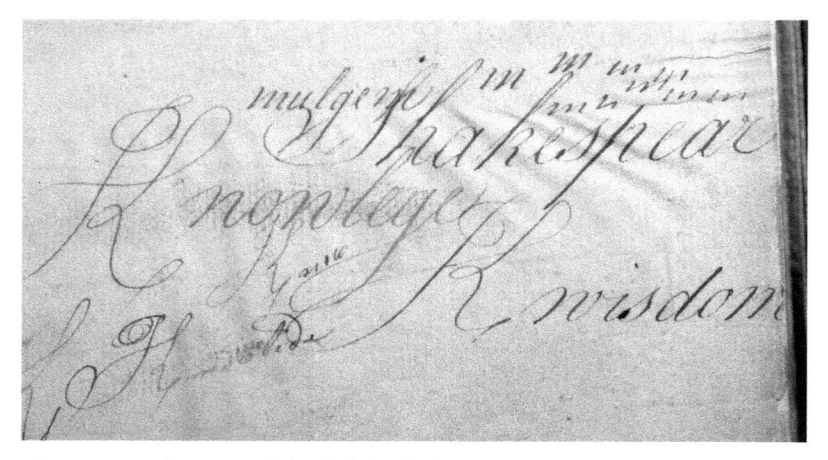

Figure 1.8 Close-up of third flyleaf of Fo. 1 no. 45. By permission of the Folger Library.

On the third flyleaf of FSL Fo. 1 no. 45, 'The incomparable Shakespear' and the dramatist's last name are elegantly calligraphed across the page in an eighteenth-century hand (Fig. 1.7).

Just under these inscriptions, the words 'Knowledge & wisdom' appear (Fig. 1.8).

A reader again celebrates what she or he regards as the intellectually empowering value of Shakespeare's works in FSL Fo. 3 no. 8. On a page of *Romeo and Juliet* (Shakespeare 1664, sig. Kkk5v), the word 'Knowing' has been calligraphed and the almost Cartesian and partly existential phrase 'Knowing so I am' appears on a page of *Macbeth* (Shakespeare 1664, sig. Ooo4v) (Fig. 1.9).

Inspired by the book's preliminaries, readers are tempted to construct a plurality of interpretations which they attribute to the author. Meaning is hence ascribed to the author in the act of engagement with the text – it is not so much a direct outcome of the text. Nevertheless, the name of the author has also a not-so-negligible effect on readers. It gives some unity to a body of otherwise disparate texts and tends to personalise the works. In this sense, '[t]he work presents itself as a metonymic fetish of the person, as a relic endowed with sacredness and treated as such' (Meizoz 2007, 42).[5] Meizoz's definition of the fetishisation of the work of art may of course be applied to Shakespeare – as well as to the way his readers construct him as an author and, as we have observed, authorise his works.

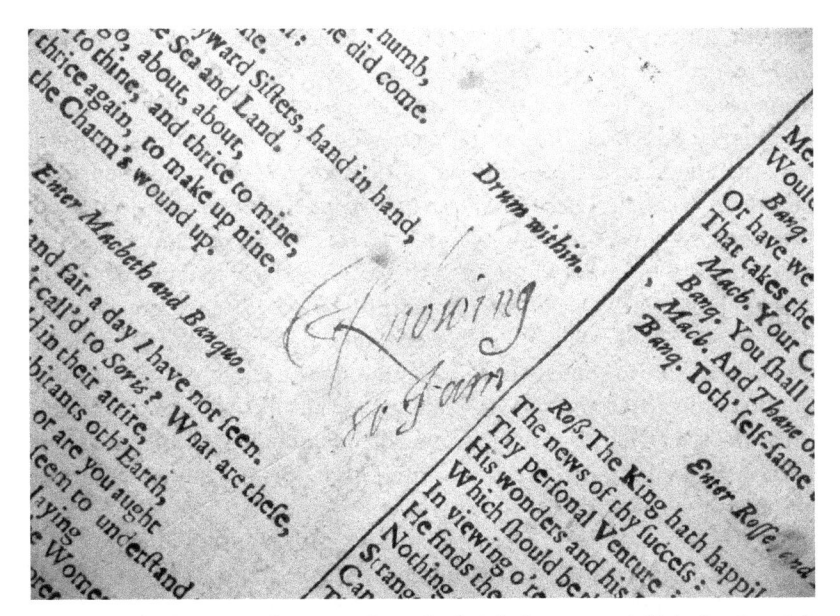

Figure 1.9 Close-up of a page of *Macbeth* (Shakespeare 1664, sig. Ooo4v) in Fo. 3 no. 8. By permission of the Folger Library.

Be that as it may, all sacred territory can be challenged by those who themselves established the boundaries. Readers never form unified communities and have various agendas. Thus one finds early examples of negation and parody of Shakespeare – and of course you only negate or parody what has already high value or is sacred. In a First Folio that was sold in 2006 at Sotheby's in London for 2.8 million pounds (now some 3.1 million euros) is a mischievous note written in an eighteenth-century hand, possibly directed at other readers, left on the last page of *Hamlet* (Shakespeare 1623, sig. qq1v): 'But I desier the readerers mougth [mouth] to kis the wrighteres [writer's] arse'.[6] One can imagine that such a phrase was even more transgressive because it was left in the volume of an already revered and fetishised author.[7]

Conclusion

'There is nothing outside the text,' wrote Jacques Derrida famously in *Of Grammatology* (1997, 158). Often misconstrued, the phrase has been frequently associated with the almost complete lack of interest in the figure of the author during the second half of the twentieth century, especially in the field of literary studies. Derrida never meant that the text should be totally paramount and completely severed from the author. His idea was rather to give readers an almost limitless freedom of interpretation of the text, even if the figure of the author remained what he called – with a degree of regret – 'this indispensable guardrail' (Derrida 1997, 158) that stopped interpretation from straying into nonsense. No one today would contest the importance of the historical or empirical author (even if, in Shakespeare's case, his *identity* is regularly but unconvincingly disputed). Dramatists counted for little in Elizabethan theatre, yet Shakespeare did have a special status – he was, to some extent, a member of the Establishment, as the Chamberlain's Men and the King's Men were hardly obscure companies. Nonetheless, all of this historical fame could not have been perpetuated without his successful entrance into the cultural realm of literary authorship.

The transmutation of the historical author into a cultural and fetishised figure has been the subject of this chapter. What I have tried to highlight is the type of cultural work that was done – and continues to be carried out – to construct Shakespeare as an author. With the preliminaries of his early editions, including the First Folio's fascinating Droeshout portrait (which continues to circulate in our cultures) and the visible and invisible work of several generations of readers, Shakespeare was 'pushed by many hands', to gloss Crites in Dryden's essay *Of Dramatik Poesie* (1668, 9). This great variety of agents and agencies – together with subsequent dramatists, adaptors, stage directors and interpreters – created and disseminated the Shakespeare we are familiar with: the omnipresent, endlessly fascinating and ever fleeting figure who is malleable and transferable to a multiplicity of contexts.

Notes

1. For more information on the design of the picture and its later adjustments see, in particular, Blayney 1991, 18–19; Blake and Lynch 2011, 26–7.
2. For an account of this copy's paratext, see its entry in the Folger Library's online catalogue: http://hamnet.folger.edu/cgi-bin/Pwebrecon.cgi?BBID=97416.
3. Sherwen gives the following reference for the Dryden extracts: 'See his Poems, Vol. II. p. 231. Ed. 1743'.
4. Lister also inscribed some eight female names (possibly family members?) on the same page.
5. Author's translation.
6. Once the property of Dr Williams's Library in London, the Folio is now in private hands in the US.
7. On the First Folio as fetish and on its place within the postmodern capitalist economy see Hooks (2016, 186, 193).

References

Akenside, Mark. 1795. *The Poetical Works of Mark Akenside*. London: printed for C. Cooke.
Barthes, Roland 1975. *S/Z*. Translated by Richard Miller. London: Cape.
Blake, Erin C. and Kathleen Lynch. 2011. 'Looke on his Picture, in his Booke: The Droeshout Portrait on the Title Page'. In *Foliomania! Stories behind Shakespeare's most important book*, edited by Owen Williams and Caryn Lazzuri, 21–31. Washington, D.C.: Folger Shakespeare Library.
Blayney, Peter W. M. 1991. *The First Folio of Shakespeare*. Washington, D.C.: Folger Library Publications.
Bourdieu, Pierre. 1993. 'The Production of belief: Contribution to an economy of symbolic goods'. In *The Field of Cultural Production: Essays on art and literature*, edited by Randal Johnson, 74–111. Cambridge: Polity Press.
Chartier, Roger. 1994. *The Order of Books: Readers, authors, and libraries in Europe between the fourteenth and eighteenth centuries*. Translated by Lydia G. Cochrane. Stanford, CA: Stanford University Press.
De Grazia, Margreta. 1996. 'The ideology of superfluous things: *King Lear* as period piece'. In *Subject and Object in Renaissance Culture*, edited by Margreta De Grazia, Maureen Quilligan and Peter Stallybrass, 17–42. Cambridge: Cambridge University Press.
Derrida, Jacques. 1997. *Of Grammatology. Corrected edition*. Translated by Gayatri Chakravorty Spivak. Baltimore, MD and London: The Johns Hopkins University Press.
Donaldson, Peter S. 2011. 'Shakespeare and media allegory'. In *Shakespeare and Genre: From early modern inheritances to postmodern legacies*, edited by Anthony R. Guneratne, 223–37. Basingstoke: Palgrave Macmillan.
Dryden, John. 1668. *Of Dramatick Poesie, an Essay*. London: Henry Herringman.
Edmondson, Paul and Stanley Wells. 2012. 'Portraits of Shakespeare'. In *Shakespeare, Satire, Academia: Essays in honour of Wolfgang Weiss*, edited by Sonja Fielitz and Uwe Meyer, 1–14. Heidelberg: Winter.
Facebook. 2018. 'William Shakespeare'. Accessed 15 April 2018. https://www.facebook.com/WilliamShakespeareAuthor.
Ferrell, Lori Anne. 2013. 'Extra-illustrating Shakespeare'. *Early Modern Literary Studies: Special Issue 21*. Online: https://extra.shu.ac.uk/emls/si-21/08-Ferrell_ExtraIllustratingShakespeare.htm. Accessed 31 October 2022.
Fineman, Joel. 1981. 'The structure of allegorical desire'. In *Allegory and Representation*, edited by Stephen Greenblatt, 26–60. Baltimore, MD: The Johns Hopkins University Press.
Hooks, Adam G. 2016. 'Afterword: The folio as fetish'. In *The Cambridge Companion to Shakespeare's First Folio*, edited by Emma Smith, 185–96. Cambridge: Cambridge University Press.
Lanier, Douglas. 2014. 'Shakespearean Rhizomatics: Adaptation, ethics, value'. In *Shakespeare and the Ethics of Appropriation. Reproducing Shakespeare: New studies in adaptation and appropriation*, edited by Alexa Huang and Elizabeth Rivlin, 21–40. New York: Palgrave Macmillan.
McHale, Brian. 2015. *The Cambridge Introduction to Postmodernism*. New York: Cambridge University Press.
Meizoz, Jérôme. 2007. *Postures Littéraires. Mises en scène modernes de l'auteur*. Geneva: Slatkine Érudition.
Schoenbaum, Samuel. 1970. *Shakespeare's Lives*. Oxford: Oxford University Press.
Scott-Warren, Jason. 2010. 'Reading graffiti in the early modern book', *Huntington Library Quarterly* 73: 363–81.
Shakespeare, William. 1623. *Mr. VVilliam Shakespeares comedies, histories, & tragedies: Published according to the true originall copies* (The First Folio). London: Printed by Isaac Iaggard and Ed. Blount.
Shakespeare, William. 1632. *Mr. VVilliam Shakespeares Comedies, Histories, and Tragedies. The second impression* (The Second Folio). London: Printed by Tho[mas] Cotes.
Shakespeare, William. 1664. *Mr. William Shakespear's Comedies, Histories, and Tragedies. Published according to the true Original Copies. The third impression* (The Third Folio, 1664 edition). London: Printed for P. C.
Schlueter, June. 2017. 'Facing Shakespeare: The Martin Droeshout engraving', *Medieval and Renaissance Drama in England* 30: 17–35.

2
Religious conflict and the return of the author in early modern dramatic paratexts
Jeanne Mathieu

> Which thing our Author marking well, […]:
> And as he mused in his minde, immediately arose,
> An History of late yeares don, which might as he suppose,
> Styrre up their myndes to godlynes, […].
>
> (Woodes 1952, 32)

Introduction

'The question of the author has never ceased to haunt the critics,'[1] Jean-Christophe Mayer writes in *Shakespeare et la Postmodernité* (2012, 6). Indeed since Roland Barthes expounded his theory of the death of the author and Michel Foucault, reacting to Barthes' theory, coined the term 'author function' in the 1960s, various critics have tried to address these two concepts, be it to confirm, refute or amend them. In 1968 Roland Barthes declared the author 'dead'. He summarised his theory in a seminal passage:

> [W]riting is the destruction of every voice, of every point of origin. Writing is that neutral, composite, oblique space where our subject slips away, the negative where all identity is lost, starting with the very identity of the body writing. […] As soon as a fact is *narrated* no longer with a view to acting directly on reality but intransitively, that is to say, finally outside of any function other than that of the very practice of the symbol itself, this disconnection occurs, the voice loses its origin, the author enters into his own death, writing begins. […] The author is a modern figure, a product of our society insofar as, emerging from the Middle Ages with English empiricism, French rationalism and the

personal faith of the Reformation, it discovered the prestige of the individual, of, as it is more nobly put, the 'human person'.

(Barthes 1977, 142–3)

A year later Michel Foucault expounded his concept of the 'author function'. According to him, the author, or the writer, did not exist as such before the eighteenth century. Despite this, Foucault remarked that

[d]iscourses are objects of appropriation. The form of ownership from which they spring is of a rather particular type, one that has been codified for many years. We should note that, historically, this type of ownership has always been subsequent to what one might call penal appropriation. Texts, books, and discourses really began to have authors (other than mythical, sacralized and sacralizing figures) to the extent that authors became subject to punishment, that is, the extent that discourses could be transgressive.

(Foucault 1998, 211–12)

The last word of this quotation, 'transgressive', seems to fit perfectly to describe both the period of the Renaissance on which this chapter focuses and the medium of drama it examines.

Confessional antagonism is at the very core of the period, forcing those confronted with a choice to take, at least in public, a clear and unambiguous stand. The playwrights and authors of the period had to position themselves ideologically. To do so, they had two options: either they appeared directly in the texts, and more particularly in the paratexts, of their plays, or they constructed a *persona* to speak in their stead. This distinction between the empirical and the fictional author is crucial, and this chapter intends to discover whether one of these prevails or both of them coexist in early modern drama.

Nonetheless, if the author is etymologically the one who causes the text to emerge, the paratext fulfils the same function. The paratext has often been discarded as a 'non-organic' element (McCaulley 1917, 253) of dramatic texts. Nevertheless, in a study dealing with prologues and epilogues in Renaissance drama, Douglas Bruster and Robert Weimann conclude that 'something like 40 per cent of the surviving playtexts feature a prologue' (2004, 3). Interestingly, many early modern prologues contain occurrences of the words 'author' or 'poet'. The word 'poet', for instance, appears in Ben Jonson's *Every Man in His Humour* (published 1601). There is a reference to 'our doubtful author' in Jonson's *Cynthia's Revels* (published 1601), to 'our author' in his *Poetaster* (published 1602) and to 'our poet' in his *Volpone* (1606), to mention just a few examples.

This chapter aims to go beyond the theory of the death of the author by trying to discover how empirical authors were constructed as literary figures and by looking at the paratexts of their plays. It follows Gérard Genette's definition of the term:

> the paratext is […] a *threshold*, or – a word Borges used apropos of a preface – a 'vestibule' that offers the world at large the possibility of either stepping inside or turning back. It is an 'undefined zone' between the inside and the outside, a zone without any hard and fast boundary on either the inward side (turned toward the text) or the outward side (turned toward the world's discourse about the text), an edge, or, as Philippe Lejeune put it, 'a fringe of the printed text which in reality controls one's whole reading of the text.' Indeed, this fringe, always the conveyor of a commentary that is authorial or more or less legitimated by the author, constitutes a zone between text and off-text, a zone not only of transition but also of *transaction*: a privileged place of a pragmatics and a strategy.
> (Genette 1997, 2)

My approach also takes into account that paratexts include 'those liminal devices and conventions, both within the book (peritext) and outside it (epitext), that mediate the book to the reader: titles and subtitles, pseudonyms, forewords, dedications, epigraphs, prefaces, intertitles, notes, epilogues, and afterwords' (Macksey 1997, xviii). However, contrary to what Gérard Genette did in his groundbreaking study, this chapter pays attention to the ways in which this wide array of paratextual material reflects historical changes – more particularly the confessional conflict. Its methodology consists in analysing historical and literary elements and intertwining them, referring at times to the author's biography.

The chapter discusses eight published plays which include paratexts and echoing issues related to the sixteenth- and seventeenth-century religious conflict. These plays, written for the public stage, can be defined as 'new media' of sorts; they were written at moments of intense domestic and international tension between Protestants and Catholics. The following analysis will mainly focus on Barnabe Barnes's *The Devil's Charter* (1607), Thomas Dekker's *The Whore of Babylon* (1607), Thomas Middleton's *A Game at Chess* (1624) and Nathaniel Woodes's *The Conflict of Conscience* (1581). *The Jew of Malta* by Christopher Marlowe (c.1589–90), Samuel Rowley's *When You See Me You Know Me* (1605), William Shakespeare's *Henry VIII* (1613) and *Henry VI Part I* (c.1592) will also be briefly mentioned.

Analysing these plays, this chapter examines the extent to which the figure of the identified author of these plays may resurface when religious issues are dealt with. Theological controversies and religious plurality may account for the emergence of the author. To what extent did early modern playwrights need to assume an ideological stance leading to their emergence as empirical authors? Another issue discussed in this chapter is the relationship between authorship and authority. To what extent does the author figure, in these liminal texts, cast himself as a source of authority and thus manipulate the audience? In conclusion, the chapter explores the relationship of the author to other agents involved in the publication of plays. To what extent is the birth of the author a mere part of the birth of the whole industry?

The return of the author: comments on religious issues

All the examined plays address religious issues in one way or another. Their authors appear to have taken the representation of highly significant events forming the plots of their plays, such as the assassination attempts against Elizabeth I or the defeat of the Spanish Armada, as their responsibility or even moral duty. For instance, Thomas Dekker's address to the reader ('Lectori') as he introduces the first edition of *The Whore of Babylon* (1607) starts with a very significant sentence:

> The generall scope of this drammaticall poem is to set forth (in Tropicall and shadowed collours) the greatnes, magnanimity, constancy, clemency and other the incomparable heroical vertues of our late Queene.
>
> (Dekker 1964, 497)

This sentence draws the reader's attention to the explicit political intention of the playwright, the 'generall scope' of his drama. At the end of his address to the reader Dekker admits that 'I may, (by some more curious in censure, then found in iudgement), be critically taxed' (1964, 497). What is worth noting here is the element of self-fashioning of the historical author. The playwright gets involved thanks to the use of the pronoun 'I' and takes responsibility for what the readers are about to dip into: a fiercely anti-Catholic play. The more the reader advances through the text, the more the empirical author seems to be present. The address proceeds from outlining the scope of a 'drammaticall poem' to the assertion of the playwright's identity. He fashions himself as the one taking responsibility for the text content and its eventual flaws.

Moreover, in his address Dekker contributes to the establishment of the dichotomy between Catholics and Protestants, very much present in 1607 and clearly visible in the anti-Catholic legislation passed after the Gunpowder Plot. Indeed, religious dichotomy is apparent in the very words Dekker uses to describe his goal in writing the play. He wants

> to set forth [...] the greatnes, magnanimity, constancy, clemency and other the incomparable heroical vertues of our late Queene and (on the contrary part) the inueterate malice, treasons, machinations, vnderminings, & continual blody stratagems, of that purple whore of Roome [...].
> (Dekker 1964, 497)

The perfect balance created in this sentence by the use of five adjectives to describe Elizabeth I, followed by five others, far more derogatory, to describe the Church of Rome, emphasises the idea of a dividing line being drawn between the two confessions. The playwright also defines his role a few lines later when he describes his task:

> In sayling vpon which two contrary Seas, you may obserue, on how direct a line I haue steered my course.
> (Dekker 1964, 497)

Such a position is completely consistent with other texts written by Dekker, including *The Double PP* (1606), the pamphlet on which *The Whore of Babylon* is based.

The paratext can thus become a *locus* where the author may insert a judgement on the story being told or on the characters being portrayed on stage. The figure of the author and that of the Chorus merge. The adjectives in paratextual material are of prime importance, often used to express what has been termed subjectivity. In a chapter entitled 'Adjectives and subjectivity', Angeliki Athanasiadou remarks:

> The choice of an adjective use in a certain position (and not only in the premodifier but also in the postmodifier and the predicative position) seems to be associated with the viewpoint of a speaker.
> (2006, 210)

A closer look at the full titles of the plays under study reveals that the use of adjectives was very widespread. This can be seen in Samuel Rowley's *When You See Me You Know Me*, which relates the reign of Henry VIII and whose full title reads: *When You See Me You Know Me; or the Famous Chronicle Historie of Henry VIII, with the birth and vertuous life of Edward Prince of Wales.*

Another significant example is the full title of William Shakespeare's *Henry VI Part I*, which reads: *The First part of the Contention betwixt the two famous Houses of Yorke and Lancaster, with the death of the good Duke Humphrey: And the banishment and death of the Duke of Suffolke, and the Tragicall end of the proud Cardinall of VVinchester, vvith the notable rebellion of Iacke Cade: And the Duke of Yorkes first claime vnto the Crowne.*

In these two long titles, the words 'virtuous,' 'good' and 'proud' seem to point out the commitment of the author to express a judgement on the characters of his play. Even though this can also be seen as part of a marketing strategy, titles may become privileged places in which the playwright comments upon the action or the characters of the play; they are spaces where his subjectivity or presence can clearly be felt. Therefore he becomes a subject to whom intentionality can be granted. This process can best be seen in Nathaniel Woodes's title, which summarises the whole story: *An Excellent New Comedie intituled: The Conflict of Conscience Contayninge a Most Lamentable Example of the Dolefull Desperation of a Miserable Worldlinge, termed, by the name of Philologvs, who forsook the trueth of Gods Gospel, for feare of the losse of lyfe, & worldly goods*. The adjectives 'most lamentable', 'dolefull' and 'miserable' reveal the presence of the author and of a moral judgement that is pronounced on Philologus's story. This is reinforced by the indication of Nathaniel Woodes's occupation on the title page of the play, stating that the story was '*compiled by Nathaniel Woodes, Minister in Norwich*' (Woodes 1952, 30).

Moreover, the historical period dealt with must also be taken into account. The early modern period was a time when, especially in these moments of crisis, strict censorship was a factor that shaped the English print market and prompted authors to invent strategies of disengagement from their plays. This is the case in Dekker's address to the readers. Indeed, he seems somehow to qualify his earlier clear-cut opinion when he remarks:

> of such a scantling are my words set downe, that neither the one party speakes too much, not the other (in opposition) too little in their owne defence.
>
> (Dekker 1964, 497)

What emerges here is the image of a neutral, obfuscated writer who takes no stance on the religious feud.

Another tool used by Thomas Dekker in order to minimise the role of authorship is the allegory which can be said to shape the whole play. On the one hand, Titania represents Elizabeth I and Fairie Land stands for England. On the other hand, the Empress of Babylon stands for Rome and the papacy. Dekker himself draws the reader's attention to that fact when he admits that he represented the religious conflict 'in Tropicall and shadowed collours' (1964, 497). The oxymoron 'shadowed collours' perfectly symbolises the ambiguous place of the author in this text. The fact that transgressive elements (especially regarding the idealised representation of Elizabeth I on stage) are present in the text encourages the author to withdraw from his text using literary strategies of obfuscation. However, at the same time he reaffirms his importance and the mastery of his art, as the word 'Tropicall' indicates. Not only does this word conjure up the idea of a tropical place (and indeed the play is set in a distant allegorical country), but it is also reminiscent of the word 'trope', which is linked to rhetoric and to the art of literature.

The transgressive nature of these plays seems to be of the utmost importance: it points back to Foucault, who envisaged the birth of the legally recognised author at the time when authors could be punished for what they wrote. Interestingly, Thomas Middleton may well have been imprisoned for his play *A Game at Chess*, which was performed in 1624. *The Oxford Dictionary of National Biography* mentions that

> Middleton went into hiding, pursued by a warrant; his son, Edward, was arrested and brought before the privy council; Middleton himself claimed, in a poem to King James, that he was imprisoned 'in the Fleet'. None of his extant plays can be convincingly dated after August 1624, and he was probably released on condition that he stopped writing for the stage.
>
> (Taylor 2008)

Taking part in a religious debate or commenting upon religious issues therefore seems to reveal traces of the empirical author because the presence of a judgement goes hand in hand with subjectivity. The emergence of the early modern author was thus significantly influenced by confessional and religious issues, and his role was altered and redefined. Yet revealing oneself could also mean assuming responsibility for the content of the play and could consequently be hazardous. Nevertheless, this threat did not lead to the disappearance of the figure of the author. On the contrary: his role was reasserted through a renewed need for control and authority.

An ever-increasing need for control and authority

In order to assert their authority over the texts they were writing, playwrights started to design a poetics of religious conflict. In the paratexts under study, they constantly emphasise that it is the responsibility of the poet to represent religious dissension. Their main purpose was to appropriate historical or topical elements used to create their own works of art. Their role as playwrights is highlighted when they state that they are capable of transforming serious matters into something entertaining. This is the idea expressed in the prologue to *The Whore of Babylon*, used to assert the powers of the playright:

> wee present / Matter aboue the vulgar Argument: / Yet drawne so liuely, that the weakest eye, […] may reach the mistery: / What in it is most graue, will most delight.
> (Dekker 1964, 497)

The discrepancy introduced by the use of two antonyms at the end of this quotation ('graue' and 'delight') shows that the playwright's task has been successfully carried out in adapting serious matters for the stage, thus achieving a literary *discordia concors* – a perfect balance of opposites. The same idea is to be found throughout Dekker's address to the reader. Significantly he states:

> I falsifie the account of time, and set not down Occurrents, according to their true succession, […] I write as a Poet, not as an Historian, and […] these two doe not liue vnder one law.
> (Dekker 1964, 497)

In this passage, Dekker accepts responsibility for any change he had to make in order to adapt his sources to fit his poetic licence. He therefore appears as a dramatist writing consciously as a playwright and shaping his identity as a poet thanks to the representation of the religious conflict on the public stage. What comes forth here is the construction of the author as a literary figure. The same idea runs again through 'The Prologue' to *The Conflict of Conscience*, where the changes introduced by the playwright are praised:

> And though the Historie of it selfe, be too too, dolorus,
> And would constraine a man with teares of blood, his cheekes to wett,

> Yet to refresh the myndes of them that be the Auditors,
> Our Author intermixed hath, in places fitt and meete,
> Some honest mirth, yet alwaies ware, DECORVM, to exceede:
> (Woodes 1952, 34)

The presence of two antithetical lexical fields, one of sadness, the other of happiness, underlines the changes needed to adapt to and entertain the audience. The role of the playwright is of prime importance; he is the one responsible for making these alterations 'in places fitt and meete'. This is also linked to the liminal position of the Prologue and eases transition between the real world and the world of the play. As Douglas Bruster and Robert Weimann argue, 'playing and playgoing at this time involved a powerful rite of passage facilitated and described by the prologue figure and by the performance of the prologue itself' (2004, viii).

A final example of this process of change and adaptation for the stage can be found in Thomas Middleton's *Game at Chess*, where the playwright asserts in the Prologue:

> What of the Game, cald Chesse-play can be made
> To make a Stage-Play, shall this day be plaid.
> (Middleton 1993, 63)

Even though the author is not directly mentioned in this example, he is the one who ensures that this transition from the 'Chesse-play' to the 'Stage-Play' is made smoothly thanks to his skilful use of poetry. He is the one who manages to turn a stage into a chessboard. As the Epilogue spoken at Court to *The Jew of Malta* by Christopher Marlowe makes clear:

> And if ought here offend your eare or sight,
> We onely Act, and Speake, what others write.
> (Marlowe 2008, 322)

Moreover, the poet can also use his power to control and manipulate the readership. As Helen Smith and Louise Wilson argue:

> paratextual elements are in operation all the way through the reader's experience of the text, not merely at the start, and they continuously inform the process of reading, offering multiple points of entry, interpretations, and contestations.
> (2011, 6)

Jean-Christophe Mayer also acknowledges the fact that paratextual elements can be used to influence the reception of the play (2012, 151). This seems to be one of the purposes of the list of characters in *The Whore of Babylon*. The first edition was published while Dekker was still alive, and he was probably involved in the editing process. The allegory on which the play is based has been mentioned. Yet in the list of characters the veil of the allegory is lifted since the identity of the two main characters is revealed. It undermines the allegory and guides the readers towards a more topical reading. The readers are told that they are about to read a play featuring 'Titania the Fairie Queene: vnder whom is figured our late Queene Elizabeth' and 'Th'Empresse of Babylon: vnder whom is figured *Rome*' (Dekker 1964, 497). Significantly, these two characters are the only ones to be linked explicitly to the readers' familiar, contemporary world. The readers are thus encouraged to understand the play as a representation of a conflict between the two antagonistic political powers and religious faiths of the period. The paratext plays an important role in shaping expectations and responses to the play. As Gérard Genette explains:

> Indeed, this fringe, always the conveyor of a commentary that is authorial or more or less legitimated by the author, constitutes a zone between text and off-text, a zone not only of transition but also of transaction: a privileged place of pragmatics and a strategy of an influence on the public, an influence that – whether well or poorly understood and achieved – is at the service of a better reception for the text and a more pertinent reading of it (more pertinent, of course, in the eyes of the author and his allies).
>
> (Genette 1997, 2)

Paratexts can be used to encourage a particular reading of the play or to manipulate the audience or reader. However, as my point regarding the list of characters in the printed play suggests, different groups of people were involved in the production and reception of a play. In the texts dealing with religious controversies, the rise of the author went hand in hand with the rise of many other agents.

Beyond the author: religious conflict, paratextual elements and multiple births

Another part of a book where the playwright could appear as part of a group involved in its publication is the dedication. Indeed, according to

Genette, dedications are almost invariably from the author (1997, 2). At the very beginning of *The Devil's Charter*, Barnabe Barnes penned a dedication to two men: William Herbert (3rd Earl of Pembroke) and Sir William Pope:

> To the honorable and his very deare friends, Sir William Herbert, and Sir William Pope Knights, associates in the noble order of the Bathe. Barnabe Barnes consecrateth his loue. Noble Gentlemen, your loue towards mee (so long time, and in so great measure continued by you, not merited by me) did tie so firme a knotte vpon the band of my dutie towards both of you, that I have lincked you both great friends in the patronage of this little Booke. And I stay well assured, that of your good affection you would in any reasonable course willingly protect him, that writte it, whose Penne and the direction thereof, with all his best faculties, hee sincerely deuoteth to your seruice, still resting yours most assured, faithfull and affectionate: Bar. Barnes.
>
> (Barnes 1970, III)

What seems most important in this dedication is the idea of protection that the two men can provide for the empirical playwright. The need for protection testifies to the fact that playwrights were responsible for the content of their texts and could be punished, which brings us back to Foucault and encourages us to make a distinction between the empirical playwright and the implicit 'author function'. This dedication thus bears witness both to the birth of the author and, as a result, to the importance of literary patronage. Moreover, from its onset, the book is placed under the authority or protection of the Protestant faith – or, at least, of an anti-Catholic position. Indeed, both William Herbert and Sir William Pope were linked to the Protestant cause. The former 'had long been associated with the anti-Spanish "protestant" faction at court' (Stater 2008), while the latter was a man whose family acquired wealth during the dissolution of the monasteries between 1536 and 1540 (Davidson and Sgroi 2010). As Genette concludes:

> The dedication always is a matter of demonstration, ostentation, exhibition: it proclaims a relationship, whether intellectual or personal, actual or symbolic, and this proclamation is always at the service of the work, as a reason for elevating the work's standing or as a theme for commentary.
>
> (1997, 135)

Finally, the visual paratext has to be taken into account. When the book was published prior to a playwright's death, the paratext could also be used to convey a religious message. *A Game at Chess* is a particularly significant example, since, as the *Oxford Dictionary of National Biography* observes, it 'was the first single play printed with engraved title-pages' (Taylor 2008). And, as Genette observes, 'once the possibilities of the cover were discovered, they seem to have been exploited very rapidly' (1997, 23). The illustration on the title page shows a visual representation of the play, bringing the idea of religious dispute to the fore.

The engraving is divided into two parts. In the upper section, the two factions are represented and the symmetry of the two sides is striking. The Black King, the Black Queen, the Black Duke and the Fat Bishop, representing the Catholics, are seated on the left-hand side; the White King, the White Queen, the White Duke and the White Bishop are seated on the right-hand side. All the characters are facing their counterparts, as if positioned for a duel.

In the lower part of the engraving, three characters are portrayed. The treachery of the Black House, a moral feature constantly emphasised in the text, is symbolised by the letter given by the Black Knight to the Fat Bishop. The caption reads 'A letter from his Holynesse'. This highlights the idea of a subterranean, or clandestine, plot being fomented by the Catholics; the political influence of the Church of Rome is indeed shown throughout the play. The end of the conflict is also suggested in this engraving, thanks to the words attributed to the White Knight: 'Chesse mate by discouery' and to the bag visible in the background. The bag, symbolising Hell, contains three defeated Black characters. Thus Middleton and the engraver ensured that both the dispute and the final victory of the Protestant side were made apparent on the title page of the play.

Conclusion

'[I]t is language which speaks, not the author,' Roland Barthes writes (1977, 143). Nevertheless, at the end of our analysis, we are very much tempted to qualify this judgement. The paratext is a liminal element thanks to which the historical playwright was able to present his religious views. The author may appear and leave traces of his religious commitment in these short texts. At the same time, he can also appear behind a mask as a mere construct.

However, the paratext is a place where the author may not be the only one expressing himself: other agents may also leave traces of their religious commitment. The cases of dedications in *The Devil's Charter* and engravings in *A Game at Chess* have been analysed in this chapter.

Finally, the paratext is still used today as a way to make demands, whether these be religious or social. For instance, in his 2014 production of *Henry VI* for the Festival of Avignon in France, which was marked by social conflict, the director, Thomas Jolly, decided to add one character to the play: a rhapsode who came on stage at the end of each of the three parts of the play, as a kind of epilogue, to reaffirm the claims of the actors in terms of social reforms. Thus Genette's definition of the paratext – 'what enables a text to become a book' (1997, 1) – may be amended: the paratext may also enable a play to become a performance. As Genette pointed out himself: 'valid or not, the author's point of view is part of the paratextual performance, sustains it, inspires it, anchors it' (1997, 308).

Note

1   Translated by the author.

References

Athanasiadou, Angeliki. 2006. 'Adjectives and subjectivity'. In *Subjectification: Various paths to subjectivity*, edited by Angeliki Athanasiadou, Costas Canakis and Bert Cornillie, 209–39. Berlin: Mouton de Gruyter.
Barnes, Barnabe. 1970. *The Devil's Charter* (1607). New York: AMS Press.
Barthes, Roland. 1977. 'The death of the author' (1968). In *Image Music Text*, selected and translated by Stephen Heath, 142–8. London: Fontana Press.
Bruster, Douglas and Robert Weimann. 2004. *Prologues to Shakespeare's Theatre: Performance and liminality in early modern drama*. London: Routledge.
Davidson, Alan and Rosemary Sgroi. 2010. 'POPE, Sir William (1596–1624), of Cogges, Oxon'. In *History of Parliament Online. Volume 1604–1629*. Accessed 29 April 2021. http://www.historyofparliamentonline.org/volume/1604-1629/member/pope-sir-william-1596-1624.
Dekker, Thomas. 1964. *The Whore of Babylon* (1607). In *The Dramatic Works*, vol. 2, edited by Fredson Bowers, 491–591. Cambridge: Cambridge University Press.
Foucault, Michel. 1998. 'What is an author?' Translated by Josué V. Harari. In *Aesthetics, Method, and Epistemology, Essential Works of Michel Foucault 1954–1984*, vol. 2, edited by James D. Faubion, translated by Robert Hurley and others, 205–22. New York: The New Press.
Genette, Gérard. 1997. *Paratexts: Thresholds of interpretation*. Translated by Jane E. Lewin. Cambridge: Cambridge University Press.
Macksey, Richard. 1997. 'Foreword'. In Gérard Genette, *Paratexts: Thresholds of interpretation*, translated by Jane E. Lewin, xi–xxii. Cambridge: Cambridge University Press.
Marlowe, Christopher. 2008. *The Jew of Malta* (c.1589–90). In *Doctor Faustus and Other Plays*, edited by David Bevington and Eric Rasmussen, 247–322. Oxford: Oxford University Press.
Mayer, Jean-Christophe. 2012. *Shakespeare et la Postmodernité: essais sur l'auteur, le religieux, l'histoire et le lecteur*. Bern: Peter Lang.
McCaulley, Martha G. 1917. 'Functions and content of the prologue, chorus and other non-organic elements in English drama, from the beginnings to 1642'. In *Studies in English Drama: First Series*, edited by Allison Gaw, 161–258. New York: D. Appleton and Co.

Middleton, Thomas. 1993. *A Game at Chess* (1624). Edited by Trevor H. Howard-Hill. Manchester: Manchester University Press.

Rowley, Samuel. 1970. *When You See Me You Know Me* (1605). New York: AMS Press.

Shakespeare, William. 2008. *The First Part of Henry the Sixth* (1592). In *The Norton Shakespeare: Based on the Oxford Edition*. Second Edition, general editor Stephen Greenblatt, 475–538. New York: Norton.

Smith, Helen and Louise Wilson. 2011. 'Introduction'. In *Renaissance Paratexts*, edited by Helen Smith and Louise Wilson, 1–14. Cambridge: Cambridge University Press.

Stater, Victor. 2008. 'Herbert, William, third earl of Pembroke (1580–1630)'. In *Oxford Dictionary of National Biography Online*. Edited by Sir David Cannadine. Oxford: Oxford University Press. Accessed 12 May 2018. https://www.oxforddnb.com/view/10.1093/ref:odnb/9780198614128.001.0001/odnb-9780198614128-e-13058.

Taylor, Gary. 2008. 'Middleton, Thomas (*bap.* 1580, *d.* 1627)'. In *Oxford Dictionary of National Biography Online*. Edited by Sir David Cannadine. Oxford: Oxford University Press. Accessed 12 May 2018. http://www.oxforddnb.com/view/article/18682.

Woodes, Nathaniel. 1952. *The Conflict of Conscience* (1581). Edited by Herbert Davis and F. P. Wilson. Oxford: Malone Society.

3
'Many more remains of ancient genius': approaches to authorship in the Ossian Controversy
Petra Johana Poncarová

The 'author function', as Michel Foucault outlines it, characterises 'the mode of existence, circulation, and functioning of certain discourses in society'. It does not 'refer purely and simply to a real individual, since it can give rise simultaneously to several selves, several subject-positions that can be occupied by different classes of individuals' (Foucault 1998, 211, 216). While Foucault acknowledges that 'it would be ridiculous to deny the existence of individuals who write, and invent', he asserts that 'some time, at least, the individual who sits down to write a text, at the edge of which lurks a possible œuvre, resumes the functions of the author' (Foucault 1972, 222). These observations provide a useful point of departure for considering one of the most heated debates about authorship in the history of European literature which has been going on for more than 250 years: the controversy concerning the poems of Ossian.

This chapter seeks to examine the controversy from the point of view of authorship, focusing on the arguments which have been used in the debate. It explores the approaches to authorship and authenticity as well as to related topics, such as literary forgery. It exposes the ways in which approaches to authorship changed throughout the eighteenth, nineteenth and twentieth centuries, and reveals how close some of the more recent critical approaches are to the original attacks on the poems – and how surprisingly 'modern' the observations of a nineteenth-century folklore collector may be. Using my recent research (Poncarová 2020, 125–33), the chapter draws largely on the works of Gaelic scholars that do not seem to be getting due space in the debate outside Gaelic academia itself – while, mysteriously enough, works of researchers more distant from both the Gaelic language and culture, pivotal as they are to the controversy, are still considered classics in the field. In more general terms the chapter also contributes to the discussion of the author function as a concept. It explores how a discourse of Ossianic literature emerged around the works of James Macpherson himself, who certainly wrote and invented, and what possible œuvres lurked at the edges of his texts.

Stories and ballads about the blind bard Ossian, his father Fingal and his warrior band had existed in Gaelic-speaking Scotland and Ireland centuries before the birth of James Macpherson (Seumas Mac a' Phearsain, 1736–96). Macpherson is sometimes considered to be their sole purveyor and the organiser of a daring cheat, sometimes their editor and translator – a writer seeking to boost the confidence of his downtrodden native culture, appeal to the taste of the period and achieve literary fame. However, it was a book published in 1760 and entitled *Fragments of Ancient Poetry. Collected in the Highlands of Scotland and Translated from the Galic or Erse Language* that brought the subject to the attention of audiences outside the Gaelic-speaking, still largely oral culture of these two countries.

The fame of Ossian spread quickly throughout Europe and translations into other languages started to emerge. The first of these was the Italian verse translation in 1763 (*Poesie di Ossian, Figlio di Fingal, Antico Poeta Celtico*), followed by the German translations of *Fragments of Ancient Poetry* (*Fragmente der alten Hochschottländischen Dichtkunst*) and *Fingal* in 1764, and then the first German rendering of *The Works of Ossian, the Son of Fingal* (1765) in three volumes in 1768–69 (*Die Gedichte Ossians*). The first complete French translation followed in 1777 (*Ossian, fils de Fingal, barde du troisième siècle*).

Since 1760 the controversy about the poems of Ossian and Macpherson's involvement with them has engaged the attention of scholars in an increasing number of disciplines. The focus of the discussion has been shifting in response to the changing paradigms of evaluation of literary works. Developing approaches to authorship have been central in many contributions to the so-called Ossianic wars, from Samuel Johnson's travelogue *A Journey to the Western Islands of Scotland*, published in 1775 (Johnson and Boswell 1924), to Thomas M. Curley's *Samuel Johnson, the Ossian Fraud, and the Celtic Revival in Great Britain and Ireland* (Curley 2009). The range of perspectives in the Ossianic debate has broadened beyond the confines of straightforward celebrations or damnations, yet approaches to the poems, even in some very recent critical works, remain coloured by the controversy over the poems' authorship and their authenticity. Yet, as Hugh Cheape argues, 'the controversy over authenticity has distorted our understanding and appreciation of the Ossian phenomenon and arguably obscured its importance and influence' (1997, 1–2).

The poems were initially published anonymously. However, it was quite soon understood that they had been translated from Gaelic into English by James Macpherson, a young Highlander and aspiring poet who at that time worked in Edinburgh as a private tutor. Macpherson grew up in a Gaelic-speaking community in Badenoch where the Ossianic tradition would have been an important part of oral culture. In Edinburgh Macpherson was introduced by the philosopher Adam Ferguson, a fellow Gaelic speaker,[1] to the famous playwright John Home and through him to Hugh Blair, Professor of Rhetoric and Belles Lettres at the University of Edinburgh. In order to comply with Home's wishes, Macpherson produced his first alleged translations of traditional Gaelic poetry into English. The enthusiasm these specimens provoked in Macpherson's patrons, some of the most influential Scottish men of letters of that time, led to the publication of *Fragments* in 1760. Their support also allowed Macpherson to embark on research trips into Gaelic-speaking areas to collect more material for further publications – and, most importantly, to 'recover' a lost Gaelic heroic epic. Already the *Fragments* were hailed as representing 'many more remains of ancient genius'[2] waiting to be unearthed in Scotland.

Whether Macpherson indeed believed there was such an epic to be recovered, or whether he mentioned it to please his noble supporters and to satisfy the contemporary ideal that required a heroic epic as the true foundation of national literature, will probably never be known with certainty. What is becoming clearer with research into period documents, however, is that Macpherson's motivation was most likely a combination of personal ambition, a desire to please his influential patrons and the public and an effort to gain more respect for his native language and culture. Both of the latter were subject to suppression following the failed Jacobite rising of 1745–6. Macpherson himself witnessed the post-Culloden repercussions in his home township of Ruthven and his broader family was severely affected by them (Stafford 1988, 6–24). The atmosphere of gloom and melancholy pervading the Ossianic publications, along with the sense of a world coming to an end, reflect the situation of the Highlands in Macpherson's time.

Macpherson drew on the ancient tradition of Ossianic lore and on manuscripts he collected during his trips. His employment of these sources was increasingly liberal and controversial, especially when compared with the present-day practice of critical editions.[3] Some situations, images and expressions have been traced in surviving ballads or have a parallel in Gaelic lore (Thomson 1952; Campbell 1984, 5–258), but other parts were apparently Macpherson's own invention. Still, it is important to realise that there is no way of establishing what exactly Macpherson heard and wrote down on his trips, and some of the manuscripts he gathered and kept have been lost.[4] He certainly had in his possession the Book of the Dean of Lismore, one of the most precious Gaelic manuscripts compiled between 1512 and 1542, and the 'Little Book of Clanranald', which has not survived in its entirety. However, he could not make full use of them given the difficulties in spelling and vocabulary. Essentially Macpherson was using his sources, more pronouncedly in *Fingal* and most obviously in *Temora*, to construct a national epic, quite possibly in co-operation with, or even under the guidance of, Hugh Blair, a celebrated expert on Homer and ancient epic poetry. The discovery of a Gaelic epic would be the very boost of confidence that Scotland (and especially Gaelic Scotland) needed.

The eighteenth century: immediate responses

Questions concerning the authorship of the material and therefore its (in)authenticity emerged immediately after the first publication. The preface to *Fragments* starts with Blair's assurance that 'the public may depend on the following fragments as genuine remains of ancient Scottish poetry' ([Blair] 1760, iii). Ossian is only mentioned as one of the characters in the preface, not as the author, and Blair states 'there can be no doubt that these poems are to be ascribed to the Bards' (1760, v). When *Fingal* was published in 1761–2, it was presented on the title page as 'An Ancient Epic Poem, in Six Books: Together with several other Poems, composed by Ossian, the son of Fingal' ([Macpherson] 1762). As Fiona Stafford notes, while *Fragments* was published without any indication of authorship, 'there was no doubt about the identity of the translator of *Fingal* and James Macpherson's name was printed under the title in bold, red capitals' (Stafford 1988, 135).

The epic was attributed to the distinct figure of Ossian, whom the readers knew from the previous volume. *Temora*, the last part of the Ossian canon associated with Macpherson, followed in 1763. In John Dunn's words,

> for the half-century that followed, the body of poetry that was eventually collected as *The Poems of Ossian* provoked the comment of nearly every important man of letters.
>
> (1966, i)

The question of authorship was vital in the appreciation of Ossian at the time, as the attribution to a living author would mark them as 'inauthentic'. A statement by Samuel Johnson is a telling manifestation of this approach:

> Had it [*Fingal*] really been an ancient work, a true specimen of how men thought at that time, it would have been a curiosity of the first rate. As a modern production, it is nothing.
> (Johnson and Boswell 1924, 320–1)

For Johnson, the value of the material depended on the authorship. Consequently, sensibilities that were so remarkable when considered the fruits of an ancient civilisation were not so noteworthy when expressed by an eighteenth-century writer. Johnson and other like-minded readers demanded a manuscript.

As Ian Haywood points out, seventeenth-century antiquarians amassed great libraries and collections of manuscripts. In the eighteenth century, as a consequence of the boom in antiquarian studies, manuscripts became 'empirical units of historical knowledge' and 'as the power of the MS was acknowledged, its authenticity became a proportionally urgent concern' (Haywood 1983, 17–20). The reception of the Ossianic poems was affected by the desire to own a tangible monument of an ancient culture. Its dynamic was long determined by the dichotomy of purity and corruption, contrasting a pristine original with the dubious copy, and oral tradition was perceived as unstable and elusive. Derick Thomson (Ruaraidh MacThòmais) notes that an account of a research tour of the Highlands by Johnson's protegé William Shaw reveals disgust at the evidence of largely oral nature:

> in place of going to their cabinet for manuscripts, or copies of them, as I expected, application was made to some old man, or superannuated fiddler, who repeated over again the tales of the 15th century.
> (Thomson 1952, 4)

Johnson was one of the most prominent participants in the Ossian pamphlet war, which raged especially in the 1760s and 1770s. In his introduction to *Ossian Revisited*, Howard Gaskill notes how later writers have persisted in adopting Johnson's views (1991, 7–8). The famous lexicographer has been considered as an authority on the matter, although he could neither speak nor read Gaelic, and many of his observations, such as that there were no Gaelic manuscripts older than one hundred years, that there had been no Gaelic bards for some centuries and that none of the Gaelic poets were literate, were proved wrong by his immediate contemporaries. These conclusions bear witness to the nature of Johnson's enquiries in the Western Isles and the people whom he met or was directed to meet.[5] His account therefore bypasses the very recent existence of Iain Lom (John MacDonald, c.1624–c.1710) or Alasdair mac Mhaighstir Alasdair (Alexander MacDonald, c.1695–c.1770), who published his collection of poems *Aiseirigh na Seann Chànain Albannaich* ('Resurrection of the Ancient Scottish Language') in 1751 (MacNicol 1779, 247).

In addition to accusing Macpherson of inventing Ossian, the debate widened to encompass an argument about the existence of written Gaelic literature in Scotland. For Johnson and many others, the debate had a prominent nationalist strain. As Burnett and Andersson note,

> Macpherson's Ossianic epics were held up to be the great literary work of the Scottish nation at precisely the moment when the very idea of Scotland, Scottish culture and Scottishness were being critiqued and questioned as never before.
>
> (2011, 27)

Generally, as Richard B. Sher explains, the latter half of the eighteenth century was a time of rampant anti-Scottish prejudice and suspicion in England (1991, 207–45). The Scots who participated in the post-Union state and culture to a greater extent than ever before, and were making their mark in a number of fields, presented a competition and a threat. The considerable unpopularity in England of John Stuart, a Scot, the third Earl of Bute and a favourite of George III, to whom Macpherson dedicated *Fingal* (covertly) and *Temora* (overtly) was another important factor. As Sher notes, there arose a notion in England that 'Scots constituted a conspiracy or a cabal to advance their own interests at the expense of all others, and, if need be, at the expense of truth itself' (1991, 213).

The nationalistic tone of the argument becomes amply visible in the exchange between Johnson and the Rev. Donald MacNicol (Dòmhnall MacNeacaill).[6] MacNicol was a Gaelic-speaking minister who, in his eloquent and indignant *Remarks on Dr Samuel Johnson's Journey to the Hebrides* (1779), vindicates the whole nation, its culture, history and achievements against the account of Scotland in Johnson's travelogue. The defence of the Ossianic poems is part of his defence of a nation and, more specifically, of the Gaelic part of Scottish culture, which MacNicol believes to have been misunderstood or ignored by Johnson. Commenting on Johnson's diatribes against Macpherson, MacNicol makes a noteworthy point concerning the authorship of the poems of Ossian when he argues that

> [I]n labouring to deny their antiquity, therefore, the Doctor [Johnson] only plucks the wreath of ages from the tomb of the ancient bard, to adorn the brow of the modern Caledonian. For the moment Macpherson ceases to be admitted as a translator, he instantly acquires a title to the original.
> (MacNicol 1779, 9)

No matter whether the author was the long-dead Ossian or the living Macpherson, the poems that enthralled some of the most powerful and educated people in Europe were a Scottish achievement. The nationalist strain of the controversy served to link the authenticity of Ossian to the national prestige of Scotland. The question of authorship was closely connected to the construction and upkeep of national identity, while the authority of the author was substituted for the authority of the nation.

The nineteenth century: ongoing disputes

In Scotland the Ossian Controversy continued to rage in the nineteenth century. As late as in 1867 a book by Rev. Peter H. Waddell was published that argued for the total authenticity of Ossian (Cheape 1997, 7). Alexander Carmichael (Alasdair Gilleasbaig MacGilleMhìcheil, 1832–1912), the famous folklorist and compiler of *Carmina Gadelica* (Gaelic poems, 1900), wrote in a letter in 1861:

> That poetry of the most magnificent description has been common throughout the Highlands from ages immemorial is unquestionable; that much of that poetry has always been ascribed to Ossian is equally certain; and that he was the author of much of it is more than probable. […] This I can testify to from personal observation. I believe in them myself – fully believe. I am literally convinced that Fingal lived and that Ossian sang.
> (Campbell 1984, 226)

For other readers, such as the historian Malcolm Laing (1762–1818), famous for his unrelenting endeavours to settle the authenticity question, the problematic authorship resulted in a schism of perception and feeling:

> From a singular coincidence of circumstances, it was in this house, where I now write, that I first read the poems in my early youth, with an ardent credulity that remained unshaken for many years of my life; and with a pleasure to which even the triumphant satisfaction of detecting the imposture is comparatively nothing. The enthusiasm with which I then read and studied the poems enabled me afterwards, when my suspicions were once awakened, to trace and expose the deception with the greater success. Yet, notwithstanding the severity of minute criticism, I can still peruse them as a wild and wonderful assemblage of imitations, with which the fancy is often pleased and gratified, even where the judgement condemns them most.
> (Laing 1805, 441)

Laing could not help enjoying the literary qualities of the poems, despite the results of his research into their origin. When he had no suspicion about their authorship, his delight was complete. After the 'detection of the imposture', the poems could only be enjoyed by the fancy and they became abhorrent to the judgement. In Laing's view, attribution to the third-century bard had marked the poems as an objective artefact, a historical account, only for the authorship of the contemporary Macpherson to transform them into fiction unworthy of rational analysis.

Other contemporary men of letters, such as the folklorist John Francis Campbell (Iain Frangan Caimbeul),[7] were trying to strike a more balanced attitude. In the preface to the fourth volume of his groundbreaking folklore collection, *Popular Tales of the West Highlands* (1860–2), Campbell discusses the Ossian Controversy at length. 'Wherein does the authority consist?' Campbell asks, 'in the story or in the words; in the rhythm or metre of poetry, or its theme, or its ornaments and illustrations? Who, for example, will be the author of "Morte Arthur" when Tennyson's poem is completed?' (Campbell 1984, 7). Campbell suggests a typology of seven classes ranging from 'close literal translation' to 'free translation' and 'paraphrase', the last class being 'compositions which seem to have scarcely any relation to any that have gone before' (1984, 7). In relation to Ossian, Campbell plainly states that 'the groundwork of much which is in Ossian certainly existed in

Gaelic in Scotland long before Macpherson was born' (1984, 8), adding that 'there is a mass of evidence to prove that he had genuine materials, some of which we also have got for ourselves, and there is a strong presumption that he had something which we have not' (Campbell 1984, 227).

When confronting the opinion that the poems are historical, written by a bard in the third century who witnessed most of the deeds described, Campbell admitted that

> [I]t is not now easy to support or refute this opinion, or prove a negative. The language of traditional poems alters, manuscripts get lost, manners change and men die; but it might be shown that, so far as anything is known of early Gaelic literature, there were no such poems, and that their language is not that of some one period between the third and the eighteenth centuries, or that some one event which is mentioned happened later than the supposed date of the poet.
> (Campbell 1984, 9)

Campbell concludes his restrained, remarkably balanced and evidence-based account of the controversy by opining that

> while MacPherson's misdeeds meet their reward, let it be remembered that others similarly tempted have fallen and failed. Chatterton had no foundation for his attempt, and failed. MacPherson had a wide foundation, and built upon it, and succeeded, and made a fortune and a name.
> (Campbell 1984, 21)

The growing scientific engagement with folklore, of which Campbell is a notable proponent, helped to spread the notion that there may be different, equally valid versions of the same story, rather than one pure original and subsequent corrupted copies. When William Sharp commented on the poems at the end of the nineteenth century, his argument was more favourable to Macpherson. Sharp took for granted that the poems were based on genuine material, pointing out that '[w]hat remains to be settled is, in what degree, to what extent, are these Ossianic poems of James Macpherson paraphrases of legendary romances and primitive ballads and folk-lore' (Sharp 1896, ix).

Sharp also argues that 'if he [Macpherson] were the sole author, he would be one of the few poetic creators of the first rank'. He went on to observe 'that no single work in our literature has had so wide-reaching, so potent, and so enduring an influence' (1896, xxiii). Finally Sharp expresses his hope that 'the day is gone when the stupid outcry against Macpherson's 'Ossian' as no more than a gigantic fraud finds a response among lovers of literature (1896, xxiii).

The twentieth and twenty-first centuries: new directions

As if to comply with Sharp's wish, Derick Thomson (1921–2012), the late Gaelic scholar, poet and cultural activist, for the first time identified the particular passages in individual ballads upon which Macpherson probably drew, and the extent to which he altered them:

> The evidence shows that Macpherson cast his net wide, and collected a large amount of Ossianic tradition. The picture emerges of an eager investigator, travelling through Inverness-shire, Perthshire, Argyll and the Inner and Outer Hebrides. He employed scribes to record oral traditions. One of these, Ewan Macpherson, went with him to Skye, Uist and Benbecula, and in a declaration which he made afterwards, he says that he understood from James Macpherson that he had collected the bulk of his material on the mainland, before he came to the islands, but that he was still anxious to collect additional matter, and various editions of the same poems. He wheedled MSS. from their owners, sometimes by personal interview, sometimes by letter, and spent hours poring over what he considered their uncouth and outlandish spelling. He was perhaps impatient, and perhaps disappointed with his finds, and he was not by training too well equipped for the task which he set himself. He could not have known the real value of much of the material which he collected. But the importance of his work in this sphere – in the collection of traditional material, and more especially in the stimulating of interest in these traditions – should not be minimised.
>
> (Thomson 1952, 81)

Furthermore, Thomson claims that 'the controversy was, in fact, misdirected for more than a century. The point at issue was taken to be whether there existed Gaelic poems, preferably in ancient MSS., composed by a bard called Ossian in the third century A.D.' (Thomson 1952, 3). The seekers of Ossianic literature were only looking for an epic, not for supposedly lesser genres such as orally transmitted ballads and stories. With his characteristic wry humour, Thomson observes that

> one may perhaps be forgiven for suspecting that the majority of them [the controversialists of the latter half of the eighteenth century] had taken up their alignment before proceeding to any careful study of the evidence, and that in many cases they found the evidence which they were most anxious to find.
> (Thomson 1952, 3)

He is accordingly unsparing in his judgement of Macpherson's achievements, although he points out the importance of his efforts for Gaelic literature and culture:

> Ii is evident that Macpherson was not satisfied with the materials which he found. He considered many of the poems corrupt copies, and in this he was correct, although not altogether in the sense that he imagined. The language has often been corrupted and at times rendered unintelligible, but in sentiment and content the ballads are probably much nearer their prototypes than is Macpherson's work to the ballads. Macpherson's refining and bowdlerising pen has often changed the atmosphere of the ballads almost beyond recognition.
> (Thomson 1952, 81)

According to Thomson, the ballads on which Macpherson drew are thoroughly native, whereas 'Macpherson's work is a blend – and seldom a happy one – of several different cultures' (1952, 84). It is precisely on this intriguing blend of different cultures, which speaks so much about the conditions of the Gaelic Scotland of Macpherson's time, that some of the recent critical approaches tend to focus.

During the latter half of the twentieth century, critical attention gradually shifted away from authorship to other paradigms, albeit with some exceptions. One of them is the recent study *Samuel Johnson, the Ossian Fraud, and the Celtic Revival in Britain and Ireland* (Curley 2009). The summary on the jacket cover points out that 'James Macpherson's famous hoax, publishing his own poems as the writings of the ancient Scots bard Ossian in the 1760s, remains fascinating to scholars as the most successful literary fraud in history' (Curley 2009). The table of contents lists chapters as 'An introductory survey of scholarship on Ossian: Why literary truth matters' (Curley 2009, 1) and 'James Macpherson's violation of literary truth' (Curley 2009, 22). The book opens with a dedication to 'my beloved wife Ann, who always tells the truth', adding 'I dedicate this book to Johnson's love of truth in life and literature' (Curley 2009, vi). The author then argues that 'coming to terms with the authenticity issue is obviously central to evaluating the Ossian controversy' (Curley 2009, x). As Niall MacKenzie put it in his review for *Scottish Gaelic Studies*, there is an 'endearing fecklessness' about a book which is obsessed with 'the line of demarcation between truth and falsehood in the world of letters' and yet opens with a misquotation of one of its sources, contains a number of basic mistakes, and calls Samuel Johnson, whose own errors and bias in *A Journey* have in the meantime been amply demonstrated, 'the great truth-teller in English literature' (MacKenzie 2010, 149). Although such reversals focusing on the 'truth' of the poems seem to be rather rare in contemporary scholarship, it is still remarkable that such a volume appeared relatively lately from a respected academic publisher.

In recent decades Ossianic research is becoming more concentrated on the relationship of Macpherson to the Gaelic world and tends to appreciate Macpherson's impulse for generating more interest in Gaelic oral tradition. This is a significant change, given the low status of Gaelic and the suppression of the language and the Highland culture in general by the British government after Culloden. Donald E. Meek (Dòmhnall Eachann Meek), who has researched Macpherson's involvement with the Gaelic ballad tradition, argues that

> Macpherson's role as a creative employer of this material has not always received the recognition he deserves. All too often he is viewed as the villain of a complex literary hoax, imposing alien structures and concepts on his original sources and hoodwinking an all-too-gullible public into believing that there were in existence complete 'epics' composed by a poet named Ossian.
> (Meek 1991, 19)

This characterisation of Macpherson as a 'creative employer' reveals a change in the conception of authorship: the use of existing material in a new work of art is not denounced, but should rather be judged according to the merit of the result and the response of the readers. A glint of the nationalist strain can be still traced in the current debates, with Gaelic scholars, as among them Meek himself, defending Macpherson against critics, most prominently Hugh Trevor-Roper (1983), who used Macpherson as an example of an inventor of tradition. Such a notion, although not intended as a compliment, can be expanded with the focus on the creative and productive dimension of Macpherson's activities, a concept that informs the most current research on the subject.

Derick Thomson, and before him John Francis Campbell, pointed out the possibility of examining similarities between the Ossian Controversy and the eighteenth-century culture of allegedly ancient works and translations without originals, such as the works of Thomas Chatterton, William Lauder and Iolo Morganwg. Haywood argues that these writers participated in the important debates of the times and offered 'bold imaginative solutions to many of the problems'; he strives to show both Macpherson and Chatterton as 'makers, not falsifiers' (1983, 12). Other studies have commented on the use of literary devices in the Ossianic poems and the sources of their imagery; they have also appreciated the poems' contribution to the development of free verse. As Dunn (1966, i–xii) points out, Macpherson was vital for inviting experiments with measured prose and one of the most daring innovators of what was to become free verse: S. T. Coleridge and William Blake were both avid readers of Ossian.

Other new approaches to Ossian have been informed by postcolonial theories and gender studies. Hugh Cheape published a study of the material culture of Ossian (1997). Margery Palmer McCulloch brought together Macpherson, Burns and MacDiarmid, commenting on the ways they responded to the national needs of their time; she argues that

> Macpherson and Burns in the period of the eighteenth-century literary revival and MacDiarmid in the twentieth share characteristics related to personal and national needs and objectives and to the methodologies they adopted to realise these.
> (McCulloch 1997, 120)

In relation to Ossian, Robert Crawford pointed out that 'the fragment is a form which speaks of cultural ruin and of potential reassembly. It is central to the development of Romanticism, Modernism and Postmodernism' (McCulloch 1997, 123). In a recent informal but informative article, Ronald Black (2021, 18–20) connects the figure of Fionn mac Cumhaill and his merry band of superhuman warriors to the legendary figures of King Arthur and Robin Hood. He also calls for a return to the practice of performing the Ossianic ballads, as far as they have been preserved, and for a rediscovery of their appeal, humour and liveliness, in contrast to the prevalent mood of Macpherson's adaptations.

The viewpoint of translation seems a fruitful way of regarding the controversy, as translation lies at the very core of the Ossian dispute. In the last decades, studies of actual translations in the Ossian corpus[8] have begun to emerge in Gaelic studies. Among these is the work by the Gaelic scholar Donald William Stewart (Dòmhnall Uilleam Stiùbhart), who has observed that some of the Ossianic texts in English are haunted by the imagined ghost of the Gaelic original and calibrated to match an original which does not exist (Stiùbhart 2015).[9] In relation to Ossian, the Icelandic academic Gauti Kristmannsson has proposed the concept of 'translation without an original' (1997, 449–62).

The Ossian phenomenon has been able to move across languages, cultures and different media. As Fiona Stafford points out, the 'substance of Ossian' must have been perceived as more than literary, for it was considered adaptable to other art techniques and translatable into different media and different cultures (1996, viii). In Stafford's view,

> Macpherson's 'translations' involved acts of interpretation not only between Gaelic and English, but also between the oral culture of the depressed rural communities of the Scottish Highlands and the prosperous urban centres of lowland Britain, where the printed word was increasingly dominant.
>
> (1996, viii)

In relation to recent trends, it is tempting to study Ossian using the critical and theoretical apparatus developed for the study of the phenomenon of fan fiction – that is, stories written by admirers of a certain work of art using the characters and settings of the original – which has become the great folklore phenomenon of the online era. As Derick Thomson proved (1958, 172–88), Macpherson indeed inspired many other 'Ossianic' collections where people used the characters and plot elements to create their own versions and new stories.

All this research puts us into a new position from which to look not only at the Ossian Controversy, but also at the poems themselves, and at their wider influence on European culture. The Ossian dispute constitutes a remarkable episode in the history of European literature, revealing how important and complex what Foucault labels the 'author function' (1998, 211) in Western culture actually is. To follow Foucault's terminology, Macpherson may, with certain reservations, be considered one of the 'founders of discursivity' who 'made possible not only a certain number of analogies but also (and equally important) a certain number of differences. They have created a possibility for something other than their discourse, yet something belonging to what they founded' (Foucault 1998, 218).

In the last decades of the twentieth century and in the twenty-first century, the problematised relationship between original and copy, the suspicious attitude to everything that claims the privilege of authenticity and a culture of unacknowledged quotations and hints, prequels and sequels written by different authors open new possibilities for approaching Ossian. In view of the changing notions of authorship in the age of new media and cultural studies, authenticity is no longer the crucial concern in the process of evaluating literary texts. This allows us to seek new approaches to Ossian and to move beyond the restrictions of the authorship debate, exploring instead along the lines Foucault suggests in 'What is an author?':

> We would no longer hear the questions that have been rehashed for so long: Who really spoke? Is it really he and not someone else? With what authenticity and originality? And what part of his deepest self did he express in his discourse? Instead, there would be others, like these: What are the modes of existence of this discourse? Where has it been used, how can it circulate and who can appropriate it for himself?
> (Foucault 1998, 222)

Notes

1 This shared Gaelic heritage led to theories of a 'Gaelic conspiracy' between Macpherson and Ferguson. This affair, one of the most vituperative conflicts in the Ossianic Controversy, is discussed in great detail by Sher (1991, 207–45).
2 [Blair] 1760, vii.
3 The evaluation of this liberal attitude still differs even in the works of one scholar. Compare, for example, the changes in Derick Thomson's evaluation of this aspect in his three studies of Ossian (Thomson 1952; Thomson 1958, 172–88; Thomson 1998).
4 It is interesting that although *Temora* is generally believed to be largely Macpherson's own invention, John Francis Campbell recognised traditional elements in the poem, although he acknowledges 'it is not the Gaelic of the 1807, nor Gaelic from which the English of 1760 could have been translated' (Campbell 1984, 75).
5 Dòmhnall Uilleam Stiùbhart and other scholars have been focusing on the role of local mediators and cultural brokers in the famous eighteenth-century tours of travellers such as Thomas Pennant and Boswell and Johnson. See the project 'Curious Travellers', https://curioustravellers.ac.uk/.
6 Donald MacNicol (1735–1802) was a minister of the Church of Scotland in Lismore. Apart from his reply to Johnson, he is also known for his association with the poet Duncan Ban MacIntyre (Donnchadh Bàn Mac an t-Saoir), whose poems MacNicol transcribed from the poet's recitation.
7 John Francis Campbell, also known by the Gaelic nickname Iain Òg Ìle (1821–1885), was a Celticist, folklore collector and editor, traveller, polymath, senior civil servant, courtier to Queen Victoria and scientific inventor with strong links to the isle of Islay. Apart from the four volumes of *Popular Tales of the West Highlands* (1860–2), Campbell also published *Leabhar na Feinne* (1872), a book of heroic Gaelic ballads.
8 The texts Macpherson published were presented as translations, then translated into Gaelic. A full Gaelic edition, supposedly 'the originals', appeared in 1807.
9 I am grateful to Dòmhnall Uilleam Stiùbhart for sharing his notes and presentation with me.

References

[Blair, Hugh]. 1760. 'Preface'. In *Fragments of Ancient Poetry*. Edinburgh: G. Hamilton and J. Balfour.

Black, Ronald. 2021. 'The case for the people's Ossian', *The Royal Celtic Society Newsletter* 6.1 (Spring 2021): 18–20.

Burnett, Allan and Linda Burnett Andersson. 2011.'The poems of Ossian – A controversial legacy'. In *Blind Ossian's Fingal: Fragments and controversy compiled and translated by James Macpherson*. Edited by Allan Burnett and Linda Burnett Andersson, 25–52. Edinburgh: Luath Press.

Campbell, John Francis. 1984. *Popular Tales of the West Highlands*, vol. 4 (1862). 2nd edition (reprinted). London: Wildwood House.

Cheape, Hugh. 1997. 'The culture and material culture of Ossian, 1760–1900', *Scotlands* 4.1: 1–16.

Curley, Thomas M. 2009. *Samuel Johnson, the Ossian Fraud, and the Celtic Revival in Great Britain and Ireland*. Cambridge: Cambridge University Press.

Dunn, John J. 1966. 'Introduction'. In *Fragments of Ancient Poetry by James Macpherson*, Augustan Reprint Society, vol. 122, i–xii. Los Angeles: William Andrews Clark Memorial Library of the University of California.

Foucault, Michel. 1972. *The Archaeology of Knowledge and The Discourse of Language* (1969, 1971). Translated by A. M. Sheridan Smith. New York: Pantheon.

Foucault, Michel. 1998. 'What is an author?' Translated by Josué V. Harari. In *Aesthetics, Method, and Epistemology, Essential Works of Michel Foucault 1954–1984*, vol. 2, edited by James D. Faubion, translated by Robert Hurley and others, 205–22. New York: The New Press.

Gaskill, Howard. 1991. 'Introduction'. In *Ossian Revisited*, edited by Howard Gaskill, 1–16. Edinburgh: Edinburgh University Press.

Haywood, Ian. 1983. *The Making of History: A study of the literary forgeries of James Macpherson and Thomas Chatterton in relation to eighteenth-century ideas of history and fiction*. London and Toronto: Associated University Press.

Johnson, Samuel and James Boswell. 1924. *Johnson's Journey to the Western Islands of Scotland and Boswell's Journal of a Tour to the Hebrides with Samuel Johnson, ll.d.* Edited by R. W. Chapman. Oxford: Oxford University Press.

Kristmannsson, Gauti. 1997. 'Ossian: A case of Celtic tribalism or a translation without an original'. In *Transfer: Übersetzen – Dolmetschen – Interkulturalität*, edited by Horst Drescher, 449–62. Frankfurt/M., Berlin, Bern, New York, Paris, Vienna: Peter Lang.

Laing, Malcolm. 1805. 'Footnote 45 to "Carrick-Thura: A poem"'. In *Poems of Ossian, &c. containing the Poetical Works of James Macpherson, Esq. in prose and rhyme: with Notes and Illustrations by Malcolm Laing, Esq.* vol. 1, 440–1. Edinburgh: Constable and London: Longman, Hurst, Rees and Orme, Cadell and Davies, and J. Mawman.

MacKenzie, Niall. 2010. 'Review of *Samuel Johnson, the Ossian Fraud, and the Celtic Revival in Great Britain and Ireland* by Thomas M. Curley', *Scottish Gaelic Studies* 26: 146–54.

MacNicol, Donald. 1779. *Remarks on Dr Samuel Johnson's Journey to the Hebrides*. London: T. Cadell.

[Macpherson, James]. 1762. *Fingal, An Ancient Epic Poem, In Six Books: Together with several other poems, composed by Ossian, the son of Fingal. Translated from the Galic language by James Macpherson*. London: T. Becket and P. A. De Hondt.

McCulloch, Margery Palmer. 1997. 'Visionaries and revisionaries: Ossian, Burns and MacDiarmid', *Scotlands* 4.1: 119–28.

Meek, Donald E. 1991. 'The Gaelic ballads of Scotland: Creativity and adaptation'. In *Ossian Revisited*, edited by Howard Gaskill, 19–48. Edinburgh: Edinburgh University Press.

Poncarová, Petra Johana. 2020. 'Derick Thomson and the Ossian Controversy', *Anglica* 29.3: 125–33. DOI 10.7311/0860-5734.29.3.10.

Sharp, William. 1896. 'Introductory note'. In *The Poems of Ossian, translated by James Macpherson*, ix–xxiv. Edinburgh: Patrick Geddes & Colleagues.

Sher, Richard B. 1991. 'Percy, Shaw and the Ferguson "cheat": National prejudice in the Ossian wars'. In *Ossian Revisited*, edited by Howard Gaskill, 207–45. Edinburgh: Edinburgh University Press.

Stafford, Fiona J. 1988. *The Sublime Savage: A study of James Macpherson and the Poems of Ossian*. Edinburgh: Edinburgh University Press.

Stafford, Fiona. 1996. 'Introduction'. In *The Poems of Ossian and related works*, edited by Howard Gaskill, v–xxi. Edinburgh: Edinburgh University Press.

Stiùbhart, Dòmhnall Uilleam. 2015. 'A Gaelic text of "Malvina's dream" in the hand of Adam Ferguson: Edinburgh University Library Laing II 51 fo. 180'. Lecture delivered at the conference 'Macpherson's Ossianic Legacy', Kingussie, 18 April 2015.

Thomson, Derick. 1952. *The Gaelic Sources of Macpherson's 'Ossian'*. Edinburgh: Oliver and Boyd.

Thomson, Derick. 1958. 'Bogus Gaelic literature c.1750–c.1820'. *Transactions of the Gaelic Society of Glasgow* 5: 172–88.

Thomson, Derick. 1998. 'James Macpherson: The Gaelic dimension'. In *From Gaelic to Romantic: Ossianic translations*, edited by Fiona Stafford and Howard Gaskill, 17–40. Amsterdam: Rodopi.

Trevor-Roper, Hugh. 1983. 'The invention of tradition: The Highland tradition of Scotland'. In *The Invention of Tradition*, edited by Eric Hobsbawm and Terence Ranger, 15–42. Cambridge: Cambridge University Press.

4
Translation of indigenous oral narratives and the concept of collaborative authorship
Johanna Fernández Castro

Introduction

Between 1911 and 1913 the German anthropologist Theodor Koch-Grünberg explored the Roraima, a border region between Brazil, Venezuela and British Guyana, where he made contact with the indigenous peoples Pemón (Taulipáng and Arecuná). During his fieldwork in this region he travelled with, among many other helpers and cultural brokers, Akuli, a shaman and narrator, and Mayuluaipu, an apprentice shaman, narrator and interpreter. He transcribed oral narratives of the Taulipáng and Arecuná,[1] as related to him by Akuli and Mayuluaipu. Upon his return to Germany, Koch-Grünberg published the indigenous narratives in the second of the five volumes of his work *Vom Roroima zum Orinoco* (Koch-Grünberg 1917–28).

In 1928 the Brazilian writer Mário de Andrade published his work *Macunaíma, o heroi sem nenhum caracter* (Andrade 1928), inspired by the indigenous narratives collected and translated in Koch-Grünberg's monograph. *Macunaíma* became the representative text of Brazilian Modernism; it is considered highly significant for Brazilian culture owing not only to its indigenous origins, but also to its hybrid character, poised between cultures and languages, including German and Portuguese. Nowadays the work of Mayuluaipu, Akuli and Koch-Grünberg, along with Andrade's adaptation of the narratives in *Macunaíma*, is regarded as part of the history of the oral tradition of the indigenous groups mentioned above.

In this chapter, the collected and translated indigenous narratives offer insights into a translation process that usually remains hidden behind scientific anthropological discourse. The concept of translation in this complex frame highlights the role of the indigenous narrators and translators as participants in a process of collaborative authorship that challenges the notion of individual authorship.

The chapter consists of five sections. In the first, the concepts of individual and collaborative authorship are defined. The second explains the role of translation in the anthropological encounter and reveals how it challenges the traditional notion of individual authorship. The third deals with the different roles or functions that participants perform in the process of textualising oral narratives, namely as anthropologists, editors/translators or narrators. A specific example of collaborative authorship in the anthropological encounter is analysed in the fourth section. Finally, the relationship between collaborative authorship and the intertextual dialogue is clarified.

Individual and collaborative authorship

As Sophie McCall reminds us,

> [h]istorically, non-Aboriginal recorders and editors have maintained tight control over the process of entextualizing Aboriginal oral forms, transcribing, translating, structuring, editing, introducing, interpreting, and publishing versions of Aboriginal oral expression under their own name.
>
> (2011, 205)

The indigenous narratives told and translated by Akuli and Mayuluaipu, translated into German, edited by Koch-Grünberg and finally published under his name are a complex form of textual production that encompasses a change in medium, from oral to written, a change in language, from Taulipáng or Arecuná to German, and the participation of many agents. Although this chapter deals with written texts, they are intermedial translations, from oral to written language. However, this chapter aims neither to deal with orality as such, analysed by many renowned scholars,[2] nor to delve into the characteristics of every indigenous oral tradition. Rather, it aims to highlight the importance of the change of medium as a type of translation that implies social interaction between narrator and listener, and thus a cultural exchange.

Considering social interaction and cultural exchange in this context questions in part the 'tight control' (McCall 2011, 205) of the anthropologist as editor-author, since these 'textualized oral narratives' (McCall 2011, 15 and *passim*)[3] arise out of a co-operation between non-indigenous and indigenous people, facilitated by translation. The translation of oral narratives told to the anthropologists challenges the '"strong" concept of authorship as autonomous agency, original creativity and intellectual ownership' (Berensmeyer, Buelens and Demoor 2012, 8), and thereby the idea of the sacralised authentic *original*, since the defining feature of oral tradition is its transmission by means of memorisation and repetition. Moreover, the presence of many agents in the production of textualised oral narratives reveals the performative activity of collaborative authorship as a '"weak" (but historically much more prevalent) concept of heteronomous authorship' (Berensmeyer, Buelens and Demoor 2012, 8). Thus collaborative authorship, understood 'as a product of cultural networks and their acts of authorization' (Berensmeyer, Buelens and Demoor 2012, 8), offers us insight into the ways in which collective indigenous knowledge has been textualised within the anthropological encounter.

Individual authorship in this chapter refers to the system in which 'work, publications, conventions and career opportunities are centered on the individual scientist' (Knorr Cetina 1999, 166). For the German anthropologists of the early twentieth century, whose discipline was just beginning to be established, it was very important to build a name in order to gain prestige and to be regarded as an 'authority'. Anthropologists, acknowledged as individual scientists, were 'collector-editors' of indigenous oral traditions; they 'submitted the oral performance to numerous changes, omissions, and manipulations [e.g. translations]' (McCall 2011, 2). Although the collaboration of indigenous informants and/or translators is acknowledged in Koch-Grünberg's preface, the anthropologist's name is credited with 'sole authorship on the title page' (McCall 2011, 2). The names of cultural brokers in the ethnographic encounter, serving as creative agents who mostly worked as translators, such as Mayuluaipu, do appear in many parts of the texts – preface, subtitles, interlingual translations and footnotes. However, in the end it is the anthropologist's name that can be found in the library catalogue and that remains directly related to publication of the textualised oral narratives.

The criticism of the sacralised original – together with the assumptions of the impossibility of a pure origin and of the omniscient (individual) author – have been placed at the core of literary and culture studies ever since Roland Barthes' statement of the death of the author,

Michel Foucault's notion of the author function and Jacques Derrida's analysis of the myth of Babel and the role of translation. For the purposes of this chapter, it is necessary to understand how the author's name, in this case the anthropologist's name, works in a given social structure and in relation to other texts. According to the notion of author function, the anthropologist's name (e.g., Koch-Grünberg) is thus related to a country (Germany), a knowledge-production tradition (German ethnological research in the Amazon), a theory about the social life of the objects of study, and so on. In this way, the author function appears as 'the interface between a text and the system of other relevant texts [in the source and target language] in which it is produced' (Compagno 2012, 44).

In texts resulting from anthropological research, individual authorship and legal ownership consequently become problematic. According to Dudley,

> [w]hat gives the author function its critical edge in oral history and ethnography [oral traditions included] is the fact that no one 'authors' the texts [...], yet the true conditions of *our discourse* require that *someone* step forward to claim that authorship, with all the legal, political and moral ramifications it entails.
>
> (1998, 165; emphasis added)

Following this line of thought, the author function notion may apply to *our discourse*, as Dudley claims, but it still does not apply to every discourse, nor to every society. As Foucault states, 'in a *civilisation like our own* there are a certain number of discourses endowed with the "author function" while others are deprived of it' (1998, 211; emphasis added). Therefore, though the author function can be found in the German scientific discourse, it is not present in every discourse of the German culture. In the same way, it cannot be applied to indigenous societies, their oral narratives or their notions of collective property, given that the concept is a Western construct, related in turn to other constructs of Western societies such as writing, text, originality, intellectual property, individual authorship, etc. Thus, when Foucault references a 'civilisation like our own', he might be referring to the Euro-American civilisation and its 'individualistic conception of authorship' (Venuti 1995, 6) and intellectual property.

Although the author function aims to decentre the romantic figure of the author as individual genius, it still presupposes individual authorship as 'the condition of being the originator of works' (Love 2002, 39). This concept of authorship defined anthropological discourse at the beginning of the twentieth century; even now it 'informs our image of science and many sciences' practices' (Knorr Cetina 1999, 166). Nonetheless, the presence of many individuals, informants and other translators in the textual production confirms that 'the producer of a text is not a unitary being' (Braz 2011, 2). Authorship in this context can thus be apprehended as 'a set of linked activities [...] which are sometimes performed by a single person but will often be performed collaboratively or by several persons in succession' (Love 2002, 39). Moreover, Koch-Grünberg's volumes reveal not only the agency of others, but also the many faces of the anthropologist, acting in many functions or '*authemes*', as Harold Love calls them (2002, 39) – namely as author, collector, translator and editor.

These last remarks are relevant in order to differentiate between the anthropologist as a recognised individual author and the indigenous people involved in the collective textual production. Although authorship in this context could be analysed through the notion of author function, the presence of the indigenous storytellers and translators such as Akuli and Mayuluaipu – for whom the notion of individual authorship is incompatible with the nature of the social relations, interactions and modes of production of their oral tradition – means that their authorship could best be understood as an instance of *collaborative authorship*. Though the idea of collaborative authorship[4] as proposed by Sophie McCall refers to contemporary literary as-told-to narratives, resulting from interaction between non-indigenous people and First Nations storytellers in Canada, it seems, given the role of social interaction, to be a pertinent point of departure for the analysis of the collective textual production process described above.

Translation and authorship

The role of translation becomes relevant in the following analysis, since it implies complex transformations that are always interrelated, being always the result of the interaction of different actors and intertwined within different media. Translation appears in Koch-Grünberg (1917–28) in many forms. The anthropologist acknowledges his lack of proficiency in many of the indigenous languages and admits the presence of interpreters during the expedition. His translations of the narratives in prose are complemented by interlinear translations, in which the indigenous languages and the indigenous narrators and translator become visible for the reader, letting 'the native texts exist strongly enough in their own right to make much of the "scientific" commentary seem redundant, or of another order of knowledge' (Sá 2002, 66).

The many forms of translation of the indigenous narratives reveal that these were objects of continuous transformation. Accordingly, translation can be apprehended in terms of 'regulated transformation' (Derrida 1985, 20) or as 'removal from one language into another through a continuum of transformations' (Benjamin 1996, 70). The written indigenous narratives are the materialisation of these approaches in the form of a 'palimpsest' (Arrojo 1997b, 33), a type of rewriting on a surface where the traces of the last writings remain, framing and therefore influencing new texts. Concepts such as transformation and palimpsest are established in the context of translation studies, challenging the dichotomy between original and translation, along with the notion of authorship. It has been emphasised that translation is a sort of 'transgression', that it is in fact 'inevitably unfaithful' given 'the impossibility of perfect repetition' (Arrojo 1997a, 27).

Such a perspective presupposes the role of the translator as a creative agent who is not subordinated to the author, insofar as she/he develops translation strategies according to her/his subjectivities and to the purpose of the translation in the target culture. Rosemary Arrojo proposes the notion of 'translator-function', borrowing Foucault's author function, in order to position the translator as a 'regulating element that necessarily and legitimately determines meaning in the relationship which a reader will establish with a translated text' (1997a, 31). The translator function contributes to the recognition of the creative work of the translator, making their name visible, as opposed to remaining unknown or hidden behind the author's name. Additionally, it highlights the role of translation in the textual production, thus unveiling the palimpsestic character of the text and the presence of the agents involved in it. However, although the translator function implies a notion of authorship in terms of creativity and legal ownership, it does not necessarily promise material benefit. Nonetheless, the translator function allows for the recognition of indigenous narrators and translators and the gain of symbolic capital.

Anthropologist – author – translator

To understand the translation and compilation of the indigenous narratives within the anthropological discourse and their later adaptations as a result of collaborative authorship does not mean forgetting that the names Akuli and Mayuluaipu fail to appear on the front page of the printed book, nor to avoid the role of the anthropologist as editor-author. I do not mean to suggest that 'collaboration' is 'a "solution" to the problem of cultural representation' (McCall 2011, 168). However, using collaborative authorship in order to explain the textual production via social interaction facilitated by translation does allow us to see how 'stories circulate in different communities, for different reasons, and to different political effect' (McCall 2011, 37). Instead of ignoring the ethical implications of the authorial act of the anthropologist, this approach highlights that, even if they were ignored as individual authors, there were indeed other participants in the production of text – those whose authorship should be acknowledged, even if it can no longer be remunerated.

In order to understand why indigenous narratives are mostly framed within the anthropological discourse, it is relevant to take a look at the context in which they were collected. By the beginning of the twentieth century, one of the main goals of German anthropologists doing research in South America was to collect objects from indigenous cultures;[5] these were then shipped to Germany, where they are still exhibited in ethnographic museums. Ethnographic research was synthesised into volumes or monographs that explained different cultural aspects of the indigenous groups. Besides the collection of anthropometrical information – including descriptions of the use of hunting and fishing instruments, cooking habits and social behaviour – the anthropologist also compiled and translated rituals, myths and every kind of oral narrative. The transcription and translation of oral narratives was a secondary task, strongly related to missionary chronicles and evangelisation endeavours. Textualised oral narratives were then part of scientific and allegedly 'objective' representations framed by the anthropologist-author in German academic discourse. As a result, oral narratives lost their original character as religious, pedagogical or historical accounts. Yet many anthropologists tried to rescue the literary value of this kind of text; they transcribed, translated and edited them in publications that sometimes even appeared as literary anthologies under the name of the anthropologist-editor.

The anthropologist, in this case Koch-Grünberg, represents an ambiguous individual worthy of attention, since neither he as author nor his texts have a fixed identity; on the contrary, his role as author is characterised by many *'authemes'*. According to Love, these are a 'set of linked activities [...] which are sometimes performed collaboratively or by several persons in succession' (2002, 39). Based on this performative model of authorship (Berensmeyer, Buelens and Demoor 2012, 5–29), activities such as collecting, editing and translating define in this case the functions as well as the ascriptions of authorship.

On the one hand, Koch-Grünberg was recognised as an author and creator (although through compilation and editing) of an original work and its legal owner. On the other, he was not recognised as translator, since the task of translation remained a secondary tool in the production of knowledge. The process was regarded as 'matching written sentences in two languages, such that the second set of sentences becomes the "real meaning" of the first' (Asad 2009, 237). Hence the figure of the anthropologist represents for the reader of the textualised narrative an invisible translator subordinated to the visible, sacralised author, even though the same person performs both functions.

The role of the anthropologist as a translator, in this case, is no less problematic than the role of the author. The authorship (of these translations and compilations) implies 'not just creativity or individuality, but also ethical responsibility' (Pym 2011, 32). Since oral narratives – sacred narratives in the source culture, for example – were transformed not only into written texts, but also through translation into popular literature in the target culture, they thereby lost their sacred meaning. During this process, in which writing appeared as a colonising instrument, indigenous narratives were adapted for the target culture (the German reader); they were 'pulled into the framework of the receptor cultural norms and the receptor literary system' (Tymoczko 1990, 54). In doing so, translators determine meaning, transforming the text on various levels. A new content thus arises in contexts that may substantially differ from the *original* context. In Koch-Grünberg's translation of the Taulipáng and Arecuná narratives,[6] for instance, complexity begins with the transformation from oral language into written language. Undoubtedly the translation from an indigenous language (using Spanish or Portuguese as a relay language) into German is already a difficult task in which information is appropriated by non-indigenous peoples. Similarly, the transcription of an oral narrative into a written text reveals the ways in which translation can be instrumentalised as a sort of colonial tool.

Two particular aspects of the Western target culture regulate the translated narrative. First, the form of the written fixed text determines the failure of a translated narrative in the target culture, since if it 'does not adapt as it does in oral traditions, translated literature becomes antiquarian or exotic' (Tymoczko 1990, 53). This is the case of many indigenous narratives collected in the early years of anthropological research. Second, the notion of individual authorship transforms the translated narratives into *originals*, which are perceived as individual creations; within the legal frame, this only generates benefit for the anthropologist-editor-author. The translation of these narratives within anthropological texts is thus not only a question of change of language and genre, but also, most significantly, one of ethics. Translation has both contributed to the exotification and romanticisation of indigenous cultures and served as a tool of appropriation of their immaterial heritage.

Collaborative authorship in the anthropological encounter

Translation cannot be understood as a one-way movement – that is, not only as a colonial tool. This is because, as social interaction, it implies the agency of many participants who do not always play the role of the victims of translation as colonisation. Another way to approach the translation of oral narratives of the Taulipáng and Arecuná, without ignoring the ethical aspects implied, is to examine the active role of participants in the anthropological encounter. The fact that Koch-Grünberg mentioned the narrators, Akuli and Mayuluaipu, by name – and especially Mayuluaipu's role as translator – and also discussed many aspects of the translation process was not typical in the anthropological discourse of the time. By revealing the agency of many participants in the production of these narratives, this strategy challenges the romanticised view of the indigenous 'voice' in translated or transcribed texts as something 'singular, unmediated, and pure' (McCall 2011, 5).

In the preface to Volume 2, Koch-Grünberg mentions the contribution of those who helped him to understand unknown cultures and explains their crucial presence in the process of collecting and translating the narratives,[7] along with his own approaches in the German translation: 'I have put in brackets the narrator's explanations and clarifications, which were not part of the text, in order to show how the people tried to explain every detail to me' (Koch-Grünberg 1917–28, 2:V).[8] In doing so, Koch-Grünberg describes his translation strategies and emphasises the pivotal role of the narrator. Of course, this also serves to justify the indigenous authenticity of the text.

Nonetheless, paying attention to the act of translation helps to expose the fiction of the 'Absent Editor' (Brumble 2008, 75). As Koch-Grünberg explains:

> The meaning of a healing ritual, whose procedure I have illustrated above, was described to me by Akuli in every detail. I reproduce his narration here, as it was translated into Portuguese by Mayuluaipu.[9]
> (1917–28, 3:211)

In this statement, not only the co-operation of the agents involved, but also Koch-Grünberg's role as editor comes to the fore. He distances himself from the authorial role and credits Akuli and Mayuluaipu with explaining the meaning of the healing ritual; furthermore, he ignores the fact that he has translated (and interpreted) the text into German. However, his responsibility in explaining the meaning of the ritual in his mother tongue is as relevant as that of his informants.

The process of translation here reveals how the textualised indigenous narratives can be the product of cultural interaction and 'mutual agreement' (Murray 1991, 6), which does not mean that both participants experienced *equal* conditions.

> Jose [Mayuluaipu] is always available to me. [...] He is modest and attentive and incessantly gives me information about the manners, customs and worldviews of his tribe. Every day he dictates Taulipáng texts to me, tales and magic spells, and we translate them together word by word into Portuguese.[10]
> (Koch-Grünberg 1917–28, 1:210)

Although from this quotation one can witness the co-operative translation at work, as well as Mayuluaipu's 'good intention' to tell stories to Koch-Grünberg, other texts' passages show that this was not always the case. Especially in difficult times, Mayuluaipu and Akuli wanted to go home. Koch-Grünberg required them to stay because that had been their agreement since the beginning of their enterprise. This means that there was indeed a 'mutual agreement', even if everyone was not always satisfied with it.

Although their contribution is not ignored, the names of Mayuluaipu and Akuli remain subordinated to the anthropologist's and are not included on the title page of the book. Even if the preposition 'of' in the subtitle of Volume 2, 'Myths and Legends of the Indians Taulipáng and Arecuná', explicitly identifies the Taulipáng and Arecuná as owners or originators (Koch-Grünberg 1917–28, 2: n.p.), the narrators do not appear as individuals. In addition, it could be argued that, since the Taulipáng und Arecuná did not have the notion of (individual) authorship that Western societies did, the subtitle points to collective legal ownership, and therefore authorship, of the narratives, although without material benefit. In spite of the fact that the notion of collective authorship did not exist at that time, Koch-Grünberg does consider the narratives 'mythological communal property' and therefore the 'original property of humankind' (Koch-Grünberg 1917–28, 2:4).[11] According to this line of reasoning, we have been dealing with authorship in terms of collective ownership, in which indigenous communities are considered the *primitive* examples of our original human condition. As one of the aims of anthropology at the time was to gather as much material as possible from these so-called *primitive* societies because they would soon disappear, questions about authorship in terms of legal ownership were irrelevant, since anthropologists were dealing with an almost 'extinct primitive people' (Bastian 1881, 181).

Even if translators and other cultural brokers remained mostly anonymous in anthropological research of the time, the agency of the individuals involved in the collection and translation of oral narratives can be traced throughout Koch-Grünberg's œuvre. The names of Akuli and Mayuluaipu appear under the titles of each narrative, revealing their pivotal role in the activity of storytelling, the key characteristic of oral tradition in the indigenous communities. This strategy demonstrates how both parties to the encounter, the narrator and the anthropologist, were involved – as well as, to a certain degree (through the information in footnotes), what the interaction between them was like. This makes it possible to trace a translation process that usually remains hidden behind the scientific anthropological discourse.

When Mayuluaipu was not translating Akuli's narrations, he was telling Koch-Grünberg his own versions of the same (or different) stories. With reference to the translation, the anthropologist explains:

> Mayuluaipu told me the myths first in Portuguese and I translated them word by word into German. Afterward he dictated the original text and helped me with the exact translation.[12]
> (Koch-Grünberg 1917–28, 2:V)

Although the interaction between Mayuluaipu, Akuli and Koch-Grünberg has been described as a sort of collaborative textual production, Akuli and Mayuluaipu could not know when they engaged in it how their narrations would be used and displayed in the future, or in what form. The notion of collaborative authorship in this case thus refers only to the creative character of the textual production and the collaborative work. During the narration, translation and compilation of the texts in the course of the fieldwork, only Akuli and Mayuluaipu gained some individual material benefit of the textual production, earning some money at the end of the expedition. After the texts were published, the creative role of the textual production and its material benefit became visible only to the anthropologist-editor-author.

Collaborative authorship and the intertextual dialogue

The numerous lectures on and interpretations of Koch-Grünberg's work, whether in academia, literature or audiovisual media, are the effects of a knowledge transformation, a process characterised by instability. Information in the form of narratives and translations, although written, is always in an instable state. An example of this can be seen in narratives about the indigenous hero Macunaíma, compiled and translated into German by Koch-Grünberg during the Roraima expedition and published in 1924. The following adaptation of these narratives in the book *Macunaíma* (Andrade 1928) raises several questions about authorship and translation.

Andrade read the indigenous narratives in Koch-Grünberg's German text and adapted the hero Macunaíma into his own literary work. One could question the authorship of both writers in legal terms, arguing that they appropriated the indigenous narratives and earned profit from them, disregarding the intellectual property of the indigenous communities.[13] Furthermore, Andrade was accused of plagiarism because he appropriated indigenous narratives and Koch-Grünberg's texts. In response to the accusations, he proudly admitted that he had copied not only the indigenous narratives and Koch-Grünberg's texts, but those of other authors as well. His authorship, following Love's classification of authorship as a performative act, is a sort of 'precursory authorship' since 'a significant contribution from an earlier writer [was] incorporated into the work' (2002, 40), which implies an intertextual relationship. In fact, Andrade considered 'his literary creation as re-creation, as copying' (Lopez 1974, 99–100) – which does not mean that *Macunaíma* (Andrade 1928) should be considered as the result of intertextual relationships alone. Rather, Andrade 'is less concerned with intertextuality as such than with the possibilities of intercultural relations opened by the intertextual dialogue' (Sá 2004, 39). *Macunaíma* (Andrade 1928) can be understood as a form of translation whose success lies in the fact that

> To remain alive and to function fully as literature – essential in oral literary systems – translated narratives *must* adapt to the standards of the receptor culture and hence *must* refract the source text.
> (Tymoczko 1990, 53)

Nonetheless, *Macunaíma* (Andrade 1928) was not initially adjusted to the standards of the Brazilian literature of the 1920s. On the contrary: it criticised and subverted them in a syncretism of indigenous narratives and European classic literature. Yet Andrade's work, in the form of written and fixed text, refracted the source text in that his version still conserves many aspects of the indigenous Macunaíma.

The question of the authorship by Koch-Grünberg and Andrade becomes especially relevant in considering the meaning of *Macunaíma* (Andrade 1928) for the indigenous cultures in Brazil and for their political struggles. In this context, the narration and translation by Akuli and Mayuluaipu – as well as the collection and translation by Koch-Grünberg and the adaptation by Andrade – can be regarded as processes of transformation of information, pivotal for the dissemination of indigenous knowledge. The meaning of this collaborative textual production has extended beyond the literary field into the political one. Regarding the conflict between indigenous and non-indigenous landowners over territory in Brazil, the significance of the indigenous narratives has gained recognition within the political debate. As the Brazilian anthropologist Eduardo Viveiros de Castro states:

> The indigenous people were decisive for Brazil to win this territory [the Roraima region], in a dispute with the Guyana, and hence England. To say that they represent a threat means at least to commit a historical injustice. Even the myth of Macunaíma, which was collected by a German, Koch-Grünberg, and transformed by a Paulista, Mário de Andrade, was told by indigenous people from that region, the Macuxi and the Wapichana. They are the *co-authors of the national ideology.*[14]
>
> (Viveiros de Castro 2008; emphasis added)

The translation of indigenous oral narratives and their further adaptations – into literary works or films, for example – show the significant role of the social interaction of the participants and the importance of 'texts, images and other cultural objects [...] in the performative processes of making meaning and of shaping identities' (Berns 2010, 14). Moreover, textualised narratives, as an important part of the indigenous peoples' cultural heritage, have become a significant tool in the demand for indigenous political rights.

Macunaíma (Andrade 1928) has been significant for more than having made an indigenous hero famous and transplanted him from anthropological discourse into literature. It has also been considered as the 'allegorical personification of Brazilian culture' (Kangussu and Fonseca 2012, 153). As Viveiros de Castro states, *Macunaíma* (Andrade 1928) is a representative text of Brazilian culture, a palimpsest, an intertextual product with traces of a German anthropologist and a writer from São Paulo. The role of the indigenous people as 'co-authors of the national ideology', following Viveiros de Castro, implies that *Macunaíma* (Andrade 1928) is a collective textual production with repercussions for Brazilian national ideology, and that it plays a significant role both for indigenous people in Brazil and for wider Brazilian culture.

Conclusion

It is through translation and the manipulation it implies that *Macunaíma* (Andrade 1928) journeyed from textualised indigenous narrative from the Brazilian rainforest to anthropological study in Germany, before returning to Brazil in the 1920s to become an enduring symbol of Brazilian literature and culture. Through translation, *Macunaíma* returned to its geographical origin and has subsequently been re-appropriated by many indigenous communities. The role of the individual author in this case has been blurred or eclipsed by the participation of narrators and translators, including a scientist and a novelist. Authorship, in terms of originality and ownership, has been challenged – not only by the intertextuality that comes with the act of translation, but also by the social interaction that it implies, giving way to an understanding of this process as collaborative authorship. Translation highlights the creativity and the function of the agents involved as transmitters of cultural heritage rather than as owners of information. Narratives such as *Macunaíma* (Andrade 1928) have gained cultural value not only because they are acknowledged as symbols of national and cultural identities, but also because they are the result of cultural exchange. As Cobley reminds us, narratives 'might represent "cultural difference" and "hybridity"' (2001, 39), both aspects that characterise *Macunaíma* (Andrade 1928) the narrative as much as they do Macunaíma the hero.

Today the role of oral narratives for indigenous peoples of the Amazon valley, their function as vehicles of knowledge transmission within their cultures, as well as the current notion of authorship they address, can be best understood in the following quote:

> Our ancestors gave their grandchildren knowledge in oral form, as a web that connects the past with the future. [...] The knowledge, in the form of narratives – called myths in the West – was appropriated by researchers, missionaries, adventurers and travellers, who did not consider the collective authorship and spread stories without concern about their true owners.
>
> ('Carta de los Kari-Oca' 2004)

This declaration about copyright and the protection of indigenous knowledge was made by the Kari-Oca people at a national convention for indigenous writers (Rio de Janeiro, 22 and 23 September 2004). In it, the narratives of an indigenous community are understood as immaterial heritage whose meanings and functions within the community should persist through narration. There is no notion of individual authorship, since the narrator does not recognise himself as the owner, originator or author of the narrative. The role of the narrator is in this case more the role of a kind of 'repeater' who, in the terms of the indigenous scholar Menezes de Souza (2015), not only repeats but also transforms the narrative in every performance. Authorship in this context can be apprehended as a process that is 'never completed […] but passed on from agent to agent, all of whom will subject it to their own forms of alteration' (Love 2002, 38). Following this idea, the narrator or translator should be perceived as more than as an author; rather as a medium of knowledge transformation and *dissemination*.

In the analysis of textual production in the framework of ethnographic research at the beginning of the twentieth century, it is evident that translation plays an essential role. Various actors take part in the translation process, which forces us to question concepts such as authorship, author function and even copyrights. In turn, the textualisation of indigenous oral narratives, their translation, edition and publication as well as dissemination, are practices that force us to rethink the notion of copyright within the framework of international legal treaties. The analysis of these practices within ethnographic scientific discourse contributes to the discussion on the construction of individual copyrights and their redefinition, particularly in the case of indigenous narratives.

Notes

1. The spelling of the indigenous groups' names varies depending on the language of research. The spelling used in this chapter is based on the Spanish and Brazilian spellings (Arellano 1986).
2. One of the most quoted works about orality is Walter Ong's *Orality and Literacy* (Ong 1982). Although his work has had a huge influence in the field, his focus is on Western orality. Other non-indigenous authors such as Jack Goody (1968), dealing with literacy and orality, base their analyses mostly on anthropological research.
3. McCall's term 'textualized oral narratives' (2011, 15 and *passim*) seems pertinent for the corpus analysed in this chapter. It also allows us to avoid the use of 'oral literatures', a term strongly criticised by Walter Ong as 'anachronistic and self-contradictory' (1982, 13). He proposes instead the term 'oral art forms' (1982, 13).

4   Harold Love refers in his study about attributing authorship to collaborative authorship as a type of authorship (2002, 33–9). For its explanation he uses examples of ancient and seventeenth-century literature.
5   See Glenn Penny (2003) for a detailed overview of the history of German anthropology.
6   Some of the texts were published in the anthology *Südamerikanische Indianermärchen* (Koch-Grünberg 1921).
7   'As a translator [Mayuluaipu] was priceless to me' (Koch-Grünberg 1917–28, 2:V). All quotations from German and Portuguese are translated by the author.
8   'Alle Erläuterungen und Erklärungen der Erzähler, die in den Text nicht gehören, habe ich in Klammern beibehalten, um zu zeigen, wie die Leute bemüht waren, Einzelheiten meinem Verständnis näher zu bringen.'
9   'Das innere Wesen einer Zauberkur, deren äußeren Verlauf ich oben geschildert habe, wurde mir von Akuli in allen Einzelheiten beschrieben. Ich gebe seine Erzählung hier wieder, wie sie von Mayüluaipu ins Portugiesische übersetzt wurde.'
10 'Jose steht immer zu meiner Verfügung. [...] Er ist bescheiden und aufmerksam und unermüdlich, mir die genauesten Angaben zu machen über die Sitten, Gebräuche und Anschauungen seines Stammes. Jeden Tag diktiert er mir Taulipáng-Texte, Märchen und Zaubersprüche, und wir übersetzen sie zusammen Wort für Wort ins Portugiesische.'
11 'Abgesehen von diesen modernen Erzeugnissen indianischer Phantasie enthalten diese Sagen viel primitives Material. Sie zeigen alle Merkmale, die Ehrenreich als Urformen bezeichnet, "als mythologischen Allgemeinbesitz", der auf primitiver Stufe den Bestand der Mythologie erschöpft und daher als Ureigentum der Menschheit anzusehen ist.'
12 'Mayüluaipu erzählte mir die Mythen zunächst in portugiesischer Sprache, und ich übersetzte sie dann wortgetreu in das Deutsche. Eine Reihe von Sagen diktierte er mir sodann im Urtext und half mir bei der genauen Übersetzung.'
13 Both texts are now copyright free. In Brazil and Germany works enter the public domain 70 years after the death of their author.
14 'Os índios foram decisivos para que o Brasil ganhasse essa área, numa disputa que houve no passado com a Guiana, portanto, com a Inglaterra. Dizer que viraram ameaça significa, no mínimo, cometer uma injustiça histórica. Até o mito do Macunaíma, que foi recolhido por um alemão, Koch-Grünberg, e transformado por um Paulista, Mário de Andrade, foi contado por índios daquela área, os macuxis, os wapixanas. Eles são co-autores da ideologia nacional.' The Macuxi and Wapichana are considered part of the Pemón ethnic group, as are the Taulipáng and Arekuná.

References

Andrade, Mário de. 1928. *Macunaíma, o heroi sem nenhum caracter*. São Paulo: Oficinas graficas de E. Cupolo.
Arellano, Fernando. 1986. *Una introducción a la Venezuela prehispánica: Culturas de las naciones indígenas venezolanas*. Caracas: Univ. Católica Andrés Bello.
Arrojo, Rosemary. 1997a. 'The "death" of the author and the limits of the translator's visibility'. In *Translation as Intercultural Communication: Selected papers from the EST Congress, Prague 1995*, edited by Mary Snell-Hornby, Zuzana Jettmarová and Klaus Kaindl, 21–32. Amsterdam and Philadelphia, PA: John Benjamins.
Arrojo, Rosemary. 1997b. 'Pierre Menard und eine neue Definition des "Originals"'. In *Übersetzungswissenschaft in Brasilien: Beiträge zum Status von 'Original' und Übersetzung*, edited by Michaela Wolf, 25–34. Tübingen: Stauffenburg.
Asad, Talal. 2009. 'The concept of cultural translation in British social anthropology' (1986). In *Critical Readings in Translation Studies*, edited by Mona Baker, 223–47. London and New York: Routledge.
Bastian, Adolf. 1881. *Der Völkergedanke im Aufbau einer Wissenschaft vom Menschen und seine Begründung auf ethnologische Sammlungen*. Berlin: F. Dümmlers.

Benjamin, Walter. 1996. 'On language as such and on the language of men' (1916). Translated by Edmund Jephcott. In *Selected Writings. Volume 1, 1913–1926*, edited by Marcus Bullock and Walter Jennings, 62–74. Cambridge, MA: Belknap Press of Harvard University Press.

Berensmeyer, Ingo, Gert Buelens and Marysa Demoor. 2012. 'Authorship as cultural performance: New perspectives in authorship studies', *Zeitschrift für Anglistik und Amerikanistik* 60.1: 5–29.

Berns, Ute. 2010. 'Solo performances: An introduction'. In *Solo Performances: Staging the early modern self in England*, edited by Ute Berns, 11–30. Amsterdam: Rodopi.

Braz, Albert. 2011. 'Collaborative authorship and indigenous literatures'. *CLCWeb: Comparative Literature and Culture*, 13.2: 1–10. Accessed 20 March 2019. https://docs.lib.purdue.edu/clcweb/vol13/iss2/5/.

Brumble, H. David. 2008. *American Indian Autobiography*. Lincoln and London: University of Nebraska Press.

Carta de los Kari-Oca desde Brasil. 'El derecho de autor y la protección de los conocimientos indígenas'. 2004. Quaderns digitals.net. Accessed 2 May 2021. http://www.quadernsdigitals.net/index.php?accionMenu=secciones.VisualizaArticuloSeccionIU.visualiza&proyecto_id=2&articuloSeccion_id=3611&PHPSESSID=440bf5a9d3de194f0fa6f9667ab73af0.

Cobley, Paul. 2001. *Narrative*. London and New York: Routledge.

Compagno, Dario. 2012. 'Theories of authorship and intention in the twentieth century. An overview', *Journal of Early Modern Studies* 1.1: 37–53.

Derrida, Jacques. 1985. 'Otobiographies: The teaching of Nietzsche and the politics of the proper name' (1984). Translated by Avital Ronell. In *The Ear of the Other: Otobiography, transference, translation: Texts and discussions with Jacques Derrida*, edited by Christie V. McDonald, translated by Peggy Kamuf, 1–38. New York: Schocken Books.

Dudley, Kathryn Marie. 1998. 'In the archive, in the field: What kind of document is an "oral history"?' In *Narrative and Genre*, edited by Mary Chamberlain and Paul Thompson, 160–6. London: Routledge.

Foucault, Michel. 1998. 'What is an author?' Translated by Josué V. Harari. In *Aesthetics, Method, and Epistemology, Essential Works of Michel Foucault 1954–1984*, vol. 2, edited by James D. Faubion, translated by Robert Hurley and others, 205–22. New York: The New Press.

Goody, Jack. 1968. *Literacy in Traditional Societies*. Cambridge: Cambridge University Press.

Kangussu, Imaculada Maria Guimarães and Jair Tadeu da Fonseca. 2012. 'Macunaíma, literatura, cinema e filosofia', *Artefilosofia* 11: 144–57.

Knorr Cetina, Karin. 1999. *Epistemic Cultures: How the sciences make knowledge*. Cambridge, MA: Harvard University Press.

Koch-Grünberg, Theodor. 1917–28. *Vom Roroima zum Orinoco: Ergebnisse einer Reise in Nordbrasilien und Venezuela in den Jahren 1911–1913*. 5 vols. Berlin: Reimer (vol. 1) / Stuttgart: Stecker und Schröder (vol. 2–5).

Koch-Grünberg, Theodor, ed. 1921. *Südamerikanische Indianermärchen*. Jena: Diederichs.

Lopez, Telê Porto Ancona. 1974. *Macunaíma, a margem e o texto*. São Paulo: HUCITEC.

Love, Harold. 2002. *Attributing Authorship: An introduction*. Cambridge: Cambridge University Press.

McCall, Sophie. 2011. *First Person Plural. Aboriginal storytelling and the ethics of collaborative authorship*. Vancouver: University of British Columbia Press.

Menezes de Souza, Lynn Mario T. 2015. 'La otra historia: La escritura indígena en el Brasil' *Povos Indigenas no Brasil*. 15 May. Accessed 2 May 2021. https://pib.socioambiental.org/es/La_otra_historia:_la_escritura_ind%C3%ADgena_en_el_Brasil.

Murray, David. 1991. *Forked Tongues: Speech, writing, and representation in North American Indian texts*. Bloomington: Indiana University Press.

Ong, Walter J. 1982. *Orality and Literacy: The technologizing of the word*. London: Methuen.

Penny, H. Glenn, ed. 2003. *Worldly provincialism: German anthropology in the Age of Empire*. Ann Arbor: University of Michigan Press.

Pym, Anthony. 2011. 'The translator as non-author, and I am sorry for that.' In *The Translator as Author: Perspectives on literary translation*, edited by Claudia Buffagni, Beatrice Garzelli and Serenella Zanotti, 31–44. Berlin: Lit Verlag Dr. W. Hopf.

Sá, Lúcia. 2002. 'Germans and Indians in South America: Ethnography and the idea of text'. In *Myth: A new symposium*, edited by Gregory Allen Schrempp and William F. Hansen, 61–71. Bloomington: Indiana University Press.

Sá, Lúcia. 2004. *Rain Forest Literatures: Amazonian texts and Latin American culture*. Minneapolis: University of Minnesota Press.

Tymoczko, Maria. 1990. 'Translation in oral tradition as a touchstone for translation theory and practice'. In *Translation, History and Culture*, edited by Susan Bassnett and André Lefevere, 46–55. London: Pinter Publishers.
Venuti, Lawrence. 1995. *The Translator's Invisibility: A history of translation*. London: Routledge.
Viveiros de Castro, Eduardo. 2008. Interview by Flávio Pinheiro and Laura Greenhalgh. 'Não podemos infligir uma segunda derrota a eles', *Estadão*, 19 April 2008. Accessed 6 June 2021. http://alias.estadao.com.br/noticias/geral,nao-podemos-infligir-uma-segunda-derrota-a-eles,159735.

5
In the name of the father: Darwin, scientific authority and literary assimilation
Niall Sreenan

Introduction: Darwin and 'author function'

In his essay 'What is an author?' Michel Foucault addresses what he calls the 'paradoxical singularity' of the author's name in literary writing and its complex role in mediating the relationship between the author and the text (1998, 209). Literary writing, or écriture in Foucault's terms, has less to do with a canon or 'literariness' than it has with a type of writing that Barthes in 'The death of the author' insists 'can no longer designate an operation of recording, notation, representation, [or] "depiction"' (1977, 145). Foucault describes écriture as being characterised by an

> interplay of signs arranged less according to its signified content than according to the very nature of the signifier […], the creation of a space into which the writing subject constantly disappears.
>
> (1998, 206)

Foucault's essay is both an expansion upon Barthes' foundational work and a critical response to it. The difference in terminology they deploy to describe the fate of the author is instructive. Where Barthes seems to insist on the author's 'death', with the implication that the author of écriture is now a non-being, Foucault prefers the term 'disappearance', enjoining the reader to pay close attention to what takes its place. 'It is not enough,' he states, 'to repeat the empty affirmation that the author has disappeared [...]. Instead, we must locate the space left empty by the author's disappearance' (1998, 209).

Central to Foucault's development of Barthes' influential essay is the notion that along with the death of the author a transposition of the 'empirical characteristics of the author into a transcendental anonymity' occurs, creating a *de facto* 'author function' without specific characteristics: an individual without individuality (Foucault 1998, 208). Barthes appears to espouse a theory of writing free from representational or signifying certainty in which the author is dissolved by the possibilities of the text. However, Foucault cautions that this assumption engenders a dynamic whereby the complexities of writing, or the text in question and its relation to an empirical author or implied author-function, become obscured by an empty space – which, in reality, is occupied by an implicitly transcendental and adaptable but invisible authorial figure. In this instance the author's name, unlike the proper name of an empirical author from which it becomes uncoupled, comes to represent an abstraction; it designates something marked only by its supposed absence. Thus the supposed 'death' of the author does not create nothingness; it rather transforms the author's name into a sign for nothingness. Furthermore, this assumed absence leaves a space in which critical and interpretive foundationalism of authorship is once more re-entrenched.

According to Foucault, then, the author and his name is not a replaceable or insignificant element in discourse; it is not capable of receding into non-being. Rather, it is a crucial but shadowy element of discourse which 'characterise[s] a certain mode of being of discourse' (Foucault 1998, 211). The author function elevates discourse beyond what Foucault terms 'ordinary, everyday speech' (1998, 211) or what Barthes might call 'ordinary culture' (1977, 142) to a discourse 'that must be received in a certain mode and that, in a given culture, must receive a certain status' (Foucault 1998, 211).[1]

Few names have been allotted such specifically extraordinary and paradoxical status as that of 'Charles Darwin', the use of which in literature and literary criticism is the focus of this chapter. Bruno Latour calls him 'Saint Darwin, this Father of the Church', suggesting that the author of *The Origin of Species* and the theory of evolution by natural selection has become a substitute for God in the largely secular, author-less, Western scientific imaginary that his work was instrumental in bringing about (Latour 2009, 467). As I have pointed out, for Foucault the 'death of the author' does not signal the actual absence of authorial power, but the creation of an implicit yet sometimes obscure author function.

According to Latour, and also to Jacques Barzun (1958, 66–7), the name 'Darwin' signifies the death of divine authority – even, Latour points out, as it acts as a metonymic placeholder for the discourse of biological evolutionary theory as such. Thus Darwin displaces the authority of a transcendent, religious God with an evolutionary scientific one, while simultaneously signifying the supreme authority of the scientific discourse that brought about the death of God. This sense of the paradoxical nature of Darwin's author function as a signifier for the divinity of scientific authority is confirmed by the various ways in which Darwin's name, and theory, are deployed in a multiplicity of discursive contexts. This chapter focuses on the use of Darwin's name and thought in literary and literary critical contexts, each of which registers the authorial significance of the named discourse they use to different degrees and highlights the specific complexities of Darwin's author function.

Foucault's notion of the 'founders of discursivity' (1998, 217–18) is a useful theoretical touchstone to describe the fate of Darwin's name in the history of scientific and literary discourses. For Foucault, the figures of Marx, Freud and Nietzsche each inaugurated exceptional forms of discursive thought – the development and transformation of which is not defined by an adherence to their inaugural concepts and authorial power, but by the fact that their names are associated with founding the conditions for the production of further creative discourse. For Foucault, therefore, one can be Freudian without simply repeating Freud's ideas, as was the case for Jacques Lacan, but by developing and transforming Freud's foundational concepts in a variety of discursive contexts – even in ways that might be implicitly opposed to Freud's psychoanalytic approach. In this chapter I shall be asking whether, or to what extent, it is possible to read the afterlife of Darwin's name and theories in the same way.

In the chapter that follows, I shall examine a number of examples of literary, literary critical and scientific usages of Darwin's name and assimilations of his theory, in dialogue with the work of both Barthes and Foucault on the author. There are two primary points that I wish to address. The first is the complex singularity of Darwin's name and writing in relation to the concept of the 'author function' (Foucault 1998, 211–19) – which, I shall be arguing, can be productively viewed, in the light of Foucault's characterisation of Marx, Freud and Nietzsche, as 'transdiscursive' (1998, 217). The second is the potential for 'non-scientific' writing, especially in the form of the novel, to demonstrate this transdiscursive possibility. Looking at works by Thomas Hardy and Émile

Zola, the novel, I shall then argue, offers us literary discursive space in which to explore the transdiscursive potential of Darwin's thought, by circumventing the epistemological demands made by scientific discourse associated with Darwin's name.

'Literary Darwinism': Darwin's name and effects of scientificity

The French writer and critic Armand Lanoux, in his influential biography of Émile Zola, describes an encounter between Zola and Edmond and Jules de Goncourt. Zola, he writes, directed an outburst at the brothers that outlined the rationale for using biological sciences as a central conceptual and methodological pillar of the literary Naturalist artwork:

> Les caractéres de nos personnages sont détérminés par les organs génitaux. C'est de Darwin! La literature, c'est ça![2]

(Lanoux 1962, 102)

[The actions of the characters we write about are determined by their genital organs. That's what Darwin says and that's what literature is!]

No mention is made of the encounter either in the Goncourt brothers' detailed autobiographical notebooks, nor in any of Zola's own correspondence. Indeed, according to David Baguley, in a study of the genetic relationship between Zola and Darwin, the story is almost certainly a fabrication, a symptom of the overweening, biographical, creative licence of Lanoux (Baguley 2011, 203). Although this seemingly innocuous anecdote reflects with a certain literary economy the reductive scientific dogmatism of Zola's thought in his literary-scientific manifesto, *Le Roman expérimental* (Zola 1880), Baguley points out that it erroneously associates Darwin with Zola's quasi-scientific realist method and greatly overstates the importance of Darwin to Zola's wider scientific idioculture. Aside from a handful of allusions in three of his novels, and a brief mention of Darwinism in the theoretical work on the Naturalist novel mentioned above, Darwin's name is largely absent from Zola's extensive œuvre. Neither his correspondence nor his voluminous preparatory *ébauches* indicate any direct or rigorous engagement with Darwin's texts (Baguley 2011, 203).

Baguley's essay suggests that the erroneous practice of making simplistic connections between Darwin and Zola, as well as the widespread and durable critical myth that the latter read the former, can be traced in part to Lanoux's biographical licentiousness. However, this anecdote also invites us to make a couple of theoretical assertions regarding the dynamics of naming and authoriality in the encounter of scientific discourse and literature. In *Le Roman expérimental*, Zola actually makes a passing allusion to Darwin: 'I ought to touch upon Darwin's theories; but [...] I should lose myself were I to enter into details' (Zola 1893, 19 [1880]).

Zola's use of Darwin's name can be interpreted in two ways. It may be viewed in Barthesian terms, asking how this apparent allusion to Darwin's science instead works as a sign for an allusion; it produces for Zola the *effect* of scientificity as much as the effect of reality, the combined outcome of which is the bolster of the pretensions of Zola's literary Naturalist method. Or it may follow Baguley's line of reasoning – as well as the critical assumptions against which he argues – and examine whether Zola's notebooks or correspondence justify this allusion. Both the Barthesian method and that of Baguley produce the same outcome: Zola seems to have been fabricating his knowledge of Darwinism. However, the latter method shows the success of Zola's gesture. Where he simply uses Darwin's name, this invites critics to attempt to take that sign as an indication of either Zola's comprehensive engagement with, or total lack of knowledge of, Darwin's actual work.

This tension in Zola's writing between its avowed scientificity and its literary materiality is also remarked upon by Thomas Hardy, Zola's contemporary. He writes in 'The science of fiction' (1891) that 'M Zola, in his work on the *Roman Expérimental*, seems to reveal an obtuseness to the disproof of his theory conveyed in his own novels' (Hardy 2001b, 107). Hardy, who criticised shallow forms of mimetic 'realism', claimed not to require the authorial prestige of scientific facticity to inject his work with a shallow sense of modernity or epistemological glamour. 'To advance realism as complete copyism, to call the idle trade of story-telling a science,' he writes of literary Naturalism, 'is the hyperbolic flight of an admirable enthusiasm', but an ultimately misguided enterprise (Hardy 2001b, 107). Rather, Hardy argued, one should actively seek to create 'the illusion of truth' which penetrates deeper into reality than the use of scientific names and allusion (2001b, 108).

Arguably, this is precisely what Zola did do. Nevertheless, Hardy was also attracted to Darwin's name, as well as the ideas to which that name was attached. In Hardy's autobiography, compiled by his second wife Florence Hardy from correspondence, notes, memoranda and other writings, Hardy is described as an 'early acclaimer' of *The Origin of Species*, and he also attended Darwin's funeral in April 1882 (Hardy 1997, 148). Elsewhere he undertakes a monumental piece of scientific and literary citation, claiming as his primary intellectual influences Spencer, Hume, Mill, Huxley and Darwin (Weber 1940, 246–7). Though perhaps done in the service of literary expediency, rather in an effort to make unjustified claims regarding his scientific erudition, this attests to the unique cultural capital associated with Darwin for Hardy, Zola and their readers.

The perceived cultural capital of Darwin's name extends also to literary criticism. In the late nineteenth and early twentieth centuries, in France and England respectively, Ferdinand Brunetière and John Addington Symonds published works of literary history and criticism that appropriated Darwin's name and, superficially, Darwin's concepts. Their works, *L'évolution des genres dans l'histoire de la littérature* (Brunetière 1890) and 'On the application of evolutionary principles to art and literature' (Symonds 1890, 1: 42–83), sought to describe, with the aid of biological evolution, the development of literature as a form of art and both the emergence and the extinction of literary genres.

For both men, Darwin's methods seem less important than the epistemological significance they ascribe to them. This allows them to wield Darwin's science as a transcendent scientific method with which to understand literary history.

It is precisely this authorial transcendence that Gillian Beer's 1983 work on the dialogue between evolutionary discourse and the nineteenth-century novel implicitly critiques by emphasising the specifically literary texture of Darwin's writing. However, this work too, entitled *Darwin's Plots,* also makes use of Darwin's name to define Beer's critical corpus and narratological approach. In so doing it implicitly places Darwin at the origin of a cluster of highly influential narratological tropes in the nineteenth and twentieth centuries.

Such has been the influence of Beer's work, and perhaps so powerful is the scientific cultural capital associated with Darwin's name, that – as George Levine points out in his Foreword to Beer's *Darwin's Plots* – it has spawned an entire 'Darwin Industry' in the humanities. For Levine, this attention to Darwin in literary criticism in particular 'expanded even beyond the imagination of those who already understood how enormously rich and fertile Darwin's thought remained' (Levine 2009, ix). However, one consequence of the growth of a 'Darwin Industry' is the return of discourses such as those of Brunetière and Symonds, in which Darwin's name represents transcendent scientific truth.

This occurs most suggestively in the development by the critic Joseph Carroll of a literary critical ethos he calls 'Literary Darwinism'. Carroll is the most prominent in a cadre of loosely affiliated literary scholars who seek to bring a synthesis of evolutionary natural selection and genetics to bear on the study of literature.[3] The fundamental critical thesis, as expressed by Carroll, is that

> all knowledge about human behaviour, including the products of the human imagination, can and should be subsumed within the evolutionary perspective.
>
> (DiSalvo and Carroll 2009)

Literature, it is argued, is an 'adaptation' to the demands of natural selection and should be understood, like other adaptations, as being produced by it. The key concept is subsumption. This methodology of adopting non-discursive 'knowledge' derived from Darwinian science is aimed at subsuming all other forms of critical thought; it is equally committed to the idea that all human behaviour, including literary discourse, is subsumed by the evolutionary demands of evolutionary survival. Such an approach derives from the work of the scientist Edward O. Wilson, who in *Consilience: The unity of knowledge* (Wilson 1998) rejects the discursive, relativist conceptions of truth espoused, according to him, by so-called 'postmodern' philosophy. Instead Wilson espouses the fusion of all forms of human inquiry under the umbrella of a rationalist, positivist, scientific epistemology.

Numerous critiques have been waged against this work. But, as with Brunetière (1890) and Symonds (1890, 1: 42–83), I am interested here in how the deployment of authorial power bolsters the epistemological aims of the literary Darwinist project. Regardless of their fealty to Darwin's thought or the veracity of their speculations, Darwin's name is used in these literary critical discourses primarily to signal a rejection of the Barthesian and Foucauldian notion of écriture, as well as the manner in which their discourse should be received. Under the rubric of 'Literary Darwinism', the name 'Darwin' is a metonymic placeholder for their use of positivist, rationalist epistemologies. Yet these, paradoxically, insist on the independent truth value of scientific discourse even as they rely on the authority of Darwin's author function and cultural capital.

Darwin, Darwinism and transdiscursivity

Barthes (1977) suggests a historical reason for the author's significance to writing prior to the authorial parricide enacted by contemporary writing (and Mallarmé in particular). He writes that

> The author is a modern figure, a product of our society insofar as, emerging from the Middle Ages with English empiricism, French rationalism and the personal faith of the Reformation, it discovered the prestige of the individual [...] It is thus logical that in literature it should be this positivism, the epitome and culmination of capitalist ideology, which has attached the greatest importance to the person of the author.
>
> (1977, 142)

The importance granted to the name 'Darwin', however, can be read as more than an exemplary instantiation of this historically produced, pre-Mallarmean reification of the individual. For Social Darwinian theorists such as Herbert Spencer, Darwin's theory of 'the struggle for life' underlined the natural authority of pre-Darwinian conceptions of capitalism and individualist market rationalism – both premised, like natural selection, on competitive relations between self-interested individuals (Hawkins 1997, 85–6). This idea gained considerable popular currency through the work of Spencer, whose capitalist adaptation of the work of Darwin, Mike Hawkins suggests, anticipated the recrudescence of neo-liberal forms of capitalist economics in the 1970s and 1980s (1997, 98).

The veneration of Darwin's name and work in contemporary pseudo-scientific literary critical discourses, then, can also be understood as a culmination or symptom of the combined intellectual currents that provided the intellectual conditions preceding the emergence of Darwinism in the nineteenth century (and the concomitant rise of capitalist ideological hegemony in Britain). Literary Darwinism is a re-canonisation of Darwin's major contribution to biology, the 'struggle for survival', which accompanies and intensifies the braided historical and intellectual forces of individualism, rationality, science, empiricism and capitalism that Barthes describes. The deployment of the name 'Darwin', then, is more than a reflexive veneration of these currents. In reifying Darwinism and its singular author, this deployment is a celebration of the primacy of the individual and its place in a naturally competitive milieu.

How is it, then, that several decades after Barthes proclaimed the death of the author, the sciences today maintain the author's existence, as well as all the ideological and historical implications this bears? Foucault's complementary historical analysis in 'What is an author?' (1998, 205–22) seems unable to account for this development. He notes how the author's role in science and literature followed divergent paths prior to the nineteenth century and the shift that occurs, in Barthes' view, with Mallarmé. Foucault notes that literary texts up until the seventeenth or eighteenth centuries were circulated, read and accepted with no issue as to the author's anonymity – or the lack of an author function with which to classify it. Scientific texts, by contrast, were only considered 'true' in the Middle Ages once the author's identity was confirmed. A reversal occurred, Foucault says, when science took on anonymity to indicate a superior, unbiased and repeatedly testable truth. Literary texts, on the other hand, have since the eighteenth century become discursively inseparable from their author function (Foucault 1998, 212 –13).

The socio-historical process that Foucault describes here, and the divergent fate of the author function in science and in literature, present themselves as contrary to the state of affairs I have described up to now. Where scientific truth takes on anonymity as its epistemological guarantor, so-called 'Darwinian' literary criticism demands the opposite: specific authorial identity.

Contrary to Foucault's schema, then, Darwin's author function is not reducible to that of a scientific discourse which disavows its author(s) in the name of anonymity and objectivity. Instead, Darwin seems to represent a singular kind of author function, offering positivist discourses the capacity to use the name 'Darwin' as a paradoxical symbol for scientific truth independent of historical and cultural indexes. However, Beer's work shows that such an attempt to abstract Darwin's work is by definition problematic, since Darwin's writing and thought are inseparable from their cultural and literary contexts. Indeed, further exploration of the various assimilations and reinterpretations of Darwin's work suggest that Darwin's thought is radically open to interpretation and transformation.

I have already gestured at the way in which Darwin's work, especially the theory of natural selection, is bound up with nineteenth-century individualism and capitalism – and I have identified Herbert Spencer's work as instrumental in solidifying this connection. However, Darwinian evolution by natural selection was equally interpreted as natural authorisation for socialist and communist ideologies.[4] Figures such as Engels (1978) and Peter Kropotkin (1972) saw in evolutionary Darwinism the confirmation that socialism and communism, rather than individualist competition, were innate in the natural order. Kropotkin, in particular, theorised that contrary to Spencer's reading of Darwin, co-operation ensured survival; socialism was thus integral to human evolution. What Freud characterised as Darwin's 'Copernican' revolution did not engender merely one type of discourse – scientific, literary or otherwise. It rather produced a diverse range of often antithetical concepts and theories, all of which emerge from a single authorial source (Freud 1963, 284).

Of the authors who write works of such discursive productivity and malleability, Foucault observes:

> They are unique in that they are not just authors of their own works. They have produced something else: the possibilities and the rules for the formation of other texts.
>
> (1998, 217)

However, he is very careful not to include scientists in this category of 'transdiscursive' texts, settling instead on the figures that Paul Ricœur calls 'masters' of the 'hermeneutics of suspicion' (1970, 30–8). Might one legitimately ask whether Darwin could not be included within this particular pantheon of transdiscursivity? Certainly, as I have briefly demonstrated, Darwin's work has engendered the possibilities for other texts – texts that we can call 'Darwinian', but which have not been authored by Darwin. However, it is clear that in the positivistic discourses of literary Darwinism, Darwin's name has fallen foul of the scientific orthodoxy his work has spawned. In these works, where Darwin's name is both repressed and revered, these critics lay claim to an authentic, scientific Darwin, while insisting that anonymity bears the guarantee of truth. It is thus towards literary writing that we should turn to illuminate the transdiscursive character and singularity of Darwin's writings.

Zola and Darwin: the case of *Germinal* (1885)

Hereditary science provides the architecture and methodological premise of Émile Zola's *Rougon-Macquart* novel series; it also, as Susan Harrow has pointed out, forms part of its thematic substrate (2010, 94). Many of Zola's characters are haunted by an atavistic, hereditary taint that prevents them from achieving their ambitions, condemns them to tragic endings and confirms the scientific determinism built into the formal impetus and thematic preoccupations of the Naturalist novel. As I have illustrated, the extent to which we can read Zola's commitment to naturalism and determinism as a corollary of an assumed interest in Darwinian evolution is arguable. However, in Zola's novel *Germinal* (Zola 1978), which takes as its theme the eternal war between capital and labour and the possibility of revolution, a discussion of Darwin by the novel's protagonist connects the British naturalist's work to a much broader theme than that of biological evolution.

Étienne Lantier, the novel's protagonist and an incipient, self-educated Marxist revolutionary, foments a worker's strike in the fictional mining town of Montsou. Having witnessed the violent and catastrophic failure of this strike, Lantier asks:

> *Darwin, avait-il donc raison, le monde ne serait-il qu-une bataille, les forts mangeant les faibles, pour la beauté et la continuité de l'espèce?*
> (Zola 1978, 490)
>
> [Was Darwin right, then? Would the world forever be a battleground on which the strong devoured the weak in pursuit of the perfection and continuity of the species?]

The question invites us to consider whether the apparently inescapably tragic character of natural selection – 'the survival of the fittest' and the death of the unfit – can be reconciled with an emancipatory politics, and whether the Naturalist novel itself can address this question.

If Zola read Darwin's work at all, it was likely to be in poorly and tendentiously translated or in significantly attenuated form (Prum 2014, 391–9). As if to anticipate the critical objections that his fact might initiate, Zola deploys a playful, metafictional gesture that acknowledges his own ignorance and addresses the reception of Darwin in France in general. Earlier in *Germinal* he writes:

> *Étienne, maintenant, en était à Darwin. Il en avait lu des fragments, résumés et vulgarisés dans un volume à cinq sous; et, de cette lecture mal comprise, il se faisait une idée révolutionnaire du combat pour l'existence, les maigres mangeant les gras, le peuple fort dévorant la blême bourgeoisie.*
> (Zola 1978, 490)
>
> [Étienne had now got as far as Darwin. He had read this and that, as summarised for a popular audience in a volume costing five sous; and on the basis of his patchy understanding he had come to see revolution in terms of the struggle for existence, the lean eating the fat, the strong people devouring the pallid middle class.]

Here Zola's assimilation of Darwin, although it seems visible only through apparently shallow nominal allusion, offers us an implicit critique of our desire to put Darwin into interdiscursive circulation without attempting first to apprehend the complexity or breadth of his work. Such a critique is, by extension, applicable to the process of authorial canonisation. Darwin's name is used just as Foucault suggests it might be: a literary abstraction devoid of empiricity, with a tenuous connection to the works associated with that author and in which the nuances and contradictions these works contain are effaced by glib, ideologically bullish assumptions. And yet Zola's naming of Darwin paints an image of the way in which nineteenth-century European audiences received his work and the way in which Darwin's paradoxical author function arose. Even as new 'texts' and new thought were being created by the nuance and malleability of Darwin's writings and theories, his name became a crepuscular entity, both radically present in a range of discourses and devoid of individuality and contradiction.

Thomas Hardy's novels: Darwin as scientific authority

Thomas Hardy's treatment of Darwinism, in contrast to that of Zola, does not engage in ironic metafictionality. In fact Hardy, despite his avowed support for Darwin, does not mention his name at any point in his fictional corpus. However, unlike Zola, Hardy does engage with the large themes of Darwin's work: man's place in nature, life as a constant struggle and the fraught dynamics of reproduction and sexual relation that mark the human as much as the animal. It is upon the last that I wish to focus here.

Numerous critics have identified in Hardy's novels a preoccupation with sexuality and the vicissitudes of courtship, the strained conditions of which in Victorian England are evoked so well by Hardy in his novels (Higonnet 1993; Wright 1988). Hardy himself affirmed that realism consisted not of the representation of the abject, as in Zola, but of the realistic representation of 'relations between the sexes', and in Darwin we find suggestive material for the way in which Hardy goes about such a representation (Hardy 2001a, 97). The mechanics of sexual selection outlined in Darwin (1871) are, briefly, as follows: the male of a species competes with other males for possession of or access to a fertile female, while the female in turn exercises a form of aesthetic judgement on the male. This results in males being bedecked with feathers and instruments of war while females remain, it is assumed (and observed), comparatively passive and unadorned (Darwin 1871, 253–320). The dynamic at play here is easily perceived in Hardy's early work, *A Pair of Blue Eyes* (Hardy 2005). In this novel, published in 1872 soon after *The Descent of Man,* the central female protagonist navigates the courtship efforts of three competing male suitors. Similarly in *The Return of the Native* (Hardy 2013) three male suitors compete for the hand of one female, Eustacia Vye.

Hardy's staging of the dynamics of sexual selection does not, however, serve to naturalise the dynamic of the male as an active agent and the female as a passive one. Rather, Hardy's dramas of sexual relation work discursively to subvert these dynamics of hetero-normativity, focusing instead on the eroticism of sexual relation rather than its instrumentality. At a ritual Christmas dance, Eustacia arrives dressed as a male character in a folk play, 'revealing herself to be changed in sex, brilliant in colours, and armed from top to toe' (Hardy 2013, 163). She conceals her face and 'natural' gender in order to observe in secret the object of her sexual desire, Clym Yeobright, the returned native, who is present at the gathering.

Already the presumed schema of agency in Darwinian natural selection is subject to a reversal. Here Eustacia does not merely perform the active 'male' role; she enacts it by inverting the subject–object relation implied by the Darwinian schema. Additionally, the role that Eustacia plays is that of the aggressor, a heavily armed knight tasked with destroying its enemy, the comparatively feminine Saracen knight. She does not only take on the agency of a sexual aggressor, but also that of the invader and of the chivalrous knight. Here sexual relation is suffused with its own performativity, with the shifting dynamics of gendered roles and, in the outrageous dress of the players, the flamboyant eroticism of these dynamics.

Hardy, explaining the ritual preparations for such a performance, remarks that the costumes the players wear are outrageously showy and unnecessarily garlanded affairs:

> They insisted on attaching loops and bows of silk and velvet in any situation pleasing to their taste. Gorget, gusset, basinet, cuirass, gauntlet, sleeve, all alike in the view of these feminine eyes were practicable spaces whereon to sew scraps of fluttering colour.
>
> (Hardy 2013, 158)

This decoration results not from the competitive male instinct to impress females, but from the aesthetic sense – and creative desire – of their female companions; they drape their lovers with ribbons, scallops and silk in a manner 'pleasing to their taste'. Such gestures suggest the agential primacy of female desire in such a schema, or at least the fluidity of agency in sexual relation. However, perhaps, more significantly, it also depicts the 'relations between the sexes' as an encounter that is experienced and made pleasurable for its own sake; for the experience of creativity, for the intensities of colour and form that it produces, not merely as a precursor or instrumental lead-in to the act of reproduction.

Such eroticism and the creative possibilities of Darwinian sexual selection in relation to a philosophy of sexual difference provides the basis for Elizabeth Grosz's radical re-working of feminism in her work *Becoming Undone* (Grosz 2011). Developing the feminism of difference espoused by Luce Irigaray, Grosz sees in Darwin's work on sexual selection the basic affirmation that sexual relation is a form of creative repetition and not merely 're-production':

> Darwin's work can be understood as an analysis of the proliferation of nothing but differences: differences without any hierarchical order, without fixed identities or biological archetypes [...] differences generated for their own sake.
>
> (Grosz 2011, 167)

Such a theoretical move is consonant with Deleuze's insistence in *Difference and Repetition* (Deleuze 2004) that it is in Darwin that the notion of 'individual difference' enters the scientific imagination. The evolutionary biologist August Weissmann, Deleuze asserts, made an 'essential contribution' to Darwinian biology when he demonstrated 'how individual difference finds a natural cause in sexed reproduction: sexed reproduction as the principle of the "incessant production of varied individual differences"' (2004, 248–9).

Hardy's scene of a Christmas folk play, read through the prism of Darwin's writing, leads us to a new Darwin – a new text, if you will. Darwin's writings were not merely productive for Hardy's literary imagination; in their assimilation through Hardy's fiction, discursive possibilities continue to proliferate. Mobilising the name 'Darwin' to denote scientific authority, rather than the totemic name attached to a radically open corpus of texts, effectively ossifies Darwin's author function. This is reserved for a mode of discourse ideologically aligned with scientific epistemologies and ontologies. In contrast, Hardy's work alludes silently to that of Darwin. Through this he allows the careful reader to see in Darwin's thought – through the quotidian drama of human life – the possibility to undermine normative modes of thought in biology.

Conclusion

Darwin's writings and the name associated with them are singularly unclassifiable according to the vulgar taxonomies of science or literature. Foucault's definition of the founders of discourse omits Darwin – and natural science more generally. The focus in Foucault on Freud and Marx seems to denote a conveniently anthropocentric conception of transdiscursive possibility, at least in the sense that neither Freud nor Marx were avowedly concerned with 'the human'. Assimilations of Darwin such as that of Elizabeth Grosz – as I have read it in Hardy – offer us a broader conception of transdiscursivity as a category, as well as suggesting a divergent, post-human trajectory for Darwin's thought in critical philosophy.

I have approached Darwin's work through the writings of Foucault and Barthes on the author – for it is the image of the author, in the past and today, which is the most visible aspect of Darwin's writing. Allusion and appropriation defines its presence in many discursive contexts. Yet when we start to excavate these allusions to and co-options of Darwin's name, we can begin to glimpse the complexity of Darwin's writing, as well as the relationship between the author and these texts. I have attempted to show that in the novel, especially in those novels written in response to the revolution in biology that occurred in Europe in the mid-nineteenth century, these complexities and paradoxes can be most suggestively articulated. For the novel – by virtue of its literariness, which can be said to have become uncoupled from the idea of expression – allows for a freer engagement with Darwin's writings, unburdened by the epistemological fantasies of positivism. Following on from this, the novel becomes a discourse on equal footing with Darwin – or perhaps vice versa – in which science and art co-mingle, producing new thought, new questions and new discursive possibilities.

However, the perils of this type of engagement have to be recognised. If it is not treated with the critical care and attention it deserves, such engagement can itself contribute to the very process of authorial abstraction, which empties the name 'Darwin' of all substantive, empirical meaning and nuance.

Notes

1 Barthes uses the term 'ordinary culture' to describe a mode of discourse and a mode of being in relation to discourse that is 'tyrannically' centred upon the figure of the author. This he contrasts with modes of being of discourse that emerge after Mallarmé, which, in contrast, suppress 'the author in the interests of writing' (Barthes 1977, 142). Foucault, on the other

hand, describes everyday speech as that which does not possess an author function, and which therefore does not possess a specific status merited by the authority of such a function (1998, 211). Both authors use the idea of banality or the quotidian to describe a discourse and a way of relating to discourse that has at its core a deep desire for authorial attribution, in order to designate an appropriate means of receiving the text.
2   All translations from French are by the author.
3   'Literary Darwinism' is the title given to the discipline by its *de facto* leader, Joseph Carroll (2004; 2011). Brian Boyd is an example of a critic whose outlook is less strident than that of Carroll and who describes himself, more reflexively, as a representative of 'evocriticism' (2009, 384–97). However, his work is guided by the same commitment to advancing human knowledge through 'Darwinian' analyses of literary works.
4   D. A. Stack's analysis of socialist responses to Darwin offers a comprehensive view of the reception of Darwin by Marxist and socialist thinkers (2000, 682–710). See also Engels (1978) and Kropotkin (1972).

References

Baguley, David. 2011. 'Zola and Darwin: A reassessment'. In *The Evolution of Literature: Legacies of Darwin in European cultures*, edited by Nicholas Saul and Simon J. James, 201–12. Amsterdam: Rodopi.

Barthes, Roland. 1977. 'The death of the author' (1968). In *Image Music Text*, selected and translated by Stephen Heath, 142–8. London: Fontana Press.

Barzun, Jacques. 1958. *Darwin, Marx, Wagner: Critique of a heritage*. 2nd edition. Chicago and London: University of Chicago Press.

Beer, Gillian. 2009. *Darwin's Plots: Evolutionary narrative in Darwin, George Eliot and nineteenth-century fiction* (1984). 3rd edition. Cambridge: Cambridge University Press.

Boyd, Brian. 2009. *On the Origin of Stories: Evolution, cognition, and fiction*. Cambridge, MA and London: The Belknap Press.

Brunetière, Ferdinand. 1890. *L'évolution des genres dans l'histoire de la littérature: leçons professées à l'École normale supérieure*. Paris: Hachette.

Carroll, Joseph. 2004. *Literary Darwinism: Evolution, human nature, and literature*. London and New York: Routledge.

Carroll, Joseph. 2011. *Reading Human Nature: Literary Darwinism in theory and practice*. Albany, NY: SUNY Press.

Darwin, Charles. 1871. *The Descent of Man, and Selection in Relation to Sex*, vol. 1. London: John Murray.

Deleuze, Gilles. 2004. *Difference and Repetition* (1968). Translated by Paul Patton. London: Continuum.

DiSalvo, David and Joseph Carroll. 2009. 'What is literary Darwinism? An interview with Joseph Carroll', *Neuronarrative*. 27 February 2009. Accessed 1 May 2020. https://neuronarrative.wordpress.com/2009/02/27/what-is-literary-darwinism-an-interview-with-joseph-carroll/.

Engels, Friedrich. 1978. *The Part Played by Labour in the Transition from Ape to Man* (1876). Translated by Dudley Hogan. Moscow: Progress Publishers, 1978.

Foucault, Michel. 1998. 'What is an author?' Translated by Josué V. Harari. In *Aesthetics, Method, and Epistemology, Essential Works of Michel Foucault 1954–1984*, vol. 2, edited by James D. Faubion, translated by Robert Hurley and others, 205–22. New York: The New Press.

Freud, Sigmund. 1963. *The Standard Edition of the Complete Psychological Works of Sigmund Freud, Vol. XVI (1916–1917): Introductory lectures on psycho-analysis (Part III)*. Edited and translated by James Strachey. London: Hogarth Press and the Institute of Psycho-analysis.

Grosz, Elizabeth A. 2011. *Becoming Undone: Darwinian reflections on life, politics, and art*. Durham, NC: Duke University Press.

Hardy, Thomas. 1997. *The Life and Work of Thomas Hardy* (1984). Edited by Michael Millgate. London: Macmillan.

Hardy, Thomas. 2001a. 'Candour in English fiction' (1890). In *Thomas Hardy's Public Voice: The essays, speeches, and miscellaneous prose*, edited by Michael Millgate, 95–101. Oxford: Clarendon Press.

Hardy, Thomas. 2001b. 'The science of fiction' (1891). In *Thomas Hardy's Public Voice: The essays, speeches, and miscellaneous prose*, edited by Michael Millgate, 106–9. Oxford: Clarendon Press.

Hardy, Thomas. 2005. *A Pair of Blue Eyes* (1872). Edited by Alan Manford. Oxford: Oxford University Press.

Hardy, Thomas. 2013. *The Return of the Native* (1878). Edited by Simon Avery. Peterborough, Ont.: Broadview Press.

Harrow, Susan. 2010. *Zola, the Body Modern: Pressures and prospects of representation*. London: Legenda.

Hawkins, Mike. 1997. *Social Darwinism in European and American Thought, 1860–1945: Nature as model and Nature as threat*. Cambridge: Cambridge University Press.

Higonnet, Margaret R., ed. 1993. *The Sense of Sex: Feminist perspectives on Hardy*. Urbana: University of Illinois Press.

Kropotkin, Peter. 1972. *Mutual Aid: A factor of evolution* (1902). Edited by Paul Avrich. New York: Allen Lane.

Lanoux, Armand. 1962. *Bonjour Monsieur Zola*. Paris: Hachette.

Latour, Bruno. 2009. 'Will non-humans be saved? An argument in ecotheology', *Journal of the Royal Anthropological Institute* 15.3: 459–75.

Levine, George. 2009. 'Foreword'. In *Darwin's Plots*, Gillian Beer, 3rd edition, ix–xiv. Cambridge: Cambridge University Press.

Prum, Michel. 2014. 'Charles Darwin's first French translations.' In *The Literary and Cultural Reception of Charles Darwin in Europe*, vol. 4, edited by Thomas F. Glick and Elinor Shaffer, 391–9. London: Bloomsbury.

Ricœur, Paul. 1970. *Freud and Philosophy: An essay on interpretation*. Translated by Denis Savage. New Haven, CT: Yale University Press.

Stack, D. A. 2000. 'The first Darwinian left: Radical and socialist responses to Darwin, 1859–1914', *History of Political Thought* 21.4: 682–710.

Symonds, John Addington. 1890. *Essays: Speculative and suggestive*, 2 vols. London: Chapman and Hall.

Weber, Carl Jefferson. 1940. *Hardy of Wessex: His life and literary career*. New York: Columbia University Press.

Wilson, Edward O. 1998. *Consilience: The unity of knowledge*. New York: Knopf.

Wright, T. R. 1988. *Hardy and the Erotic*. Basingstoke: Macmillan.

Zola, Émile.1978. *Germinal* (1885). Paris: Gallimard.

Zola, Émile. 1893. *The Experimental Novel and Other Essays* (1880). Translated by Belle M. Sherman. New York: Cassell.

6
Dead Shelley
Mathelinda Nabugodi

'Let the dead bury their dead', Jesus says (Luke, 9: 60; cf. Matthew, 8: 22). The statement is commonly taken to mean that we should concern ourselves with salvation of the living rather than salvaging the dead. And yet such salvage is often the literary critic's domain. Stereotype has it that the canonical author is a dead white man, and that said man lives on through his works. In this chapter I consider the modalities of literary afterlife through the figure of one dead man, the Romantic poet Percy Bysshe Shelley (1792–1822). My focus is on Shelley's death by drowning in a shipwreck off the coast of Spezia in Italy and the poem he was working on at the time of death, serendipitously titled 'The Triumph of Life'.

Shelley had made himself known for radical opinions and misguided atheism, and many contemporary critics dismissed his poetry because they were appalled by his politics. Even Lord Byron, probably his most liberal friend, distanced himself from Shelley's 'speculative opinions' (Byron 2015, 407). After Shelley's death, his widow Mary Shelley and other friends, including Thomas Jefferson Hogg, Leigh Hunt, Thomas Medwin and Thomas Love Peacock, set about securing for Shelley the recognition that he never had in his lifetime, a process that required clearing him of his reputation as immoral atheist and political radical. This was primarily achieved through an intensive emphasis on the ideal, tender and delicate elements of his verse.

The project to rehabilitate Shelley's public image was continued throughout the nineteenth century by his daughter-in-law Jane, Lady Shelley and The Shelley Society. So successful were they that, in the words of Marilyn Butler, 'Shelley has not been the same man in our century since posterity in his own transformed him into Ariel: beautiful, ethereal, with the waves washing or wind blowing through his hair' (1981, 3). The posthumous idealisation of Shelley became the subject of controversy in the 1940s, when Robert M. Smith published *The Shelley Legend* (1945). Smith accused Shelley's critics and biographers of being deluded by the cult of the poet that developed under the auspices of The Shelley Society. Scholars such as Newman Ivey White (1946) and Frederick L. Jones (1946) took the book seriously enough to refute it at great length, which indicates the stakes which Shelley's reputation had for critics of his life and work. With hindsight, however, the most remarkable thing about the controversy may well be that Shelley's reputation seemed a relevant subject for dispute at a time when Europe was still counting the dead from the Second World War. Shelley's afterlife was next investigated by Sylvia Norman in *Flight of the Skylark* (1954), a more balanced study of the posthumous construction of Shelley's authorial persona. In the same decade an up-and-coming critic, Harold Bloom, made Shelley the subject of his doctoral dissertation, later published as *Shelley's Mythmaking* (1959), which carefully unpicked Shelley's relationship to his poetic forebears.

By the 1970s Bloom was working at Yale University alongside Geoffrey H. Hartman, Paul de Man and J. Hillis Miller; they were occasionally joined by Jacques Derrida, who gave a yearly seminar there. These five critics did not share a unified critical programme but, being distinguished by their introduction of new methods into literary study, they become known as the Yale School. Bloom's theory of poetic influence was in many ways furthest from the deconstructive approaches of the other four Yale critics; nonetheless he suggested that they publish a collection of essays that would showcase their approach to criticism. Shelley's poem 'The Triumph of Life' was chosen as the subject for all contributions, which eventually appeared in the collection *Deconstruction and Criticism* (1979). In the end only three of the five contributions contained extended readings of Shelley's poem: de Man's 'Shelley Disfigured', Derrida's 'Living On: Border Lines' and Miller's 'The Critic as Host'. These three essays are the focus of the present chapter. By examining how they imagine 'Shelley', the chapter suggests some broader reflections on how the image of an author continues to be renegotiated by his readers long after their death.

Disfiguration in 'The Triumph of Life'

'The Triumph of Life' opens at dawn.[1] While nature wakes, the poem's narrator falls into a trance in which he sees a series of dream visions. The content of each vision is by and large the same: it reveals a procession that is led by the triumphal chariot of Life. The great personages of European history take part alongside anonymous masses of people whose names are unrecorded. As the chariot rolls on, the crowds milling around it become disfigured – they are transformed into old, disabled, inhuman shadows of themselves. Before long, they collapse in the chariot's wake leaving desiccated remains, sucked dry of life. The imagery is commonly interpreted as a critique of Western history: rather than a march of progress, it is a process of progressive dehumanisation.

Early on in the poem, the narrator finds himself by the wayside, witnessing the triumphal procession passing by. Not understanding what it is that he is seeing, he wonders aloud: 'And what is this?' (177). This question is met with the unexpected reply 'Life' (180). Hearing this human voice, the narrator realises:

> That what I thought was an old root which grew
> To strange distortion out of the hill side
> Was indeed one of that deluded crew,
>
> And that the grass which methought hung so wide
> And white, was but his thin discoloured hair,
> And that the holes it vainly sought to hide
>
> Were or had been eyes.
> (182–8)

These eyes turn out to belong to the French philosopher Jean-Jacques Rousseau, who will come to act as the narrator's commentator and guide. For Shelley's generation, Rousseau's name is primarily associated with the ideals and failures of the French Revolution, which provides the immediate context for the poem's cynical take on European history. Orrin N. C. Wang has noted that by representing Rousseau, 'the radical all Europe and England knew', as a strangely distorted root Shelley puns on *radix*, the Latin word for root, which is also the root meaning of radical (Wang 1991, 644). The disfigured Rousseau enters the poem as a representative for an entire historical moment. 'The presence of Rousseau links the poem's visions to the status of Romanticism itself,' Forest Pyle suggests, 'by enjoining the fallen image of Rousseau [...] Romanticism is simultaneously implicated as one more broken monument of the Western cultural shrine' (1995, 102). In 'Shelley Disfigured', de Man appropriates Shelley's image of the fallen Rousseau for his own rhetorical reading: 'The erasure or effacement is indeed the loss of a face, in French *figure*. Rousseau no longer, or hardly [...] has a face. [...] he is disfigured, *défiguré*, defaced' (1979, 46).

The translation of 'face' into the French *figure,* and then implicitly back into 'figure', allows de Man to associate disfiguration with rhetorical figures. Since there is no etymological connection between the English 'figure' in the sense of rhetorical trope and 'disfiguration' as physical disfigurement, it is only by 'bringing in the French *figure* [that] de Man links Rousseau with language – the question of figure – and names the main action of that language as disfigurement' (Wang 1991, 637). In other words, de Man's concept of disfiguration is a pun in translation comparable to Shelley's pun on *radix* in representing Rousseau as a root. The detour into French enables a move from the physical alteration of facial features towards the conceptual and semantic distortion of linguistic figures: from the image of Rousseau's disfigured face to the rhetorical figure, and from there to its disfiguration – the latter being de Man's term for the process through which rhetorical figures undercut the epistemological content of any linguistic statement.

Despite the focus on rhetorical reading, de Man's discussion of disfiguration is haunted by the appearance of Shelley's drowned corpse, which washed up on shore in a state of such decomposition that it could only be identified by Shelley's clothing and a book in his pocket – a historical accident that cuts across the workings of language. Towards the end of his reading of 'The Triumph of Life', de Man concludes:

> The poem is sheltered from the performance of disfiguration by the power of its negative knowledge. But this knowledge is powerless to prevent what now functions as the decisive textual articulation: its reduction to the status of a fragment brought about by the actual death and subsequent disfiguration of Shelley's body, burned after his boat capsized and he drowned off the coast of Lerici. This defaced body is present in the margin of the last manuscript page and has become an inseparable part of the poem.
> (de Man 1979, 66–7)

While Shelley's death is obviously unrelated to the rhetorical structures operative in the work, it nonetheless functions as the poem's 'decisive textual articulation'. How can we parse this relation between historical events and the meaning of a literary work? Of course, one could argue that Shelley's death has itself, in the form of biographical myth, become a textual event. For instance, Joseph A. Dane, in a study of the accounts of Shelley's death and cremation given by Medwin, Hunt and Trelawny, has noted that the 'problem with these various accounts is not only that they are incompatible, but that they are largely fictional' (Dane 1998, 68). Kim Wheatley has furthermore demonstrated how the ways in which the three witnesses misrepresent the facts 'show the influence of Gothic and sentimental fiction as well as of Shelley's own poetry' (2000, 163). In other words, Shelley's friends fictionalised his death in line with generic conventions also at work in Shelley's own writings. Since any informed reader is likely to be aware that 'The Triumph of Life' is Shelley's last work, the biographical circumstances surrounding its composition can be said to frame and thus become part of the poem.

Nonetheless, it is notable that de Man's argument distinctly foregrounds the physicality of Shelley's decomposing corpse – he refers to 'the actual death *and* subsequent disfigurement of Shelley's body' (de Man 1979, 66; emphasis added). Placing Shelley's disfigured corpse in the margin of a poem that performs rhetorical disfiguration on both deictic and formal levels, de Man implies that all texts are shaped by events, accidental or otherwise, that lie beyond the bounds of the text and yet serve as their decisive articulations. The figure of the dead Shelley thus becomes the emblem of a certain conception of literary writing as inherently mutilated by historical accident. 'The final test of reading, in *The Triumph of Life*, depends on how one reads the textuality of this event, how one disposes of Shelley's body', de Man writes, adding immediately that this 'challenge' is 'in fact present in all texts' (1979, 67).

Rather than being an aberration, the way in which Shelley's death fragments 'The Triumph of Life' is representative of how history fragments literary writing.

> For what we have done with the dead Shelley, and with the other dead bodies that appear in romantic literature [...] is simply to bury them, to bury them in their own texts made into epitaphs and monumental graves. [...] They have been transformed into historical and aesthetic objects.
>
> (de Man 1979, 67)

This tendency is at work in de Man's own reading, which turns Shelley's corpse into an aesthetic object: a sentimental spectacle in the tradition of posthumous representations of Shelley initiated by his widow and his friends.

Editing Shelley

De Man's rhetorical reading of 'The Triumph of Life' neglects a crucial fact about the poem – namely, its textual status. While he does comment on variant readings, de Man disregards the fact that the holograph MS that contains 'The Triumph of Life' is so incomplete and chaotic as to be barely identifiable as a poem (1979, 41). Paying attention to the mass of papers that Shelley left behind, Ross Wilson has rightly questioned the 'decisiveness' with which de Man offers 'a critical encapsulation' of the work that was left unfinished (2013, 147). The poem was first published in Mary Shelley's edition of *Posthumous Poems of Percy Bysshe Shelley* (1824) and reprinted in *The Poetical Works of Percy Bysshe Shelley* (1839). In a letter to Edward Moxon, the publisher of the later edition, Mary Shelley writes:

> The M.S. from which it [*Posthumous Poems* of 1824] was printed consisted of fragments of paper which in the hands of an indifferent person would never have been decyphered – the labour of putting it together was immense – the papers were in my possession & in no other person's (for the most part), the volume might be all my writing (except that I could not write it).
>
> (Shelley 1964, 2: 300)

While Mary Shelley is arguing for the copyright in her husband's work, it is no exaggeration to say that a draft such as 'The Triumph of Life' did not exist as a poem until she edited it into shape. The same applies to many of the unfinished pieces that she included in her editions of Shelley's poetry. As amanuensis and editor Mary Shelley participates in the composition of Shelley's works. She uses her editorial commentary to reinforce that claim, explaining that her late husband's papers constituted 'so confused a mass, interlined and broken into fragments, so that the sense could only be deciphered and joined by guesses, which might seem rather intuitive than founded on reasoning' (Shelley 1839, 4: 226).

Some of the 'poems' that Mary Shelley constructed were little more than fragmentary jottings and abandoned scraps. Michael Rossington, one of Mary Shelley's successors as editor of Shelley's work (including 'The Triumph of Life'), notes that

> [o]nce published, fragmentary drafts of verse can hardly be demoted from their status as 'poems' in the Shelley canon [...]. Is it possible, let alone prudent, to manufacture reading texts out of rough holographs that are in many cases far from being finished, label them as 'poems', then present them as part of the Shelley canon?
> (Rossington 2013, 652)

Prudent or not, Mary Shelley's editorial labours have salvaged the Shelley textual corpus that we have today out of his chaotic manuscripts. Acknowledging the importance of posthumous editing in the creation of Shelley's poetry, however, gives rise to a further question: who is the author of 'The Triumph of Life'? Mary Shelley arguably has a share in the poem's composition – to paraphrase her own words, the poem is her own writing that she 'could not write'.

Derrida's reading of Shelley, 'Living On: Border Lines' (Derrida 1979, 75–176), does not consider the poem's textual history. However, in its focus on the manner in which texts 'live on' indirectly raises the question of posthumous editorial labour. Derrida is interested in the extent to which any act of reading demands a signatory of the text being read – demands, in other words, that we fashion an image of the author. 'But who's talking about living?' the essay opens (Derrida 1979, 75). One possible answer is Shelley, the poet who wrote a poem called 'The Triumph of Life' – a poem, so the narrative goes, left unfinished by the death of its author. But while the process of composition ends with Shelley's death, that is not the end of the poem itself, which lives on in every act of reading it. Hence Derrida speaks of 'the supposed unfinished quality' of 'The Triumph of Life' which 'separates it from its ending', and which in its turn can be further separated from 'its supposed signatory and his drowning' (1979, 83). But, we may now add, that which separates us – the readers of 'The Triumph of Life' – from the last words that Shelley wrote before drowning is Mary Shelley's editorial labour on the poem. Another possible answer to Derrida's opening question, then, is that it is Mary Shelley who is talking about living – not least because, on a personal level, the act of editing Shelley appears to have been an act of bringing him back to life.

In one of the first entries in her 'Journal of Sorrow', begun a few months after Shelley's death, Mary Shelley sets herself a task to 'commemorate the virtues of the only creature on earth worth loving or living for' (Shelley 1987, 2: 434). In this gesture, she turns her husband's afterlife into her own life's work. Her achievement in the Shelley editions goes beyond establishing reliable texts: she summons his presence by restoring his words. Michael Gamer places Mary Shelley's editions 'at the center' of posterity's image of Shelley: 'For it was in the *Posthumous Poems* that Mary Shelley presented for the first time a recollected, reconstituted literary corpus – and through it, a posthumous portrait of its author' (Gamer 2008, 24). For similar reasons Neil Fraistat, another of Shelley's editors, states that 'of the 170 years that have passed since Shelley's death, the two most crucial ones for *establishing his texts, textualizing his life,* and *securing his reputation* were 1824 and 1839, the years of Mary Shelley's magisterial editions' (1994, 410; emphasis added).

Importantly, the three facets – establishing a text, creating a narrative about Shelley's life and securing his reputation – are all intertwined in the task that Mary Shelley set herself. Sir Timothy Shelley, Shelley's father, forced Mary Shelley to withdraw the *Posthumous Poems* and banned her from bringing Shelley's name in front of the public in his lifetime. As he reached an unusually old age, she had to wait almost twenty years for an opportunity to complete her task. After Sir Timothy's death, she prepared the four-volume *Poetical Works* (1839), in whose preface she acknowledges:

> I hasten to fulfil an important duty, – that of giving the productions of a sublime genius to the world, with all the correctness possible, and of, at the same time, detailing the history of these productions, as they sprung, living and warm, from his heart and brain.
> (Shelley 1839, 1: vii)

Working through Shelley's literary corpus, Mary Shelley reanimates her husband's bodily corpse – here seen in the emphasis on his productions springing 'living and warm from his heart and brain'. Referring to what she terms Mary Shelley's 'project of writing him [Shelley] back into life', Julian North suggests that her editorial labour was 'motivated by twinned desires: to restore her husband to life, in an intimate, loving relationship with the reading public and with herself' (2010, 753). This implies a complete identification of life and work, so that editing the latter becomes a way of restoring the former: Shelley lives on in his words. Eric O. Clarke notes how the Shelley who emerges through Mary Shelley's acts of reanimation is a sexually attractive man, so that 'the question of Shelley's cultural value and his erotic value were in many ways one and the same' (1995, 188).

It is therefore important to acknowledge the extent to which our image of Shelley is a product of Mary Shelley's work. She is, after all, the author who became famous for writing *Frankenstein*, a novel centred on the reanimation of a creature cobbled together from dead body parts – in a comparable way she cobbled together a poetic oeuvre from fragmentary scraps and, in the process, crafted a persona for the poet. Samuel Lyndon Gladden highlights Mary Shelley's authorship in her editions of Shelley's poetry: 'Mary Shelley's notes to her husband's poems mark out a space for the editor herself as a thinker and as a writer of individual autonomy' (2005, 183). Mary Favret likewise draws attention to how Mary Shelley's editorial commentary creates a semi-fictional portrait of Shelley. She argues that his 'biography becomes increasingly the property of Mary Shelley (her fiction), supplanting the influence of the poetry itself. As the widow's emotional story grows more and more poignant, the poet and his work become increasingly ethereal and insubstantial' (Favret 1993, 19). Michael O'Neill has questioned Favret's assertions about the extent to which Mary Shelley wilfully seeks to overwrite her late husband's life and work, but he, too, acknowledges her editorial achievement (O'Neill 2010). In light of this textual history, Mary Shelley may well be seen as the authoritative signatory of Shelley's posthumously published writings.

Living on

Let's return to Derrida's question 'But who's talking about living?' One of the answers that Derrida himself offers is:

> *The Triumph* talks about living. But what does it say about it? A great deal, far too many things, but this much at least, in its writing-on-living: it *is* […] it lives on. But – I must say this in the syntax of my language to defy the translators to decide, at each moment – *in/after whose name, or the name of what*, does it live on? Does it live on in/after Shelley's name?
>
> (Derrida 1979, 79–80)

Paying attention to the poem's editorial history suggests the answer that it is Mary Shelley who is talking about the living Shelley; in her writing-on-Shelley, he lives on. But Derrida is not only interested in Shelley's posthumous life. 'Living On: Border Lines' is also a reading of Maurice Blanchot's *L'arrêt de mort* (1976, 379–403). As Geoffrey Hartman has noted in his introduction to Lydia Davies's translation of the novella, *arrêt de mort* translates as 'death sentence' as well as 'suspension of death' (1976, 379). Derrida's piece takes note of Hartman's translation (Derrida 1979, 109) and extends the translation process, showing that *L'arrêt de mort* also translates into 'The Triumph of Life': life's triumph over the living manifests itself in their death, and so the triumph of life is a form of death sentence. On the other hand, a triumphant life can also be understood as a triumph over death, pointing towards a suspension or arrest of death that opens onto posthumous survival.

Derrida's 'coupled pretexts of *The Triumph of Life* and *L'arrêt de mort*' prompt a meditation on life and death that unfolds into a consideration of textual survival (1979, 77). Texts live on by being read, interpreted, translated. Possibly they are never so much alive as in the kind of transformative translation exemplified by Derrida's reading of 'The Triumph of Life' as an *arrêt de mort*:

> Hence the triumph as the triumph of translation. [...] A text lives only if it lives *on* {*sur-vit*}, and it lives *on* only if it is *at once* translatable *and* untranslatable [...] Thus triumphant translation is neither the life nor the death of the text, only or already its living *on*, its life after life, its life after death.
>
> (Derrida 1979, 103)

In addition to the texts of Shelley and Blanchot, another text is woven into Derrida's triumphant translation: Walter Benjamin's essay on 'The task of the translator', which defines the life of a literary work as its afterlife among future readers. Benjamin uses the three terms *Fortleben*, *Nachleben* and *Überleben*, all of which resonate in Derrida's essay. *Leben* translates as either 'life' or 'to live', whereas the prepositions *fort* and *über* can be rendered as 'on' so that *Fortleben* and *Überleben* are quite literally living *on*, or, in French, *sur*-vivre, surviving – the very idea of an *after*life, *Nachleben*. Benjamin considers the translator's task to be literal word-by-word translation; Derrida translates words literally and, in so doing, establishes connections between the works of Shelley, Blanchot and Benjamin through which these texts live on. That is, in taking three texts that thematise the life and survival of writing, and by translating them into one another, Derrida lets them live on within his own critical reading, aptly titled 'Living On' (1979, 75).

The question of inter-translation also raises the question of boundaries: if one text translates into another, where does one end and the other begin? (Just as aptly, Derrida's second title is 'Border Lines' (1979, 75).) Moreover what does it do to an author, to the value of his signature, when one text – 'The Triumph of Life', for instance – can be read as a translation of another, such as *L'arrêt de mort*, published 106 years after Shelley's death? The question of textual afterlife is implicitly one of demarcation, of how to draw the line that delimits one text from another. 'If we are to approach [*aborder*] a text, for example, it must have a *bord*, an edge' (Derrida 1979, 81). The French word *bord* translates as 'edge', 'brink', 'verge', 'border', 'boundary', 'bound', 'limit' or 'shore' – meanings that connect the boundaries (*bords*) of Shelley's text with the shore (*bord*) on which he wrote his last poem and off which he drowned, a drowning that leaves his final poem without an ending, causing

> a sort of overrun [*débordement*] that spoils all these boundaries and divisions [...] a 'text' that is henceforth no longer a finished corpus of writing, some content enclosed in a book or its margins, but a differential network, a fabric of traces referring endlessly to something other than itself.
>
> (Derrida 1979, 83–4)

Once more, Shelley's drowning invades the text of his last poem. It opens 'The Triumph of Life' onto historical events, as well as significant translations and transitions (edge, *bord*, shore, *débordement*) that are evidently beyond the text and yet constitutive of its unfinished quality.

Living off

It is not only in critical, transformative translations between texts that their boundaries are effaced. The same thing occurs within a text, through its allusions to and citations of other works. For Shelley, any given poem is but one of the 'episodes to that great poem, which all poets, like the co-operating thoughts of one great mind, have built up since the beginning of the world' ('Defence of Poetry' 2002, 522) – an idea that, in representing all poets as co-authors of one universal work, negates the very notion of an authorial signatory. In his contribution to

Deconstruction and Criticism, 'The Critic as Host', J. Hillis Miller considers the intertextual relations between texts through the figure of parasitism. Although Miller refers to Bloom's reading of the influences that go into 'The Triumph of Life' in *Shelley's Mythmaking* (Bloom 1959, 220–76), the focus of his piece is not on Shelley's particular sources but a more general reflection on how the critical text is like a parasite living off the literary work, which, in its turn, lives off prior texts. What Derrida, following Benjamin, terms survival or 'living on' can also be seen as a parasitic consumption of predecessor texts.

Viewing the text as a host for intertextual parasites offers another way of questioning the identity of the author of 'The Triumph of Life':

> Who, however, is 'Shelley'? To what does this word refer if any work signed with this name has no identifiable borders, and no interior walls either? It has no edges because it has been invaded from all sides as well as from within by other 'names', other powers of writing – Rousseau, Dante, Ezekiel and the whole host of others [...] Though the word 'Shelley' may be printed on the cover of a book entitled *Poetical Works*, it must name something without identifiable bounds, since the book incorporates so much outside within its inside.
>
> (Miller 1979, 243)

The relations between texts mean that no authorial signatory is a boundary that cordons off a text from other writings. Rather, the life of literature is such that texts live on as they are being transformed by future readers, even as each individual text itself participates in the afterlife of prior works. Parasite and host survive in symbiosis. Furthermore, as becomes evident when considering Mary Shelley's role in the manufacture of Shelley's poetry, the authorial signature, even when printed on the cover of a book, may just be the shorthand for a composition process that involves multiple authors and editors.

Coda

This chapter was drafted in 2015 and retouched for publication in 2022, the year that marked the bicentenary of Shelley's death. The date yielded a number of events and publications that testify to the power of an anniversary: death days, like birthdays, invite us to reflect on an author's life and their posthumous influence. On a personal level, returning to this chapter at this point in time was also an invitation to take stock of my development as a critic in the last seven years. I consider this reading of 'The Triumph of Life' and its reception in twentieth-century criticism to be flawed, marred by a blindness to the racial calculus at work in the romantic era that it shares with the materials it reads. Like too many canonical texts of its time, Shelley's 'The Triumph of Life' has nothing to say about the systematic destruction of Black life that took place across the Atlantic, and yet its very silence serves as its most clamorous indictment. I address this issue in a more recent piece, 'A triumph of Black life?' (Nabugodi 2021), that attempts to identify our ethical responsibilities in engaging with the literature produced during the long centuries of racial slavery. I opened this chapter with a biblical citation: 'Let the dead bury their dead'. But the dead will never be truly dead as long as the evil that killed them lives on. It is our task to put it to rest.

Note

1   References to 'The Triumph of Life' are made by line numbers in brackets and follow the text of Neil Freistat and Donald H. Reiman's edition of *Shelley's Poetry and Prose* (2002, 481–500).

References

Arac, Jonathan. 1980. 'To regress from the rigor of Shelley: Figures of history in American deconstructive criticism', *boundary* 2, 8.3: 241–58.
Arnold, Matthew. 1977. 'Shelley'. In *The Last Word*, edited by R. H. Super, 305–27. Ann Arbor: University of Michigan Press.
Benjamin, Walter. 1968. 'The task of the translator'. In *Illuminations*, edited by Hannah Arendt and translated by Harry Zohn, 69–82. New York: Harcourt Brace Jovanovich.
Blanchot, Maurice. 1976. *Death Sentence* (1948). Translated by Lydia Davies. *The Georgia Review* 30.2: 379–403.
Bloom, Harold. 1959. *Shelley's Mythmaking*. New Haven, CT: Yale University Press.
Bloom, Harold, Paul de Man, Jacques Derrida, Geoffrey H. Hartman and J. Hillis Miller. 1979. *Deconstruction and Criticism*. New York: Seabury Press.
Butler, Marilyn. 1981. *Romantics, Rebels & Reactionaries*. Oxford: Oxford University Press.
Byron, Lord, George Gordon. 2015. Letter to Thomas Moore, 4 March 1822. In *Byron's Letters and Journals: A new selection*, edited by Richard Lansdown, 406–7. Oxford: Oxford University Press.
Clarke, Eric O. 1995. 'Shelley's heart: Sexual politics and cultural value', *The Yale Journal of Criticism* 8.1: 187–208.
Dane, Joseph A. 1998. 'On the instability of vessels and narratives: A nautical perspective on the sinking of the "Don Juan"', *Keats-Shelley Journal* 47: 63–86.
de Man, Paul. 1979. 'Shelley Disfigured'. In Harold Bloom et al., *Deconstruction and Criticism*, 39–73. New York: Seabury Press.
de Man, Paul. 1984. 'Preface'. In *The Rhetoric of Romanticism*, vii–ix. New York: Columbia University Press.
Derrida, Jacques. 1979. 'Living On: Border Lines'. Translated by James Hulbert. In Harold Bloom et al., *Deconstruction and Criticism*, 75–176. New York: Seabury Press.
Esch, Deborah. 1989. 'A defence of rhetoric / The triumph of reading'. In *Reading de Man Reading*, edited by Lindsay Waters and Wlad Godzich, 66–81. Minneapolis: University of Minnesota Press.

Favret, Mary. 1993. 'Mary Shelley's sympathy and irony: The editor and her corpus'. In *The Other Mary Shelley: Beyond Frankenstein.*, edited by Audrey A. Fisch, Anne K. Mellor and Esther H. Schor, 17–38. New York: Oxford University Press.

Feldman, Paula R. 1978. 'Biography and the literary executor: The case of Mary Shelley', *The Papers of the Bibliographical Society of America* 72.3: 287–97.

Fraistat, Neil. 1994. 'Illegitimate Shelley: Radical piracy and the textual edition as cultural performance', *PMLA* 109.3: 409–23.

Gamer, Michael. 2008. 'Shelley incinerated', *The Wordsworth Circle* 39.1–2: 23–6.

Gladden, Samuel Lyndon. 2005. 'Mary Shelley's editions of "The Collected Poems of Percy Bysshe Shelley": The editor as subject', *Studies in Romanticism* 44.2: 181–205.

Holmes, Richard. 1995. *Shelley: The pursuit*. London: Flamingo.

Jones, Frederick L. 1946. 'The Shelley legend', *PMLA* 61.3: 848–90.

Miller, J. Hillis. 1979. 'The Critic as Host'. In Harold Bloom et al., *Deconstruction and Criticism*, 217–53. New York: Seabury Press.

Nabugodi, Mathelinda. 2021. 'A triumph of Black life?', *Keats-Shelley Journal* 70: 133–41.

Norman, Sylvia. 1954. *Flight of the Skylark: The development of Shelley's reputation*. London: Max Reinhardt.

North, Julian. 2010. 'Shelley revitalized: Biography and the reanimated body', *European Romantic Review* 21.6: 751–70.

O'Neill, Michael. 2010. '"Trying to make it as good as I can": Mary Shelley's editing of Shelley's poetry and prose', *Romanticism* 3.2: 185–97.

Pyle, Forest. 1995. *The Ideology of the Imagination: Subject and society in the discourses of Romanticism*. Stanford, CA: Stanford University Press.

Rossington, Michael. 2013. 'Editing Shelley'. In *The Oxford Handbook of Percy Bysshe Shelley*, edited by Michael O'Neill and Anthony Howe, 645–56. Oxford: Oxford University Press.

Shelley, Mary. 1987. *The Journals of Mary Shelley: 1814–1844*, 2 vols. Edited by Paula R. Feldman and Diana Scott-Kilvert. Oxford: Clarendon Press.

Shelley, Mary. 1980. *The Letters of Mary Wollstonecraft Shelley*, 5 vols. Edited by Betty T. Bennett. Baltimore, MD and London: The Johns Hopkins University Press.

Shelley, Percy Bysshe. 1824. *Posthumous Poems of Percy Bysshe Shelley*. Edited by Mary W. Shelley. London: John and Henry L. Hunt.

Shelley, Percy Bysshe. 1839. *The Poetical Works of Percy Bysshe Shelley*, 4 vols. Edited by Mary Shelley. London: Edward Moxon.

Shelley, Percy Bysshe. 1964. *The Letters of Percy Bysshe Shelley*, 2 vols. Edited by Frederick L. Jones. Oxford: Clarendon Press.

Shelley, Percy Bysshe. 2002. *Shelley's Poetry and Prose*. Edited by Neil Freistat and Donald H. Reiman. New York and London: Norton.

Smith, Robert M. 1945. *The Shelley Legend*. New York: Scribner.

Wang, Orrin N. C. 1991. 'Disfiguring monuments: History in Paul de Man's "Shelley Disfigured" and Percy Bysshe Shelley's "The Triumph of Life"', *ELH* 58.3: 633–55.

Wheatley, Kim. 2000. '"Attracted by the body": Accounts of Shelley's cremation', *Keats-Shelley Journal* 49: 162–82.

White, Newman I. 1946. '"The Shelley legend" examined', *Studies in Philology* 43.3: 522–44.

Wilson, Ross. 2013. *Shelley and the Apprehension of Life*. Cambridge: Cambridge University Press.

Woodman, Ross. 2001. 'Figuring disfiguration: Reading Shelley after de Man', *Studies in Romanticism* 40.2: 253–88.

7
The author as agent in the field: (post-)Bourdieusian approaches to the author

Josef Šebek

Introduction

One of the ways in which the author has vigorously returned into contemporary literary theory is through the new sociology of literature, a discipline that has flourished since the end of the 1970s, especially in France. This approach considers the analysis of the authorial figure indispensable, including its biographical dimension. Certain scholars see the author as the focus of the mediation between the social and the textual, which is of special importance for literary sociology (Sapiro 2014, 8).

The present chapter shows how the author is understood in several recent sociologically oriented approaches to literature. This metatheoretical perspective may help to illuminate notions that are not always explicit and clearly defined, as well as some tensions that are typical of them. I have chosen what is perhaps the most innovative and influential sociological theory of literature of our time – that of Pierre Bourdieu – as the point of departure.[1] This theory will remain the point of reference throughout this chapter which, however, is dedicated to post-Bourdieusian thought (the 'post' here means both elaborating Bourdieu's concepts further and transcending them). This chapter initially outlines the central features of Bourdieu's approach and his notion of the author. It then focuses on two different, although interconnected, post-Bourdieusian approaches, those of Gisèle Sapiro and Jérôme Meizoz.

The underlying thesis is that in the recent, mostly Francophone, sociology of literature, Bourdieu's theory of the literary field, as well as his notion of the author, are undergoing an important – and in my view necessary – transformation. Evidently some of his crucial theses need revaluation, especially the concept of the autonomy of the literary field and the 'refraction effect' (Bourdieu 1996, 220–1) that exists on the interface between the literary field and the broader social space, as well as the idea of 'homology' between positions and position-taking in the field (Bourdieu 1996, 161–6).

Contemporary post-Bourdieusian approaches range from applications of Bourdieu's field theory through its revisions, which do not abandon its general framework, to new and critical projects of literary sociology. The present chapter focuses on the first two modalities, represented here by Sapiro and Meizoz. The chosen approach results from the conviction that the basic idea of Bourdieu's field theory is still inspiring.[2]

In addition, to balance out the predominantly metatheoretical character of this chapter – and to illustrate the three concepts of authorship that I am going to discuss – I will sketch an analysis of the position of the Czech writer Ladislav Fuks (1923–1994) in the Czech literary field in the 1970s, the so-called 'normalisation' period of the communist dictatorship. In this I seek to demonstrate that for a thorough analysis it is necessary to expand the Bourdieusian framework, as well as to supplement it with related concepts; I divide the analysis into three parts, connected respectively to the methodologies of Bourdieu, Sapiro and Meizoz.

Bourdieu: the literary field, its autonomy and the 'new science of works of art'

There is certainly no need to repeat Bourdieu's arguments in detail here. For the present purpose, three closely interconnected basic notions have to be emphasised.

The first is the concept of the literary field as a social micro-world with its internal rules of functioning (although it belongs to the less institutionalised fields and is characterised by the 'anomie', the absence of explicitly formulated and requisite set of rules; Bourdieu 1996, 63). Its agents are literary 'specialists' and its fundamental feature is historicity: at any given moment the field presents itself as 'accumulated history' (Bourdieu 1986, 241). The relation of the literary field to other social fields and the broader social space is not direct: a 'refraction effect' (Bourdieu 1996, 220–1) is in operation here.

Another crucial notion is 'autonomy', which has several different although interconnected meanings in Bourdieu's theory. Three of them seem to be the most important:

1 Autonomy is a constitutive feature of the field: the literary field is (relatively) independent of other fields including the 'metafield' of power (Bourdieu 1996, 47–112; 215–23).
2 Aesthetic autonomy, i.e., the refusal of economic, political, pedagogic and other non-aesthetic functions of literature, is a specific value and internal structuring principle of the literary field and its fundamental trait, since its emergence in the second half of the nineteenth century (Bourdieu 1996, 77–85; 105–9; 121–7).
3 The autonomy of motivation (*illusio*) of the agents of the game played in the field is typical also of other social fields and of human practice in general: it is the maximisation of profits in terms of the capital specific of the given field (Bourdieu 1996, 227–31; cf. Bourdieu 1986, 241–58). As a result, the literary field is both autonomous (due to its relative independence of other fields) and heteronomous (in view of the motivation of its agents).

To these three aspects can be added a fourth, the critical meaning of 'autonomy'. It is discussed in Bourdieu's writings on the literary field, especially in his critique of the theory of the 'pure' work in text-oriented literary criticism and the discourse of the author as a 'pure' creator (Bourdieu 1996, 193–205; 285–312). This understanding of 'autonomy' is central, especially in Bourdieu's texts on cultural reproduction and consumption, in which the notion of aesthetic autonomy is criticised as an effective means of social separation and domination.

The objective of Bourdieu's theory is very ambitious: to become the 'new science of works of art' (Bourdieu 1996, 177–213).[3] With the help of this 'new science', he intends to bridge the gap between the 'internal' (e.g., formalist, structuralist) and 'external' (especially Marxist sociological) approaches to literature and art, and to show how social reality is inscribed in the literary work and vice versa. Since the figure of the author is in many respects crucial to this project, Bourdieu's theory may be seen as an aspect of the new 'sociology of authors' (Baethge 2005, 118).

It is the interconnection of these three aspects – the notions of literary field, autonomy as its principle and the proposed 'new science' – that makes Bourdieu's approach so innovative. Demonstrating the mechanisms and dynamics of autonomy and heteronomy in the microworld of the literary field, Bourdieu's system, his 'new science of the works of art', reveals the links between literary text and social context. In post-Bourdieusian research, this project has been tested and amended. From a certain point of view, the new research can be understood as an implicit critique of the possibility of such a strong nexus of the three basic assumptions, as will become evident later.

What is the concept of the author in Bourdieu's theory? Generally the author is defined as the most important agent in the literary field, guided by their *habitus* which co-determines the particular way of their position-taking and their trajectory in the field. The counterparts of *habitus* and field (as the subjective and objective structure) are enriched here by a third factor – the work. It can be said that the centrality of the author means that they stand precisely in between the work and the field (the text and the context) and mediate between them. As Bourdieu writes, even '"the action of works upon works" […] is only ever exercised by the intermediary of authors' (1996, 199). Another possible view would be that the work mediates between the author and the field, however: it is primarily through their works that authors become recognised in the field; see below.

Partly due to its virtual omnipresence in his writings on literature, Bourdieu's use of the concept of the author is many-faceted and not always clear. Two questions may appear especially important. What kind of entity is the author? What is the relation between individual agency and predetermined position-taking in the field?

Bourdieu's notion of 'author' ranges from the biographical person endowed with a particular social history to the organising principle and origin of choices made in the process of creation of the work and 'inscribed' in it (Bourdieu 1996, 214–82). No division of 'roles' of the author (known, for example, from Eco's influential semiotic approach) is applied. Yet, as discussed below, these 'roles' reappear in certain post-Bourdieusian approaches.

Bourdieu distances himself from the biographical criticism which looks for the logic of the authorial personality (and the work) in the story of their social provenance and idiosyncrasies. Sartre's biography of Flaubert is a cardinal example for him: Sartre tries to find the logic of the literary personality where it (according to Bourdieu) cannot be localised – namely outside the literary field. Bourdieu's notion of the author is more restricted and focused: the author is constituted only through their relation to the field. More rigorously expressed, the author becomes themselves via position-taking (in the space of their works: that is, choosing a specific genre, form, etc.; Meizoz 2005, 185–94). This taking of positions in the social field of production is mediated – in the mind and behaviour of the author – both by their dispositions (*habitus*) and the space of possibles, that is, by the field (Bourdieu 1996, 233–4, 256–7). All information about their life is filtered through the prism of its relevance in the field.

In his discussion of the opposition of the internal and external criticism, Bourdieu sketches the space of concrete possibilities in recent and contemporary literary theory (1996, 177–208). However, the passages dedicated explicitly to the authorial figure do not take into account the important caveats of literary theory concerning the biographical notion of the author, such as the 'intentional fallacy' of Wimsatt and Beardsley, the questioning of the author's role by Barthes and Foucault, or the distinction between the author in real life and in a fictional text in narratology, semiotics and reception aesthetics. In the context of Bourdieu's theory, this neglect is quite understandable: for his approach, an authorial subject that exists both in the social world (although primarily in the restricted sense of the literary field) and in close relation to the internal structure or world of the work is absolutely crucial. Such a subject can interconnect the text and the context; it can also generate the diachronic dynamics of the field and even of the texts themselves, since

> [t]he principle of change in works resides in the field of cultural production and, more precisely, in the struggles among agents and institutions.
>
> (Bourdieu 1996, 234)

Bourdieu thus adopts a kind of intentionalism: when producing the work, the author makes particular choices to achieve certain effects or to avoid some relations – generic, stylistic, etc. – to the competing positions in the field. To analyse the work, we have to take these choices, as well as the whole field, the 'space of possibles' (Bourdieu 1996, 234), into account. Bourdieu is convinced that it is possible, though not easy, to reconstruct the author's point of view at certain moments (1996, 87–112) and that '[b]iographical analysis thus understood can lead us to the principles of the evolution of the work of art in the course of time' (1996, 260).

The question is what kind of authorial intention this implies. Bourdieu maintains that it is at least partially unconscious or covered by the interest in the action itself (as the concept of *habitus* suggests – 1996, 179, 272). Still, it is the author's relation to the work that makes it meaningful. The author is ultimately inseparable from the work and vice versa. In this sense, it is also possible to say that 'the social' – the field – mediates between the author and the work, at least in the moment of the work's production but also in its interpretation (see below).

This leads to the problem of the author's agency. According to Bourdieu, some authors (such as Flaubert, Baudelaire or Sartre) are endowed with special power; they are thus able to produce rather than to adopt positions (1996, 60–8). Nevertheless, generally the author is the one who primarily relates themselves to and chooses from the repertoire available in the field (including negative choices, for instance the rejection of certain thematic, stylistic or other possibilities). The problem of the creative freedom of the author thus seems to be answered rather ambiguously. On the one hand, Bourdieu distances himself from the structuralist notion of strictly predetermined position-taking (1996, 195–206): in the field, there is always 'an objective margin of freedom' (1996, 239) for the author. On the other hand, to become an author means to grasp the literary field as a 'space of possibles' (in the sense that Bourdieu gives to this term: that is, as the space of available choices including their social 'meaning' – 1996, 234–9) and to locate oneself in this space, since there can be no position or strategy without the context of the possible choices.

The questions of individual agency and the deliberate presentation of the self are revived and emphasised in some post-Bourdieusian approaches to the author. In the following sections of this chapter, Bourdieu's three main notions – field, autonomy and 'new science of works' – and his concept of author will be correlated with two rather distinct, although interconnected, trends of contemporary post-Bourdieusian research. These trends are represented by Gisèle Sapiro and Jérôme Meizoz.

Case study: the fiction of Ladislav Fuks I

Before that, however, I will turn – in the first part of the case study – to the position of Ladislav Fuks in the Czech literary field in the 1970s. With four novels (*Mr Theodore Mundstock*, 1963, in English 1968; *Variace pro temnou strunu*, *Variations for a Dark String*, 1966; *The Cremator*, 1967, in English 1984; *Of Mice and Mooshaber*, 1970, in English 2014) and two collections of short stories (*Moji černovlasí bratři*, *My Black-Haired Brothers*, 1964; *Smrt morčete*, *The Death of a Guinea Pig*, 1969) published in the course of the 1960s, Fuks became one of the authors most praised by critics as well as the reading public. His position was strengthened by translations of his works into ten languages and the international acclaim for his debut novel, *Mr Theodore Mundstock*. Regarding the characteristics of his position in the field, the style of Fuks's prose works occupied the space at the intersection of literary experiment and more widely acceptable style of writing. He often played – in a rather pre-postmodern manner – with popular genres, such as detective novel, horror and science-fiction, and addressed significant, serious issues of recent history, especially the persecution of the Jews during the Second World War and the holocaust.

Except for two months in 1968, Czech literature of the 1960s was still subject to state censorship, yet the literary field had been gradually returning to its former plurality and diversity of subjects and styles of writing. In other words, after the Stalinism of the 1950s, it tended to regain the position of an autonomous field of cultural production as defined by Bourdieu. At the same time this field occupied a relatively privileged position in the overall social space as one of the chief sources of public opinion. In the years following the Prague Spring and the invasion of the Warsaw Pact armies in August 1968, this plurality came to an end. The literary field split once again into official, prohibited/*samizdat* and émigré sectors.[4]

Fuks had never been a member of the Communist Party and, unlike many important Czech authors who sympathised with the reformist movement, he rarely commented on politics. After 1968 he decided to remain in the official sector. His new books continued to be published, his works from the 1960s were re-edited and he maintained a public presence in the media, as well as through direct interactions with his readership at public readings and debates. Simultaneously, regarding the subjects of his works, Fuks had been gradually pushed to focus on themes promoted by the regime. These included the agricultural collectivisation at the turn of the 1950s (*Návrat z žitného pole*, *Return from the Rye Field*, 1974) and the life of the communist hero and martyr Julius Fučík (*Křišťálový pantoflíček*, *The Glass Slipper*, 1978). Fuks's style also tended towards a less experimental, (social) realist idiom.

As for the literary field itself, although the opposition of the economic and cultural capital – central in Bourdieu's model – certainly did not lose its structuring power, the pivotal axis of the autonomy/heteronomy distinction once again became politics. Since the literary field became thus structurally complex and layered (involving more sectors and more structuring oppositions), we must seek for an adequate extension of the primary model of the field in the specific situation of the intervening heteronomous factors. This will be discussed in the second part of the case study.

The empirical study of literary fields and the question of autonomy

The notion of the 'field' has become part of general usage and is often applied out of the context of Bourdieu's theory or used rather metaphorically. Scholars who have used field theory rigorously and extensively, even before the publication of the French original of Bourdieu (1996) in 1992, include Alain Viala (1985) and Anna Boschetti (1985). Among those using the theory after the publication of Bourdieu (1996) are Gisèle Sapiro (1999) and Pascale Casanova (2004), as well as the more 'heterodox' scholars, Nathalie Heinich (2000) and especially Bernard Lahire (2006). The 'amendments' and extensions of Bourdieu's theoretical framework have taken several directions. In the geographical and cultural sense, field theory is applied to literary fields in different historical conditions and degrees of constitution.[5] Another extension is the investigation of supra-national literary fields in certain larger language areas, such as 'world literature' (Casanova 2004) or intellectual fields (Sapiro 2009). In addition, the dynamics of autonomy and heteronomy are very different in diverse national fields or at certain stages of the history of a field (e.g., at the time of national emancipation movements or under the twentieth-century dictatorships).

Two tomes on the French literary field by Gisèle Sapiro exemplify current analysis of historical literary fields. The first book deals with the Second World War and the post-war years and the second one with the topic of authorial responsibility in the nineteenth and twentieth centuries. Their titles – *The War of Writers, 1940–1953* (Sapiro 1999) and *The Responsibility of the Writer* (Sapiro 2011) – already suggest how prominent they make the figure of the author, indicating that the question of the literary field's autonomy and heteronomy will be of fundamental importance.

Sapiro's point of departure (1999) is the framework of field theory with its binary oppositions – of the dominant and dominated, for instance, and of the types of capital (economic plus social vs. cultural). The central notion becomes the author's 'trajectory', since Sapiro is interested in the way in which the conditions 'external' to the literary field have influenced the behaviour of authors, as well as how these conditions have changed their literary careers and positions they took in the literary field under the given circumstances. The analysis is partially based on the statistical processing of data (by means of factor analysis), in which characteristics such as the social and regional origin of authors become important, together with genres used by particular authors or the literary milieu in which they were socialised.

It is evident that authors are construed here as central 'units', characterised by aspects relevant in the literary field. However, the logic of their other behaviour and attitudes becomes pertinent, since the dynamics of autonomy and heteronomy during and after the German occupation of France and the dichotomy of collaboration and resistance influenced the literary field. Sapiro shows that (at least temporarily) the politically engaged standpoint of an author could be identified with the 'autonomous pole' of literary production (Bourdieu 1993, 45–6). In the works referred to above (1999 and 2011), Sapiro thus analyses the relation between the literary field, other fields and wider social (especially political) phenomena; in so doing she construes writers as agents of the literary field as well as citizens with social – and legal – responsibility. What theoretically follows from this investigation is a more sophisticated view of the opposition between autonomy and heteronomy in the literary field. The result is also a more nuanced approach to the question of the relation of literary field and other social fields, and of the 'refraction effect' (Bourdieu 1996, 220–1) the field exerts on any external stimulus.[6]

After her second book, Sapiro published an article entitled 'The strategies of writing and the authorial responsibility' (2013, 163–81) devoted to questions of authorial strategy and intentionality, based mainly on the material she used in a previous work (2011). She pointed out that the universally prevailing (economic) concept of fully rational intentions and strategies is not applicable in the literary domain; Bourdieu's concept of *habitus* as the incorporated and not exclusively conscious set of dispositions is in fact more appropriate.

Furthermore, it is necessary to take into account the inner autonomy of literary fields defined, since the end of the eighteenth century, precisely through *disinterestedness* (that is, the refusal of other than aesthetic functions of literature). Nonetheless, the notion of authorial strategy (in this extended sense) remains relevant here in many ways, one of them being the necessary self-presentation of the author. Sapiro also distinguishes between the 'strategy of writing' and the 'social strategy of an author', linked with 'semantic intension' and 'psychological intention' respectively (2013, 180). The two types of strategy are dissociated, although they remain connected. The writing process transcends the conscious strategy of its author, while the meaning of the work depends heavily on its reception. As a result, it is more appropriate for the sociology of literature to focus on the social strategies of the author (Sapiro 2013, 180).

It is interesting to compare this statement with the 'new science of works of art' proposed by Bourdieu: while his project is meant to become a universal hermeneutic of literary works, we can here observe a more differentiated approach. Although Sapiro's work is Bourdieusian in its premises, concepts and methodology, she performs the task of a literary historian to apply the field theory in a very detailed way to a particular period or problem. Her practice can be interpreted as a move towards a more refined approach to the problems of autonomy, relations of the literary field to other social fields and authorial strategies.

Case study: the fiction of Ladislav Fuks II

Returning now to the position of Ladislav Fuks in the literary field of the 1970s, we can observe that we are dealing here with questions of politics and responsibility of the writer – or, in other words, of the relation of the literary field to the primarily external, heteronomous forces thoroughly investigated by Gisèle Sapiro. In this respect, the situation of Czech literature under the communist dictatorship can be compared to that of French literature during the Second World War. As Sapiro points out, the analytical focus has to be not only on the straightforward political 'distortion' of literary strategies and choices of the authors, but also on the way in which the literary field refracts and accommodates these influences and strives to retain its autonomy. It is certainly beyond the scope of this paper and the short case study fully to account for the complex structural changes in the Czech literary field of the period. In relation to Ladislav Fuks's trajectory in the field in the 1970s, I will add just a couple of remarks that point to the pertinence of Sapiro's reworking of the Bourdieusian framework.

The structure of the Czech literary field during the 'normalisation' period, especially regarding the heteronomous factors, became more complex; the same can be said about all national literary fields of the Soviet bloc, although there were important differences. On the one hand, each sector of the field – the official, prohibited/*samizdat* and émigré literature – might be studied on its own: for instance, the official sector certainly had its inner oppositions and stakes, with its agents forming a relatively self-enclosed social space. Yet it is absolutely critical to conceive the divided literary field precisely as a split whole, since the positions in the field adopted by the authors can be fully accounted for only in structural relations to all sectors of the field.

The perception of the literary field by the agents of the field themselves became highly politicised. In all three sectors – representing specific communication circuits – the evaluation of works was related to the political position and reputation of the author; yet in all three there also existed discussions about the difference of the autonomous ('strictly literary') and heteronomous (political, moral…) values. During the 'normalisation' period Fuks was highly praised by the official critique; by contrast, in the other two sectors of the literary field his reputation was damaged. This became especially evident after the Velvet Revolution in 1989 and the subsequent 'integration' of the field. In particular, the critics endowed with the highest amount of symbolic capital (that is, those resistant to the official sector in the previous two decades) were hesitant about or directly critical of Fuks – unlike the general audience who kept its predilection for the author, as is also evidenced by new editions.[7]

The 'social strategies of the author' came to the forefront. Deciding to remain in the official sector and to go on publishing, Fuks had to adopt a series of strategies, not only implemented in his newly written texts (their subject and style), but also regarding his very existence in the social field of literature (abstaining from expressing certain opinions, becoming a member of the official writers' syndicate, etc.). On the one hand, this led to an interesting and even subtly subversive way of writing;[8] on the other, it engendered certain strategies of his self-presentation and 'framing' of his works, as, for instance, in the case of reprints of his older texts from the 1960s. I will follow up on this aspect in the last part of the case study.

The 'new science of authors'

Bourdieu's 'new science of the works of art' can be interpreted as a 'new science of authors'. The figure of the author is also central in the works of some of his followers (mainly Gisèle Sapiro). However, the 'turn to the author' is fully accomplished in the recent theory of 'author's posture' proposed by Jérôme Meizoz (2004; 2007; 2010, 81–93; 2011; see also Meizoz and Martens 2011, 199–212). Bourdieu's field theory is the point of departure for Meizoz; other important sources include Dominique Maingueneau's theory of literary discourse (1993), the concepts of literary *ethos* (Viala 1985) and the 'presentation of the self' (Amossy 2010). Like Bourdieu's 'new science', the concept of author's posture is meant to overcome the gap between the social and the textual as well as, on the methodological level, between literary sociology and text-centred approaches. Thus the author not only gets back to the fore, but is also supposed to become the remedy for the problems that literary theory has been trying to solve for a long time.

Following Viala's older definition (1985), Meizoz defines posture as 'a singular manner of occupying a "position" in the literary field' (2007,

18). It is the self-presentation of the author not as a biographical 'person' but primarily as an agent in the literary field. The author's posture consists of 'textual effects and social behaviour' (Meizoz 2007, 21) and their interrelations. The behavioural aspect of posture covers bodily action and appearance in public, the media, etc. The second aspect, under the notion of *ethos*, consists of the author's self-presentation in their primarily non-fictional, (auto)biographical texts. The relative relevance of different kinds of discourse is discussed below.

Literary posture is therefore 'the literary identity constructed by the author himself or herself' (Meizoz 2007, 18). However, Meizoz emphasises that it is necessarily an 'interactive' category: it is co-created by the promotional, critical or journalistic discourse (Meizoz and Martens 2011, 207). In this sense the author is just one, although the most important, of the agents that participate in the creation of their posture. In this way, literary posture embraces the person as well as the text.[9]

Meizoz follows Dominique Maingueneau's division of authorial roles into three instances (1993): *personne* (the 'real person'), *écrivain* (agent in the literary field) and *inscripteur* (the role of the author in the text) (Meizoz 2007, 43). He relates the 'literary posture' primarily to *écrivain* and *inscripteur*. However, posture also has an important historical dimension: here Meizoz adopts Nathalie Heinich's (1995, 513–17) distinction of the 'community regime' and 'singularity regime' of the authorial figure (Meizoz 2007, 40–2). The latter begins in the eighteenth century and means that from this moment authors have to 'show off' and 'fabricate' themselves, to find their own unique way of presenting their personality. This is the period in which Meizoz begins to analyse specific literary postures – with Rousseau's inaugurating postural act. Since then postures have become increasingly present as a repertory that authors can adopt and adapt. Therefore, according to Meizoz, there can be no author without posture, without the 'presentation of the self': authors are intelligible through their postures (2007, 19). The following four remarks illuminate the shifts represented by Meizoz's approach.

1. According to Bourdieu, the formal and generic choices the author makes (their position-taking) are influenced by, and at the same time generate, their position in the literary field. Without a thorough analysis of the author's position, we are not able to understand the work. Meizoz's approach seems to be more restricted, or even reversed, since he focuses primarily on the author and her self-presentation; the work and field are secondary. His interpretations of texts are concentrated on the selected aspects relevant for

reconstructing the author's *ethos*. But since the posture permeates extra-textual as well as textual aspects of the author's production and behaviour, the interconnection of text and context is secured. It is the author who mediates between the text and the context.

2. The second point is the question of the relation between the position in the field and posture. Since posture is defined as a *singular* manner in which a position in the literary field is adopted by an author, it should offer a wider scope for the author's individuality or 'singularity'. However, posture is at the same time a choice from a certain repertory which at least partially pre-exists. Furthermore, Meizoz emphasises that the notion of posture helps to avoid the concept of identity: there is no 'authentic' author, as posture is always already a 'mask' or ancient *persona*. Singularity is never 'authenticity' (Meizoz and Martens 2011, 202–3). What we receive, then, is a double structure of positions in the field, along with a perhaps looser but still differential set of postures.

3. As for the problem of intention and strategy, in the theory of literary postures authorial tactics seem to be assumed: the presentation of the self is predominantly deliberate and conscious, unlike the not always calculated strategies of *habitus*. Yet, as I just remarked, the possibilities are never entirely open: for a posture to become intelligible, there has to be a certain repertory of postures that the author has to take into account.

4. As mentioned above, there are considerable genre limitations in Meizoz's theory. Meizoz asks if *ethos* can legitimately be analysed in a fictional text where the 'autobiographical pact' cannot help us to identify the subject of the work with the author 'outside' the text (Lejeune 1975, 13–46). Primarily he works with non-fictional texts and wonders whether fictional text can also be analysed in this way. While for Bourdieu the distinction between the biographical and the fictional does not seem important, Meizoz addresses the problem explicitly. On several occasions he proposes the notion of 'tone' of a work as a way in which the *ethos* might be present in the fictional texts, but primarily he focuses on non-fictional or directly autobiographical texts (Meizoz 2004). Of course, this complicates the mediating role of the author's posture since most texts are predominantly fictional.[10]

What may be crucial from the theoretical point of view is the return of the author into the centre of literary study – even the long-time disqualified empirical author, now divided into 'person' and 'agent in the literary field' (Meizoz 2007, 43). On the one hand, the notion of 'author's posture' is grounded in the tradition of rhetoric, especially in the Aristotelian terms employed by Amossy (2010, 13–43, although *ethos* has somewhat different meanings here than in the classical rhetorical triad *logos – pathos – ethos*). On the other hand, one cannot fail to notice that the theory of literary posture can help us to describe current literary fields and their relation to the media landscape: the 'branding' of authors (Coker 2018), the necessity of working with their media image, etc. In this way, the theory also questions the assumption of the (relative) autonomy of literary fields.

Case study: the fiction of Ladislav Fuks III

Now I want to demonstrate the necessity of analysing Ladislav Fuks's textual strategies of self-presentation in order to understand his 'social strategies of the author' and to develop a clearer picture of his actual position in the literary field. Meizoz's concept of the author's posture seems to be an ideal operational tool for this purpose. I will demonstrate this on a preface written by Fuks for the second edition of his novel *Of Mice and Mooshaber* (1977), a work first published in 1970.

The novel is a dystopic narrative set in an unnamed large city, in whose historical-futuristic fictional world horse-drawn carriages co-exist with spacecraft, the legitimate monarch, Princess Augusta, is missing and the government is controlled by the loathed chairman Albín Rappelschlund. It abounds with allegorical overtones regarding the socialist (or other) dictatorship. In order for the novel to be published in the changed circumstances of the 1970s, Fuks endowed it with a six-page preface in which he was supposed to project the posture of a loyal socialist writer and to provide the potentially subversive text with an appropriate 'neutralising' interpretation (Fuks 1977). However, the rhetorical strategies of the preface are based on blurring all unambiguous statements and declarations, of an appropriate 'name dropping' (Marx and Engels, Gorky) and mentioning of the required themes (e.g. the critique of fascism, the style of socialist realism) without explicitly declaring that these are indeed the author's own opinions (for instance, the use of passive constructions and equivocal use of pronouns *I – us – one*).

Rhetorical analysis of the author's posture in the preface reveals the actual textual strategies of the author's self-presentation and of enveloping the literary work by this image in a rather intricate way. Such a method would certainly remain incomprehensible without the correlation with

Fuks's position in the literary field, the dynamics of political stakes and the writer's status as an official author who nonetheless tried to maintain some distance in regard to the required ideological positions.[11]

Conclusion

As stated at the beginning, the question of mediation between the text and the social context is crucial for any sociologically oriented approach to literature. In Bourdieu's theory, and in post-Bourdieusian research, this mediation takes several directions. If we take just the basic elements at play in these exchanges – the author, the work and the social context represented here by the literary field – three points of view are possible:[12]

1. The field mediates, or is a necessary intermediate factor, between the work and the author. This can also be regarded as the perspective of the work's production: the work can come into being only by means of the choices from the repertory the field offers or in relation to these possibilities.
2. The work mediates between the field and the author. The author can become themselves primarily through their works that position them in the field. In this sense, the work is equivalent to the position-taking that occurs within the field.
3. Finally, the author mediates between the work and the field. The author is present or makes themselves visible in both realms, in texts as well as in the social space. Both forms are of semiotic nature, but the semiotic systems involved differ.

In his 'new science of the works of art', Bourdieu aspired to a universal theory of the literary text as well as the social context and their interrelation. Contemporary research, while not rejecting his idea completely, points at the possible obstacles of this approach and sometimes openly limits itself only to selected aspects. Thus Sapiro distinguishes the 'strategies of writing' (2013, 163–81) that are less accessible to research than the 'social strategies of the author' (2013, 180), while Meizoz highlights the problems one encounters when trying to study the author's posture in fictional texts.

The question of autonomy is connected to the problem of the more adequate description of how specialised fields, including the literary field, relate to other fields and the wider social space. In current research the 'interface' of the literary field and other fields is examined and the ways in which the 'refraction effect' works are investigated – be it by analysing the influence of politics or social responsibility in Sapiro or by taking into account the 'presentation of the self' in the broader social space in Meizoz's texts.

As I have attempted to illustrate in the case study of the trajectory of Czech author Ladislav Fuks in the 'normalisation' literary field in the 1970s, the seminal post-Bourdieusian approaches can be highly useful for the analysis, without requiring one to abandon the fundamental framework of the field theory.

Notes

1. Sketched for the first time in Bourdieu (1966) and later presented systematically in Bourdieu (1993) and Bourdieu (1996).
2. Perhaps the most important critique of Bourdieu's literary sociology has been formulated by Bernard Lahire, who attacks many of Bourdieu's central notions and comes up with an alternative theory of 'literary game' (see especially Lahire 2006 and Lahire 2010, 143–54). Also very sceptical is Geoffroy de Lagasnerie (2011), whose analysis of the weak and controversial aspects of the field theory is referred to in endnotes below. For a brief overview of recent critical arguments see Glinoer (2011), Kohler (2010, 11–38) and more than a dozen articles on Bourdieu's literary sociology in Martin (2010). For an interesting critical socioanalysis of the group of Bourdieu's collaborators and pupils and his position as a master see Heinich (2007).
3. For Lagasnerie (2011) the 'science of works' becomes the label of Bourdieu's theory of literature as a whole.
4. To account for the Czech literary field during the communist dictatorship (1948–1989), it would in fact be necessary to start before the Second World War, when the structural politicisation of the field began, and to continue until the Velvet Revolution of 1989. For the 1960s and the 1970s it is important to bear in mind that the split of the Czech literary field into three sectors occurred after 1948 (if not, in a different political context, at the beginning of the war); we should therefore speak rather about a changing scale of split, from a strong separation to a relative structural convergence. On the other hand, these three sectors were not isolated one from another. They were associated not only in time – regarding the trajectories of authors – but also synchronically, as when an author existed on the brink of the official and prohibited spheres, especially in the so-called 'grey zone'.
5. According to Viala (1985), the French literary field came into being as early as the seventeenth century.
6. However, Lagasnerie (2011, 75–6) criticises Sapiro precisely for her lack of sense of the mutual interdependence of the literary field and other fields, as well as for construing the literary field as depoliticised: politics always enters the field as an external influence. According to him, this could be considered as the inherently problematic political stance of the field theory. Although Lagasnerie's observations on the isolation of specialised fields and depoliticisation in the field theory are important, I still believe that Sapiro's empirical analyses (1999) have made the field theory develop in a less unilateral direction.
7. However, Fuks published his last novel *Vévodkyně a kuchařka* (*The Duchess and the Cook*) in 1983; after the Velvet Revolution he authored just one work, the peculiar memoir *Moje zrcadlo* (*My Mirror*, 1995). To illustrate further the intricate political positioning of Fuks: his novel *The Cremator* (1967) was made into a film by Juraj Herz, who also co-authored the screenplay with Fuks; the film premiered in 1969, but was immediately banned and was not screened until 1990. In 2018 it was voted the best Czech film of the last 100 years (encompassing the existence of the Czechoslovak/Czech republic, 1918–2018) by the audience of Český rozhlas Vltava (Czech Radio). See https://web.archive.org/web/20181028225609/https://www.irozhlas.cz/kultura/kanon100-ceske-umeni-anketa-veletrzni-palac-praha_1810281450_ado.

8   In his article 'Remaining on the threshold: The cunning of Ladislav Fuks', Rajendra Chitnis (2004) presents a detailed close reading of Fuks's novels from the 1970s and argues for their sophisticated subversivity in line with his writings from the 1960s.
9   For a detailed discussion of the notions of ethos and posture, their mutual interrelation and genealogy in French discourse analysis, see Korthals Altes (2014, 51–73). According to Korthals Altes, both categories are fundamentally interactive, depending heavily on diverse frames and value regimes activated by participants in the literary interaction.
10 However, according to Korthals Altes (2014, 53), the posture is expressed or constructed in paratexts by and about the author, in their 'public self-fashioning' as well as in the 'style of writing and choice of genre, register, and themes' of literary work. To analyse the authorial posture in literary texts obviously requires subtle hermeneutical tools.
11 For a detailed rhetorical reading of the preface see Šebek (2019, 121–34), on which this summary is based.
12 A fourth term is apparently missing here, namely the reader and the reception. The theory of Bourdieu (as well as of Sapiro and Meizoz) is predominantly a sociology of *production* and the omission of reception is certainly symptomatic. For Bourdieu, the readers on the 'autonomous pole' (Bourdieu 1993, 45–6) of the literary field are in fact authors (or possibly also other cultural producers) themselves, so the relationship between production and consumption has a rather circular structure. For the critique of this view see Lagasnerie (2011, 94–126). However, it should be noted that in her recent introduction to literary sociology Sapiro devotes one of the four chapters to the 'sociology of reception' (2014, 85–106).

References

Amossy, Ruth. 2010. *La présentation de soi: Ethos et identité verbale*. Paris: PUF.
Baethge, Constanze. 2005. 'Une littérature sans littérarité: Pour une autonomie de l'œuvre d'art'. In *Le symbolique et le social: La réception internationale de la pensé de Pierre Bourdieu*, edited by Jacques Dubois, Pascal Durand and Yves Winkin, 117–25. Liège: Université de Liège.
Boschetti, Anna. 1985. *Sartre et les temps modernes: Une entreprise intellectuelle*. Paris: Minuit.
Bourdieu, Pierre. 1966. 'Champ intellectuel et projet créateur', *Les temps modernes* 246: 865–906.
Bourdieu, Pierre. 1984. *Distinction: A social critique of the judgment of taste*. Translated by Richard Nice. Cambridge, MA: Harvard University Press.
Bourdieu, Pierre. 1986. 'The forms of capital'. Translated by Richard Nice. In *Handbook of Theory and Research for the Sociology of Education*, edited by John G. Richardson, 241–58. Westport, CT: Greenwood Press.
Bourdieu, Pierre. 1993. *The Field of Cultural Production*. Edited by Randall Johnson. Oxford: Polity.
Bourdieu, Pierre. 1996. *The Rules of Art: Genesis and structure of the literary field*. Translated by Susan Emanuel. Stanford, CA: Stanford University Press.
Casanova, Pascale. 2004. *The World Republic of Letters* (1999). Translated by M. B. DeBevoise. Cambridge, MA: Harvard University Press.
Chitnis, Rajendra A. 2004. 'Remaining on the threshold: The cunning of Ladislav Fuks', *Central Europe* 2: 47–59.
Coker, Mark. 2018. 'Seven author branding tips', *Publishers Weekly*, 16 November. Accessed 1 September 2021. https://www.publishersweekly.com/pw/by-topic/authors/pw-select/article/78616-seven-author-branding-tips.html.
Fuks, Ladislav. 1977. 'Několik poznámek autora k *Myším Natálie Mooshabrové* a k literatuře a umění vůbec' [Notes of the author to *Of Mice and Mooshaber* and literature and art in general]. In *Myši Natálie Mooshabrové* [Of Mice and Mooshaber], 7–12. Prague: Odeon.
Glinoer, Anthony. 2011. 'De quelques critiques récentes adressées à la science des œuvres de Pierre Bourdieu', *COnTEXTES*, 6 November. Accessed 29 May 2021. https://journals.openedition.org/contextes/4881.
Heinich, Nathalie. 1995. 'Façons d' "être" écrivain. L'identité professionnelle en régime de singularité', *Revue Française Sociologique* 36: 499–524.
Heinich, Nathalie. 2000. *Être écrivain: Création et identité*. Paris: Découverte.
Heinich, Nathalie. 2007. *Pourquoi Bourdieu*. Paris: Gallimard.

Kohler, Gun-Brit. 2010. 'National disposition and the author's trajectory: Reflections on Polish and Croatian literature'. In *Authorship Revisited: Conceptions of authorship around 1900 and 2000*, edited by Gillis J. Dorleijn, Ralf Grüttemeier and Liesbeth Korthals Altes, 11–38. Leuven: Peeters.

Korthals Altes, Liesbeth. 2014. *Ethos and Narrative Interpretation: The negotiation of values in fiction*. Lincoln and London: University of Nebraska Press.

Lagasnerie, Geoffroy de. 2011. *Sur la science des œuvres: Questions à Pierre Bourdieu (et à quelques autres)*. Paris: Cartouche.

Lahire, Bernard. 2006. *La condition littéraire: La double vie des écrivains*. Paris: Découverte.

Lahire, Bernard. 2010. 'Le champ et le jeu: La spécificité de l'univers littéraire en question'. In *Bourdieu et la littérature*, edited by Jean-Pierre Martin, 143–54. Nantes: Cécile Defaut.

Lejeune, Philippe. 1975. *Le pacte autobiographique*. Paris: Seuil.

Maingueneau, Dominique. 1993. *Le contexte de l'œuvre littéraire: Énonciation, écrivain, société*. Paris: Dunod.

Martin, Jean-Pierre, ed. 2010. *Bourdieu et la littérature*. Nantes: Cécile Defaut.

Meizoz, Jérôme. 2004. '"Postures" d'auteur et poétique (Ajar, Rousseau, Céline, Houellebecq)', *Vox-Poetica* : Lettres et sciences humaines. Accessed 10 March 2021. http://vox-poetica.org/t/articles/meizoz.html.

Meizoz, Jérôme. 2005. 'Pierre Bourdieu et la question de la forme: Vers une sociologie du style'. In *Le symbolique et le social: La réception internationale de la pensé de Pierre Bourdieu*, edited by Jacques Dubois, Pascal Durand and Yves Winkin, 185–94. Liège: Université de Liège.

Meizoz, Jérôme. 2007. *Postures littéraires: Mises en scène modernes de l'auteur*. Geneva: Slatkine.

Meizoz, Jérôme. 2010. 'Modern posterities of posture: Jean-Jacques Rousseau'. In *Authorship Revisited: Conceptions of authorship around 1900 and 2000*, edited by Gillis J. Dorleijn, Ralf Grüttemeier and Liesbeth Korthals Altes, 81–93. Leuven: Peeters.

Meizoz, Jérôme. 2011. *La fabrique des singularités: Postures littéraires II*. Geneva: Slatkine.

Meizoz, Jérôme and David Martens. 2011. 'La fabrique d'une notion: Entretien avec Jérôme Meizoz au sujet du concept de la "posture"', *Interférences littéraires/Literaire interferenties* 6: 199–212.

Sapiro, Gisèle. 1999. *La guerre des écrivains, 1940–1953*. Paris: Fayard.

Sapiro, Gisèle, ed. 2009. *L'espace intellectuel en Europe: De la formation des États-nations à la mondialisation, XIXe–XXIe siècle*. Paris: Découverte.

Sapiro, Gisèle. 2011. *La responsabilité de l'écrivain: Littérature, droit et morale en France (XIXe–XXIe siècle)*. Paris: Seuil.

Sapiro, Gisèle. 2013. 'Stratégies de l'écriture et responsabilité auctoriale.' In *On ne peut pas tout réduire à des strategies*, edited by Dinah Ribard and Nicolas Schapira, 163–81. Paris: PUF.

Sapiro, Gisèle. 2014. *La sociologie de la littérature*. Paris: Découverte.

Šebek, Josef. 2019. *Literatura a sociálno: Bourdieu, Williams a jejich pokračovatelé* [Literature and the social: Bourdieu, Williams and their successors]. Prague: Univerzita Karlova, Filozofická fakulta.

Viala, Alain. 1985. *Naissance de l'écrivain: Sociologie de la littérature à l'âge classique*. Paris: Minuit.

8
Autofiction as (self-)criticism: suggestions from recent Brazilian literature
Sonia Miceli

Introduction

Recently Brazilian writers, critics and scholars have been widely concerned with autofiction, which has been the subject of articles, books and doctoral dissertations. On the one hand, this concern was an inevitable response to the growing publication of autobiographically based texts. On the other, it has stimulated the reaction of writers, who, taking advantage of the interest of readers and critics in writers' lives, have written professedly autofictional texts with the aim, in some cases, of criticising and even parodying the concept. The purpose of this chapter is to shed a light on these dynamics and, specifically, on the critical and theoretical reflection promoted by autofictional works, with a focus on the complex questions about authorship that some of these works pose.

Opinions about autofiction are significantly diversified. Indeed, although some critics look at autofiction as a massive phenomenon and consider it *the* literary genre of the twenty-first century, others simply deny it. In spite of this, autofiction has stimulated a prolific discussion about authorship, readership and literature in general.

For this reason, the works examined here do not exactly fit the definition of autofiction as a genre. They are parodies or fictional experiments whose purpose is precisely to criticise the concept of autofiction, challenging the expectations of both readers and critics.

Nevertheless, in doing so, these works enter the game, creating a fascinating interplay between literature and critical thought, and posing new questions about classical literary problems.

This commitment to theory and criticism is neither a complementary aspect of autofiction nor a Brazilian specificity; it is constitutive of it since its origin. The progenitor of the term was Serge Doubrovsky, a French writer and professor of French literature at New York University. On the back cover of his novel *Fils* (Doubrovsky 1977), he wrote a few lines that stated the official birth of a new genre, the autofiction:

> Autobiography? No, that is a privilege reserved for the important people of this world, at the end of their lives, in a refined style. Fiction, of events and facts strictly real; autofiction, if you will, to have entrusted the language of an adventure to the adventure of language.
>
> (Doubrovsky 1977; McDonough 2011, 7)

I will not discuss this definition, which is only the first of many, as the concept and the very existence of autofiction have been constantly discussed since then. The idea that autofiction is fictional only in terms of form, as 'the adventure of language', is no longer accepted, not even by Doubrovsky himself. Despite the multiple views of this matter, it can be said that autofiction, according to the general opinion, is, as Vincent Colonna put it, a 'fictionalisation of the self', which might even be fantastic (1989, 9).[1]

Yet the discussion of autofiction along these lines would miss the purpose of this chapter. What seems more important is that, when inventing the term, Doubrovsky was consciously looking for a concept to fill a gap in Philippe Lejeune's theorisation of autobiography. Indeed, in a letter to the pioneer of autobiographical studies in France, Doubrovsky reveals that he wanted 'very deeply to fill that square that your analysis left empty, and it is a true desire which has suddenly bound your critical text and what I was writing' (Lejeune 1986, 63). The case to which Doubrovsky refers is a blank in a scheme elaborated by Lejeune to illustrate possible relationships linking author, narrator and character. This scheme appears in the essay in which Lejeune exposed his well-known theory of 'the autobiographical pact' (Lejeune 1975, 28). Showing how this pact works and how it differentiates itself from 'the fictional pact', he stated that it was theoretically possible, although highly unlikely, to find a work based on a fictional pact in which author, narrator and character had the same name (Lejeune 1975, 31–2).

Lejeune's essay will not be discussed here, because his initial propositions have been substantially revised. In a lecture given at the Ain Shams University (Cairo), Lejeune spoke about his foundation of autobiographical studies. He admitted that some of his initial assumptions were too strict, but observed that they were motivated by the necessity of delineating a new field of study, drawing its borders and its basic principles:

> My first book, *L'Autobiographie en France*, used the definition in a rather normative way. This naiveté was no doubt a youthful mistake, but it may have been a necessity for a book that was mapping the French autobiographical landscape for the first time: a center, suburbs, borders had to be indicated. From my second book, *Le Pacte autobiographique*, onwards, the definition was no longer a tool, but became an object of study in its own right. I began applying to it an analytical method that had certainly been inspired by my reading of Gérard Genette, of Jakobson and later of the Russian formalists. I made distinctions between all the parameters entering the definition (pact, enunciation, types of language, time, thematic contents, etc.). For each of them I considered all possible solutions and then displayed them in double-entry tables, taking the hierarchy of their features into account. I am, in a way, a do-it-yourself man, trying all combinations, the ones that exist as well as the potential ones. One day Serge Doubrovsky, as he was looking at one of my tables, saw a box which I had rather *rashly* declared empty, and he had the idea to fill it with the combination he called 'autofiction'.
>
> (Lejeune 2005; emphasis added)

In writing his novel, Doubrovsky deliberately contributed to a theoretical discussion not by conceptual but by fictional means. He proved that what Lejeune considered unlikely was, in the end, possible and even desirable. As a result, he inaugurated a dialogue between writers and critics which has been a permanent characteristic of autofiction, both in France and in the other countries where the concept spread, such as Spain, Mexico, Argentina and Brazil.

Three examples from Brazilian literature

In order to show the wide range of this phenomenon, three cases will be presented in which this interplay between writers and critics is particularly clear. Two of them will be discussed rather briefly here; the third one will be examined in more depth.

In 2011 Bernardo Carvalho, one of the best-known contemporary Brazilian writers, published an article entitled 'Em defesa da obra' (In defence of the work). In this he deplored that literature nowadays seems to be more concerned with the figure and the life of the writer than with the work *per se*. It was not the first time that Carvalho showed his concern with what he considered to be an increasing narcissism in contemporary literature, as well as in society. Indeed, some years before he had published *Nove noites* (Carvalho 2004, Carvalho 2007), a novel inspired by historical facts. In this work Carvalho deliberately challenged an audience increasingly obsessed with the search for (historical) truth and with the relationship between reality and fiction.

The novel is centered on the story of an American anthropologist, Buell Quain, one of a group of young researchers who came from Columbia University to do fieldwork in Brazil in the 1930s and 1940s. Quain was only 27 years old when he killed himself after a short period of fieldwork in the state of Tocantins (northern Brazil). Like Bernardo Carvalho, the narrator-character of *Nove noites* (2004) is a journalist; he gets interested in the story and tries to find clues to solve the mystery of Quain's suicide.

Although the novel is clearly a work of fiction, Carvalho did significant research in the archives in order to reconstruct the story and the personality of Quain, as well as the circle of professional and personal relationships he belonged to. Moreover, some original documents (letters and pictures) are included in the book.

For this reason, many readers looked at Carvalho's work (2004) as a mix of journalistic reportage and fiction, even if he repeatedly stated that it was *just* a novel. Indeed, the use of non-fictional materials does not change the fictional status of a novel: once a document, be it a letter or a picture, enters a fictional world, it becomes fiction as well.

Writing a book inspired by a verifiable story and inscribing the figure of the author within it (the narrator shares several things with the author and, more importantly, the back cover shows a picture of him as a child), Carvalho accomplished a curious experiment. While challenging a naïve readership, whose interest for the book was mainly determined by the appeal of a true story, he has actually contributed to autofiction: the very kind of literature he explicitly condemned in his critical texts and in several interviews.

The second case is that of André Sant'Anna, whose short story, called *Autoficção* (Sant'Anna 2014; Autofiction), was published in a collection of digital books. The collection published a short story every week and sold it for 1.99 Brazilian reals (at that time, about 0.60 € or 50p).[2] The story does not have a proper plot: it is rather a stream of memories of a character, told in the third person by an unknown narrator. Since some of these memories might be attributed to the writer André Sant'Anna, the reader can reasonably presume that the character coincides with the author; this would serve as a justification for the title. Indeed, the essential requirement for autofiction, at least according to the traditional elaboration of the concept, is the coincidence between author, narrator and character – it does not matter if he actually is the protagonist or not. Even so, the final sentence of the story suggests that there is a deeply ironical intention behind it. Indeed, the concluding words are '*Literatura, o caralho*', which means 'Literature, my ass!' (Sant'Anna 2014, 83). This sentence obviously leads readers to infer that what they have just read is not proper literature.

If we therefore assume that there is a connection – as there usually is – between the title and the text, we could possibly infer that, in Sant'Anna's view, autofiction is not literature at all. Another interpretation could be that a certain way of looking at autofiction – according to which writing based on personal memories is enough to produce a literary text – is not literature. In the first case, the very concept of autofiction is dismissed. In the second case, a frequent phenomenon of contemporary literature, that is, the increasing importance of the writing of the self, is being criticised – not *per se*, but in situations where it leads to an impoverishment of the possibilities of fictional writing. In both cases, the point is that both Sant'Anna and Carvalho are concerned about the popularity of autofiction among writers and scholars. They consequently choose to write a literary text that is critical of either the concept or of a specific cultural practice associated with it. In this way, the text criticises and actually negates itself.

The third case is that of a younger writer, Ricardo Lísias, whose work is the main concern of this chapter. *Delegado Tobias* (Lísias 2014; Detective Tobias) is a set of five serials (*feuilletons*) in a digital format. The serials were published in the same collection in which Sant'Anna's short story had appeared. The serials describe the murder of the writer Ricardo Lísias by another character, also named Ricardo Lísias. The investigation, led by the detective Paulo Tobias, involves journalists, critics and scholars, seeking clues in the writer's works. The most astonishing and inexplicable detail is that the suspect shared everything with the murdered – not only his name, but also personal details of his life, except something crucial: his physical appearance. The plot thus mingles crime fiction and fantastic features, recalling the well-established connection between investigation of a crime and metatextual reflection.

Indeed, it is no coincidence that a writer who made wide use of this kind of procedures, the Argentinian Ricardo Piglia, is mentioned at a certain moment in the story, as if Lísias wanted to make excessively clear – an excess that is, of course, fully intentional – what game he is playing. In Piglia's words:

> In more than one sense, the critic is the detective and the writer is the criminal. The crime novel might be considered the great fictional form of literary criticism. […] the paranoid representation of the writer as a criminal who erases his traces and encodes his crimes, pursued by the critic, a riddles decoder.
>
> (Piglia 1986, 15)

The day after the publication of the first serial, Ricardo Lísias posted on his Facebook profile, adding documents as evidence, that a man called Paulo Tobias had lodged a complaint and was trying to stop the circulation of the e-book. This act was obviously condemned by Lísias and by many readers, who were commenting on what had happened on social networks and criticising it. Lísias's reply to the attacks of Tobias, both on Facebook and in the serials, was always the same: he thinks he is a person, but he is only a character. However, in the last serial, the author revealed that it was a *mise-en-scène* since the beginning: detective Tobias was actually a fictional character, but the responses produced by the texts exceeded the material limits of the book's support. Indeed, on the one hand, Tobias had a Facebook profile, so he did exist, if only virtually. On the other hand readers were involved in the fictional game and eventually played an active role in it.

Although the story is obviously a game, as well as a parody of journalese (the narrative is told in the third person and sounds like a reportage), it is, nevertheless, autofictional and needs to be read within the critical and theoretical context that made it possible. Indeed, this is what the three mentioned cases share. All these works are part of a collective dialogue that involves several cultural agents: readers, journalists, academics and so on. It shows that the most important feature of autofiction is its openness. On the one hand, autofiction is porous to other genres: it enters not only narratives, such as novels and short stories, but also essays, visual arts, etc. On the other hand, autofiction produces a fertile space of discussion and interchange – which, of course, is now widely stimulated by the possibilities offered by the new media.

It is not irrelevant that this feature of autofiction is reproduced and parodied in Lísias's story. In fact, the police investigation involves not only the dead writer's family and friends, but also other writers and critics who have written about Lísias's works. Their experience is summoned not to talk about literary works, but to give some clues about the writer's life and personality, which *might* be found in his work. In other words, they are invited to join the autofictional game from the point of view of critics or, generally speaking, of readers. This helps us to understand what role is played by these cultural agents in the construction of the figure of the author. In the end Lísias (2014) makes it clear that authorship is constructed at the intersection of several discourses: that of the writer, certainly, but also those of media, readers, academics and so forth.

A performance of writing

It is not important that many writers despise, or even deny, the existence of autofiction. As shown above, some major writers of contemporary Brazilian literature repeatedly negate their links to it, yet they do so precisely by playing the autofictional game. Even if criticising the genre from within, they conform to two main autofictional requirements: the creation of characters or narrators who speak on behalf of the author, and the triggering of a reflection about literature inside the text that is being written. Furthermore, they get engaged in a dialogue with readers, literary critics and theoreticians – a decisive component of autofiction since the elaboration of the concept by Doubrovsky.

In light of these remarks, autofiction should be considered as 'cultural performance' of authorship (Berensmeyer, Buelens and Demoor 2012, 5–29) – that is, a conscious enactment of the production of an authorial instance. If it is commonly agreed that author and writer do not coincide, the former being a literary instance strictly connected to a work and a signature, while the latter is a person in flesh and blood, it is also clear that the increasing presence of writers in public life leads us to perceive a sort of overlapping between writer and author, reality and fiction. This in turn inevitably determines the way in which these works are read. Berensmeyer, Buelens and Demoor (2012, 8) have described this as 'heteronomous authorship as a product of cultural networks and their acts of authorization'. Autofiction can be used to challenge and, ultimately, to reject these Cartesian dualisms (chiefly the opposition between the 'autonomous', or 'strong', and 'heteronomous', or 'weak', notions of authorship; Berensmeyer, Buelens and Demoor, 8),[3] for instance by producing a deliberate confusion to show that the borders between all these oppositions do not exist. Autofiction is therefore also a performance of writing, which has to make the reader enter the fictional game.

This is what the readers of Lísias (2014) did, when they expressed their opinions on Facebook and, by doing so, influenced the development of the story. Of course, this was made possible by the experimental nature of Lísias's work. According to Fernando Cabo Aseguinolaza, the relationship with readers should be considered one of the most relevant features of autofiction. Although Cabo does not refer to performativity but rather to the concept of theatricality used by the art historian Michael Fried (1980),[4] his propositions are relevant to this discussion. Indeed theatricality 'refers to the exercise of a particular activity subject to the anticipation of the spectator's reactions, and therefore to the expectations that the examined behaviour awakes in him/her' (Cabo 2014, 31).

As Cabo points out, theatricality is a hallmark of contemporary literature,[5] since it is no longer possible to disregard the reader's presence, even if this presence is obviously latent. In more general terms, this is even more true of autofiction – and, in general, of any form of literary self-representation – because the act of self-nomination, determining a rupture with the theatrical absorption (based on pretending that the reader or the spectator does not exist), has an effect of self-exhibition, 'so that the reader "is being shown" the author's figure in various postures' (Cabo 2014, 33). The expression 'being shown', which appears in English in Cabo's article, is contrasted to 'seeing', in order to emphasise the awareness of the writer or the artist of the reader's or spectator's presence. When something is 'being shown', it means that the writer or artist made it purposefully to be seen by the reader.

Moreover, Cabo argues that some contemporary art and literature responds to this theatricality, emphasising their anti-theatrical nature. Nonetheless, this gesture, paradoxically, uses theatrical strategies – for instance, including the reader (or the spectator) in the text (or painting). Accordingly, the novel by Lísias (2014) is intended to provoke a specific response among its readers. As a consequence, this work is deeply theatrical and performative, creating an impression as if the author were on a stage, constantly looking at the reader and aiming to affect him/her in specific ways.

Ricardo Lísias achieved a significant popularity on the Brazilian literary scene following publication of his novel *O céu dos suicidas* (Lísias 2012; The Suicides' Heaven), which narrates the experience of the suicide of one of his best friends. The following novel *Divórcio* (Lísias 2013; Divorce) is based on a real and painful experience, dealing with the author's divorce from a well-known São Paulo journalist. Even if the journalist's real name is never mentioned throughout the novel (the narrator refers to her as 'X'), it was easy to identify her. This caused a real scandal, since several intimate details about her were revealed in the book. More importantly, the novel includes excerpts from her personal diary, in which she denigrates her husband and writes about her infidelity. As a result, she took a legal action against Lísias, but he was able to prove that everything was just fiction and defended the right of literature to be free and independent. Although the entire matter addresses serious ethical dilemmas which are usually taken into account by scholars who deal with autofiction, the present approach is focused on other aspects of the novel, especially on its reflection on writing and on its connection with the production of the authorial instance.

The construction of authorship in Ricardo Lísias's works

A statement usually made about autofiction is that the subject inside the text is not something that precedes it, but a literary creation (Klinger 2008, 20). In other words, and in contrast to autobiography whose aim is to reconstitute a personal life and attribute a specific meaning to it, autofiction does not verbally represent someone who already exists. It is not a copy of something that comes first: not a re-creation but a creation, since the very concept of original is rejected. This is not, of course, a peculiarity of autofiction, but of modern literature in general. As Barthes argues,

> The Author, when believed in, is always conceived of as the past of his own book: book and author stand automatically on the same line divided into a *before* and an *after*. The Author is supposed to *nourish* the book, which is to say, he exists before it, thinks, suffers, lives for it, is in the same relation of antecedence to his work as a father to his child. In complete contrast, the modern scriptor is born simultaneously with the text, is in no way equipped with a being preceding or exceeding the writing, is not the subject with the book as predicate; there is no other time than that of the enunciation and every text is eternally written *here and now*. The fact is (or, it follows) that *writing* can no longer designate an operation of recording, notation, representation, 'depiction' (as the Classics would say); rather, it designates exactly what linguists, referring to Oxford philosophy, call a performative […].
>
> (Barthes 1977, 145)

Moreover, Wolfgang Iser compares the text to a 'game' performing 'a transformation' of the text's 'referential worlds'. Such a transformation

> gives rise to something that cannot be deduced from these worlds. It follows that none of these worlds can be the object of representation, that the text is in no way confined to being the representation of something given in any case, there can be no representation without performance and the source of performance is always different from that is to be represented. If representation means mimesis, it always presupposes something that is to be presented in an act of depiction, and so the question arises whether the state of affairs to be depicted has an existence of its own, independent of the representation. So long as representation was equated with mimesis, the answer was generally affirmative.
>
> (Iser 1993, 281)

The problem that autofiction poses is that, while it takes up this modern idea of literature, it nevertheless produces works which create an overlap between the world of the text and the world that the writer and readers share – where they can even meet and talk, be it on Facebook or at a literary event. The public life of the author should therefore also be considered as part of a performance of authorial production: the increasing presence of writers on television and social networks, in newspapers and so forth, makes the author not only the result of a literary creation, as Barthes argued, but the outcome of a complex network of events, both textual and extra-textual.

If autofiction is the only autobiography possible in a post-Freudian and post-deconstruction world, it is interesting to see that in Lísias (2013) this lack of the original is actually literal. The narrator reveals that he had started to rewrite his ex-wife's diary, of which he owned a photocopy, to include it in the book. Once he was told that she had thrown out the original, however, he decided to transcribe it without changing a word. Although this was clearly motivated by practical and legal reasons (if there had been an original, it would have been easy for her to demonstrate that he had invaded her privacy), the implications for literary theory are obviously rich: a part of the novel, supposed to be documentary, is a copy of a copy of a non-existent text. This has allowed Lísias to defend his book from the attacks of those who consider it a non-fictional work. He repeatedly stated that he has published a novel and that his ex-wife is just a character in it.

On the other hand, there is a clear inscription of the author in the novel. The narrator refers to himself several times as Ricardo Lísias and offers easily verifiable details about his life – names of friends, profession, etc. He also mentions episodes from his past, which were already part of the short stories Lísias had previously published. Some paragraphs of these stories have been included in the novel, almost without change. They are mainly about painful memories, sexual experiences and episodes from his childhood and youth. Moreover, Lísias included in the book some pictures of him and his family.[6] Finally, the book ends with a letter, the reply to a legal summons signed by Ricardo Lísias.

The book is composed of 15 chapters, each corresponding to one kilometre of a running route taken by the narrator on New Year's Eve. The physicality of writing is increased by another, more powerful metaphor – that of a skinless body. If the trauma leaves the character Ricardo Lísias without a skin, the process of writing the novel, together with the run, helps him to recover it. Although this can obviously be read in a therapeutic key,[7] the connection between writing or, in a more general way, between language and skin is worthy of deeper examination.

'In flesh, I was waiting the whole time for someone to come closer and give me an explanation. A skinless body cannot find any answer,' says the narrator (Lísias 2013, 119). Does he find an answer at the end of the book? Does he find any explanation for what happened to him? He does not: the novel does not investigate the reasons why events unfolded in a certain way, nor does it seek explanations. Its main concern is the (re)construction, after the experience of trauma, of the figure of the author, Ricardo Lísias. Indeed, this is the major achievement of the novel. If this is what every book does, the characteristic of autofiction is that it is done explicitly and performatively.

The narrator deliberately points to a confusion between what is supposed to be real and what is deemed fictional throughout the novel. Since the very beginning he is suggesting that he might be a character from one of his short stories. He discovers similarities between what is happening to him and two characters of his stories, insinuating that he must be living within one of his fictional texts and might be losing his mind. How to keep a sense of reality, how to set a limit between the real and the fictional world when one is passing through such a bewildering experience?

In Lísias's novel *Divórcio*, the answer is to be found in physicality. The first time that the character of the author is finally sure that he is not fictional is when he is sexually aroused and feels that his feet have recovered their skin: 'My body is going to help my head: I am not inside a book I wrote' (Lísias 2013, 100). The achievement of the novel coincides with the full recovery of his skin – that is, with the production of the author as a physical body. In this sense, writing – and, in this specific case, autofictional writing – does not expose the writer: on the contrary, it helps to establish a distance, a skin, between him and his experience, precisely through the fictionalisation of the latter. The result of this process is the construction of authorship, where the author is, together with the characters, a fictional entity.

In order to illustrate this aspect, an example provided by Lísias himself is used: a short film by Ben Aston, entitled *He Took His Skin Off For Me*. By a curious coincidence the film came out in 2013 as well, but Lísias appears to have heard about it only in 2015, when he shared it on a Facebook post entitled 'To the readers of *Divórcio*'. This post suggests that he could envisage a connection between this film and his novel. The film, an adaptation of a short story by Maria Hummer, a young American writer, is centered on a man who takes off his skin for his girlfriend's sake. The idea behind it is that in this way he would be completely exposed to her; she would be able to see everything. Hummer's text, faithfully reproduced in the film, reads:

> People commented on his different appearance, but they couldn't quite put a finger on it. Have you lost weight? they'd ask, scratching their chin. In a way, he'd say. Smiling a red smile at me. Such a short sentence was unlike him. He loved words, loved using different ones to say the same thing again and again until he was sure he was fully understood. But he either had less to say now, or he felt that he was already saying it.
>
> (Hummer 2013)

Using different words to say the same thing again and again is perhaps one of the most eloquent ways to define what some writers do, and this is undoubtedly what Lísias does. His writing, in fact, is known for being repetitive and for focusing upon a relatively small set of topics and episodes from his past life. Having a skin, in Hummer's tale, is connected to language and to the possibility of saying something with many different words, just as writers do. In *Divórcio* (Lísias 2013), the metaphor of the skinless body is decisive to understand Lísias's purpose: the recovering of the skin once the writing of the novel is completed represents the self-affirmation of Lísias as an author.

However, this act of self-affirmation is never fully attained. In a short story called '*Fisiologia da dor*' (Physiology of pain), included in *Concentração e outros contos* (Lísias 2015), the metaphor of the skinless body is already present, connected with pain and artistic failure. In this case, the narrator talks about an experience he had as a plastic artist and comments it with these words:

> I put too many expectations in this work. With literature, I already know that I will not be able to say what I want in the way that I consider ideal. Therefore I will have to make repetitions. Although I reach, in doing so, a sort of continuous relief for the uneasiness I feel, on the other hand, the certainty of the incompleteness of writing also distresses me.
> (Lísias 2015, 70)

In another short story, '*Fisiologia da solidão*' (Physiology of solitude),[8] also included in Lísias (2015), we find a similar statement:

> I feel alone [...] because I am never capable of expressing exactly what I want, and not even in the way that I am sure is the most adequate.
> (Lísias 2015, 77)

Both these texts, especially the second one, deal with Lísias's reflection on literature and, specifically, on his own writing. They tackle the classic topic of the limits of language and of the gap between a project and its result – the literary work. In this sense they are undoubtedly critical and, as an obvious consequence, self-critical. Moreover, the frequent use of physical metaphors – not only that of the skinless body, but also the very titles of these and other texts, the *physiologies* – calls for an inscription of the writer within his own writing, a commitment to it. What is more important in these texts, which, due to their content, might be labelled 'autofictional', is not the reconstruction of a subjective experience, but rather the construction of a skin that is, ultimately, the result of a writing experience: authorship. Therefore the prefix 'auto' in autofiction does not refer to the self as a person, but to the self as an author. It is not the account of one's life, but rather of the experience of being or becoming an author. In Doubrovsky's words, it is 'an adventure of language'.

Indeed, although the novel *Divórcio* (Lísias 2013) narrates a series of past events (the story starts four months prior to the time of the narration), the reconstruction of that past happens more by making use of all sorts of written texts that the narrator had been producing during those months than through a mere act of remembering. In fact, more than once, the narrator relates events he says he does not remember which are based on his own notes. Therefore notes, lists, emails, drafts of other texts and the very book perused by the reader[9] provide a ground for a narrative that, otherwise, could not have been written and are repeatedly mentioned by the narrator:[10]

> I do not remember the following days. I signed the divorce on Tuesday and, according to the school register, I gave a class on accents on Friday. I looked for the manuscripts of the story 'Divorce', which I would publish three months later, and understood that the first drafts date back to Saturday. The other days are a riddle: I did not live them.
>
> (Lísias 2013, 77)

In this way, Lísias shows the offstage of his book, fulfilling another frequent requirement of autofiction: metaliterary reflection.

A dramatisation of literary theory

Evidently, this kind of critical and theoretical reflection is not exclusive of autofiction. However, it is important to stress that, as the subsection headed 'Three examples from Brazilian literature' shows, the very debate about this concept has been fuelled by writers who, with different purposes, have thought and written about or against it; in doing so, they have contributed to a discussion about literature, fiction and, of course, authorship. Moreover, as previously argued, the increasing visibility of writers on media and social networks produces a shuffling between writer, author and characters that was inconceivable in the past.

The case of *Delegado Tobias 1–5* (Lísias 2014) is very illustrative of this and the detail that distinguishes the two figures of Ricardo Lísias is far from being irrelevant: the murdered and the suspect share everything except their physical appearance. Significantly, the people whom the police interrogated were able to identify only the murdered: no one knew the suspect. Once again a physical metaphor is used, suggesting that a writer cannot be reduced to a literary instance. Even if s/he is clearly connected with it, s/he is an untranslatable body. The fourth serial reinforces this idea. Entitled 'Lísias's case is real', it provoked great astonishment among readers who found blank pages instead of a text: some of them even complained, thinking that it was a printer's error. Nonetheless, Lísias's blank pages indicate that reality, as well as the writer's body, is not translatable into literature. Clearly this does not mean that the world of fiction is separate from the real world. It suggests that fiction cannot provide us with answers about the real world – of which the writer, as a human being, is a part.

The serials perform a *mise-en-scène* of literary instances and the result is a sort of dramatisation of a literary theory. The performative aspect of this process is based on an apparently paradoxical assumption. On the one hand, the author points to his own self and life; on the other, he clearly shows that becoming an author is precisely the result of the process of writing represented in the narrative. In this way, the constructed nature of the literary text and of its author is clearly emphasised. Indeed, this is the peculiarity of performance: the performers play a role that explicitly points to the fictional nature of what they are doing. As a result, the double nature of the performers, who, simultaneously are and are not themselves, is exposed.[11]

In this process, the reader may be either explicitly addressed by the author, as happens in *Delegado Tobias 1–5* (Lísias 2014), or thought of as a latent presence – an invisible spectator who is being shown, as Fernando Cabo suggested, a literary enactment (2014, 25–44). This happens because, as I have stressed, it has now become clear that authorship is produced both within the literary text and outside of it – not only in interviews and other kinds of oral and written texts produced by writers, but also in texts produced by other people: readers, academics, journalists, etc.

Due to the reflection of literary writing and, more specifically, of their own author's writing which they set forth, it can be suggested that the works previously examined, as well as other autofictional texts, are close to critical and self-critical essays. Indeed, because of its controversial status, autofiction has promoted a renewed discussion on concepts such as fiction, authorship and readership, as well as on the old and new dynamics that tie these instances together.

The notions of autofiction oscillate between those of a new genre, which would occupy an intermediate position between fiction and non-fiction (novel and autobiography) and which is still in the process of formation (Martins 2014, 136), and a downright denial of its existence, reducing it to a postmodern variation of classical autobiographical genres (Grell 2014, 13). Although autofiction is often considered an empty concept, it works nonetheless as a theoretical device, capable of posing the problem of the relationship between fiction and reality in often paradoxical terms (all this is and is not fictional). In so doing it makes readers reach the ultimate conclusion that, if a boundary between fiction and reality exists, it is not to be found in a work of literature.

Notes

1. Colonna who, in a pioneering study, made an effort to broaden the concept of autofiction, proposed that, based on the criterion of the homonymy (between the author, the narrator and the main character), works such as the *Divine Comedy* should be considered autofiction as well (1989, 29). Unless mentioned otherwise, all translations into English are by the author.
2. This detail is worth mentioning because it accounts for the broad circulation of this collection of short stories.
3. Not surprisingly, Berensmayer, Buelens and Demoor (2012, 5–29) do not refer to the authorship of autofiction at all. As a result, their performative model of authorship excludes an important performative form of authorship.
4. Similarly, Berensmeyer, Buelens and Demoor (2012, 5–29) do not mention theatricality in their discussion of the performative model of authorship. The game-like aspects of performativity (emphasised, for instance, by Iser (1993, 283), see below, or later by Cheng 2019, 172: 'They produce an uncanny sensation of the theatricality of the real-life writing site, a space of quotidian reality turned stagelike') appear very useful for the discussion of the performativity of autofiction.
5. On the limits of the use of the term 'performativity' and its replacement with 'theatricality' in Hispanic cultural theory, see Reinelt (2002, 210–11). Her conclusions follow the work of Taylor and Villegas (1994).
6. The same is typical of some of the short stories included in *Concentração e outros contos* (Lísias 2015; Concentration and other short stories).
7. Autofictional works often deal with traumatic experiences, such as loss, illness, death of a beloved person, etc. Moreover, the genre has been associated, since the beginning, with psychoanalysis (Doubrovsky 1980, 87–97). As Isabelle Grell puts it: 'since Freud, the self escapes itself. Memory mixes reality and fiction, the I is deconstructed. From its origin, autofiction has been conceived as autobiography revisited by psychoanalysis, implying that any self-image is a more or less fictitious construction whose reasons for being we must try to understand' (2014, 7–8). For similar reasons, because of its concern with language and its fundamental assertion about the impossibility to reach a definite and stable meaning, deconstructive thought is equally important.
8. Both these stories, as well as others included in a section called precisely 'Fisiologias' (Physiologies), were written several years before the publication of Lísias (2015). They either circulated in non-commercial editions or appeared in literary magazines (Lísias 2015, 170).
9. In the thirteenth chapter, the narrator states he has just read the first 12 chapters of *Divórcio* (Lísias 2013) and lists some problems he detected in it. Here again we find the topic of the intrinsic incompleteness of literature, of the book as a (permanent) failure, mentioned above in relation to the short stories in *Concentração e outros contos* (Lísias 2015), 'Fisiologia da dor' and 'Fisiologia da solidão'.
10. Indeed, this is something he considers necessary: 'At the current stage of literature, the skeleton of a novel must be totally exposed' (Lísias 2013, 189–90). 'The skeleton of a novel' is composed of words; by exposing it, the narrator stresses precisely the role of language as a tool that does not help to explain reality – on the contrary, it makes it more opaque.
11. Diana Klinger argues that while in theatre actors must identify themselves with the characters they are playing and, as a result, put aside their personal identities: 'The performer is present more as a person and less as a character. Like in performance, in autofiction the writer-actor and the character-author live together. […] In the autofictional text, understood in this way, the naturalised character of autobiography is broken into a discursive form which, at the same time, exhibits the subject and questions it. In other words, it exposes subjectivity and writing as processes under construction. Therefore, the autofictional work may also be compared to the art of performance, as long as both present themselves as unfinished, improvised, work-in-progress texts, as if the reader were seeing the writing process "alive"' (Klinger 2008, 26).

References

Barthes, Roland. 1977. 'The death of the author' (1968). In *Image Music Text*, selected and translated by Stephen Heath, 142–8. London: Fontana Press.

Berensmeyer, Ingo, Gert Buelens and Marysa Demoor. 2012. 'Authorship as cultural performance: New perspectives in authorship studies', *Zeitschrift für Anglistik und Amerikanistik* 60.1: 5–29.

Cabo Aseguinolaza, Fernando. 2014. 'Teatralidad, itinerancia y lectura: sobre la tradición teórica de la autoficción'. In *El yo fabulado. Nuevas aproximaciones críticas a la autoficción*, edited by Ana Casas, 25–44. Madrid: Librería Iberoamericana.

Carvalho, Bernardo. 2004. *Nove noites* (2002). Lisboa: Cotovia.

Carvalho, Bernardo. 2007. *Nine Nights*. Translated by Benjamin Moser. London: William Heinemann.

Carvalho, Bernardo. 2011. 'Em defesa da obra', *Revista Piauí* 62. Accessed 29 August 2021. https://piaui.folha.uol.com.br/materia/em-defesa-da-obra.

Cheng, Li Feng. 2019. 'Author as performer', *Modern Chinese Literature and Culture*, 31.1: 161–91.

Colonna, Vincent. 1989. *L'autofiction, essai sur la fictionalisation de soi en littérature*. École des Hautes Études en Sciences Sociales. PhD thesis, 1989. Accessed 29 August 2021. https://tel.archives-ouvertes.fr/tel-00006609/document.

Doubrovsky, Serge. 1977. *Fils*. Paris: Galilée.

Doubrovsky, Serge. 1980. 'Autobiographie / vérité / psychanalyse', *L'Esprit créateur* 20.3: 87–97.

Fried, Michael. 1980. *Absorption and Theatricality. Painting and beholder in the age of Diderot*. Berkeley and Los Angeles: University of California Press.

Grell, Isabelle. 2014. *L'autofiction*. Paris: Armand Colin.

Hummer, Maria. 2013. 'He took off his skin for me', *Devil's Lake* (Spring Issue). Accessed 29 August 2021. https://dept.english.wisc.edu/devilslake/issues/2013_spring/hummer.html.

Iser, Wolfgang. 1993. *The Fictive and the Imaginary: Charting literary anthropology* (1991). Baltimore, MD and London: The John Hopkins University Press.

Klinger, Diana. 2008. 'Escrita de si como performance', *Revista Brasileira de Literatura Comparada* 10.12: 11–30.

Lejeune, Philippe. 1975. *Le pacte autobiographique*. Paris: Seuil.

Lejeune, Philippe. 1986. *Moi aussi*. Paris: Seuil.

Lejeune, Philippe. 2005. 'De l'autobiographie au journal, de l'Université à l'association: itinéraires d'une recherche'. Identité et altérité conference, 28 March 2005, Ain Shams University, Cairo, Egypt. http://www.autopacte.org/Itin%E9raires_d'une_recherche.html. Accessed 29 August 2021.

Lísias, Ricardo. 2012. *O céu dos suicidas*. São Paulo: Alfaguara.

Lísias, Ricardo. 2013. *Divórcio*. Carnaxide: Objectiva.

Lísias, Ricardo. 2014. *Delegado Tobias 1–5*. São Paulo: e-galáxia.

Lísias, Ricardo. 2015. *Concentração e outros contos*. Carnaxide: Objectiva.

Martins, Anna Faedrich. 2014. *Autoficções. Do conceito teórico à prática na literatura brasileira contemporânea*. PhD thesis, Pontifícia Universidade Católica do Rio Grande do Sul. Accessed 29 August 2021. https://repositorio.pucrs.br/dspace/handle/10923/5746.

McDonough, Sarah. 2011. *How to Read Autofiction*. PhD thesis, Wesleyan University. Accessed 29 August 2021. https://digitalcollections.wesleyan.edu/object/ir-909.

Piglia, Ricardo. 1986. *Crítica y ficción*. Barcelona: Anagrama.

Reinelt, Janelle. 2002. 'The politics of discourse: Performativity meets theatricality', *SubStance* 31.2–3: 201–15.

Sant'Anna, André. 2014. *Autoficção*. São Paulo: e-galáxia.

Taylor, Diana and Juan Villegas (eds). 1994. *Negotiating Performance: Gender, sexuality, and theatricality in Latin America*. Durham, NC and London: Duke University Press.

9
Latin American autofiction authors as *trans*formers: beyond textuality in Aira and Bellatin
Gerardo Cruz-Grunerth

Introduction: autofiction in the works of César Aira and Mario Bellatin

Autofiction is a phenomenon which has gained importance in contemporary literature. Its origin as a literary concept is due to Serge Doubrovsky, author of the novel *Fils* (Doubrovsky 1977), which he called 'autofiction'. Along with Doubrovsky, other theorists, such as Philippe Lejeune (1975), approached the phenomenon and attempted to define it. More recently a French scholar, Philippe Gasparini, presented his own view in *Est-il je?* (Gasparini 2004) and this chapter largely follows his approach. Gasparini suggests that there are certain 'procedures', going beyond the use of the proper name, which lead us to consider a narrative autobiographical and autofictional (2004, 14). Furthermore, he has opened the way of studying autofictional texts which generate their own instability. Developing this feature of Gasparini's approach, this chapter will explore the crisis of autofiction caused by its complexity and specific limitations.

In contemporary Latin American narrative, two authors in particular have exacerbated the exercise of autofiction – to the point of implementing it as a fundamental element of their poetics. This is the case of the Argentinian César Aira and the Mexican Mario Bellatin. This chapter will examine books by both authors: *Cómo me hice monja* (Aira 1993; Aira 2006) and *El gran vidrio. Tres autobiografías* (Bellatin 2007; Bellatin 2015). These works are relevant not only because they establish a link between the author and the narrator through the proper name, but also because both of them, despite their numerous differences, can be studied as works of autofiction.

Aira and Bellatin have not been chosen merely in order to discuss the present status of autofictionality. The selection is rather because their works call into question the principles formulated by Lejeune (1975), Doubrovsky and Manuel Alberca (2007), all of whom follow the idea of autobiographical pact. As a result, the narratives of these Latin American authors contain mechanisms of authorial identification, as well as moments of denial, concealment and crisis of autofiction caused by autofiction itself.

Another common feature can be found in the aesthetics of these authors. Both writers, in different terms and scopes, maintain their own separate literary projects with a similar objective. César Aira has presented his aesthetic proposition mainly in literature. Here he tends to develop what he has called *the novel of the artist*, following the phases of Borges and aiming to construct a Borges myth. This myth can then be understood as a project in which the author wishes to construct himself as a fictional character; this amplifies his real persona by transforming it during the re-creation of his identity.

This process has a similar manifestation in Bellatin, who actually refers to his own project as 'the hundred-thousand books of Bellatin' (2014, 653–64). The profound point of agreement is that both authors conceive these works as their own *corpus*, that is, both a textual corpus and a physical body. What each of them forms through his writing, besides a work of art, is a figure as a human representation; a persona that is formed or performed as much through the textual medium as through public lectures and performances. These phenomena will be read in association with the term '*trans*former' that Jean-François Lyotard (1990) uses to explain the autofictional mechanism implied in the works of Marcel Duchamp. This will allow us to adopt a complex view of autofiction, expanding our understanding of these authors as performers or *trans*formers.

It is necessary to understand how each author achieves the complexity of his autofiction. First, in Aira's novel (1993; 2006) the main character is a child; he and his family have moved from Coronel Pringles to Rosario, Argentina, exactly as the author did in his childhood. Early in the novel we find ambiguities and contradictions, for example the fact that the title refers to becoming a nun, which certainly never happens. There is also a promise derived from the title and the first paragraph, which supposedly speak in a confessional way about the hero's transformation into a nun.

> My story, the story of 'how I became a nun', began very early in my life; I had just turned six. The beginning is marked by a vivid memory […]. Before, there is nothing, and after, everything is an

extension of the same vivid memory, continuous and unbroken, including the intervals of sleep, up to the point where I took the veil.

(Aira 2006, 3)

This passage can be interpreted as a promise. As Derrida said, '[e]very title has the import of a promise' (1992, 86). Here the promise is to make someone, namely César Aira, present. The novel tells of his becoming a nun and also about the ways in which he talks about himself, both as an author and a character. The complex performance of the narrative can be described as *how to (avoid) speak(ing) about how I became a nun*. This implies a double articulation.

The above promise is also challenged by the clash between the author's masculine name, César Aira, and the feminine voice of his character. Despite the other characters relating to the protagonist as a boy, César speaks about himself as a female: 'She kept cuddling me and saying my name: César, César, César […] she had mixed me up with another girl, who had the same name as me' (Aira 2006, 100–1).

In short, in this novel the expected confession is delayed until the end of the text – yet at that point there is no confession and Aira is not present. As Derrida puts it:

the promise has seized the *I* which promises to speak to the other, to say something […] or to confirm by speech at least this: that it is necessary to be silent; and to be silent concerning that about which one cannot speak.

(1992, 84)

Another disruption appears when the end of the novel exposes the character's death. The reader must assume that the voice telling the full story comes from the realm of death: 'my brain, most loyal of my organs, kept working for a moment longer, just long enough for me to think that what was happening to me was death, real death' (Aira 2006, 115).

As a consequence a flaw appears, pointing out how and where the spatial and temporal elements are displaced. Following Derrida, this can be interpreted as the *differance* in two ways: firstly as a temporal/spatial deferral, but also, secondly, as a chance for otherness or alterity. The authorial voice of Aira – the boy/girl who utters the speech – can be deferred in three ways: spatial, temporal and in the alterity of his own identity. This is the 'game' of differance, which, as Derrida has observed, 'in no way implies that the deferred presence can always be recovered'

(1973, 151). In a similar way, the novel expresses the promise to present the author's presence, so that he can develop and display it later on. This is how César Aira constructs an autofictional discourse. Mariano García, the Argentinean specialist in Aira's narratives, considers this short-novel as a textual space in which the 'autofiction remains destroyed' (2006, 252).[1]

The following part of this subchapter discusses Bellatin's short 'experimental' novel (2007; 2015). The book is divided into three parts, each being an autobiography. In the first of these, entitled 'My skin, luminous', the text is disarticulated. On each page of the first edition in Spanish (Bellatin 2007) we find only a single numbered sentence. To follow the narrative, we need to turn the page. All sentences together form the autobiography. It is a game of textual disarticulation which corresponds with the dissolution of the author-character's identity. The main character is also ambiguous; he is a boy suffering from a mental illness. He has extremely big testicles and a luminous skin, and is displayed by his mother as a prodigy. He also has no name, nor is he named by the author: this gesture can be understood as a mark of distance. Bellatin's narrator is an anomaly. He cannot authenticate his possible fictional world because of his illness and the frequent contradictions which this world expresses.

The second autobiography, 'The sheikha's true illness', tells the story of an author-narrator who never mentions his name and lives in a Sufi Muslim community. This story, which tells the author's mystic dream about the sheikha, is narrated in his last book and also in a short story in *Playboy* magazine, both possessing the same title 'The sheikha's illness'. The narrative implies problematic issues in the society where the author lives. None of the characters are happy with the manner in which they are presented in fiction.

In the last autobiography, 'A character in modern appearance', there are three protagonists. The first one is a young man who has a German girlfriend, the second an adult woman who looks like a young girl, or rather a pretty marionette, and the third the well-known author Mario Bellatin. All of them offer an insight into their lives.

The novel's structure is complicated because in the second autobiography the author includes a kind of metafictional narrative. According to the Czech theorist Lubomír Doležel, possible fictional worlds are multiple; they can be connected through metafiction, which has a rhizomatic structure. According to Deleuze and Guattari (1987, 3–25), the rhizome is de-centred. It has no beginning and no end, and can be accessed from any point. Moreover, the actions in these fictional worlds are recursive: what happens in one happens at the same time in many others. There are many moments in the plot where the actions in one fictional world have repercussions in the other. As a result, the narrative expands from the fictional worlds, linking them to the author's real, or seemingly real, world and the reader's world. This happens when the fictional author, nameless in the narrative, is assumed to be the same person represented both in the text read by actual readers and the text written by him. It is not important to know about Bellatin's private life: readers do not need to know, for instance, that he was born without an arm. It is the virtue of this metaleptical and metafictional narrative, which includes the reader in the frame of fictionality.

The ideas of metalepsis and metafiction were proposed by the French theorist Gérard Genette. He explains that metalepsis is a process that allows ontological entities, such as characters, to migrate from a fictional world into another fictional world (Genette 2004). This transfer, known as metalepsis, makes it possible for characters like the factual Bellatin, the fictional Bellatin and the metafictional Bellatin, as well as their actions, to travel through interconnected fictional worlds. This leads to a synthetic approach proposed in Doležel's *Heterocosmica* (Doležel 1998), distinguishing factual world (FW), possible fictional world (PW1) and possible world existing in the possible fictional world (PW2), while also describing how characters and their actions in these worlds maintain contact and communication.

In Bellatin's third autobiography, the process is even more complex. In the first paragraph the reader assumes that the narrator is a young man who has a German girlfriend and is looking forward to buying a car. However, in the second paragraph, the male voice is changed to a female one which refuses to accept that she had a German girlfriend in the past. Both narrators refer to some aspects of the plot; sometimes they agree about them and sometimes they do not. For example, the man says: 'At that time, I don't remember the reasons why this happened, I had a German girlfriend' (Bellatin 2007, 103).

Then the next paragraph starts with: 'Although, as things have occurred, it is impossible that at that time I could have had a German girlfriend. Especially considering […] I am the youngest daughter of the family' (2007, 104).

A third identity in the story is a mixed one: it is that of the recognised author Mario Bellatin. The young man with a German girlfriend says:

My girlfriend had to play the role of the nurse [...] I do not understand why, but at that moment, standing on the other side, was a journalist from the cultural section of the major newspaper [...]. I was assisted [*asistida* is feminine in Spanish] by a beautiful woman, in the proscribed area of the subway. My reputation was at stake before this reporter.

(Bellatin 2007, 108–9)

The first edition in Spanish includes an additional sentence, missing in the English translation. This sentence is important because it increases the narrative's complexity:

He [the reporter] will be able to discover that he was not in the presence of a little marionette in company of his German girlfriend, but in the presence of the writer Mario Bellatin.

(Bellatin 2007, 146)

Here the presence of the author's proper name, the role played by this character in the first autobiography and a strong implication of gender issues (due to the twist of the feminine insinuations) are united.

In this way, the narrative transgresses the boundaries of fictional worlds. In the second autobiography the metafiction emphasises that the boundaries of fictional worlds have been transgressed. The third autobiography reveals other boundaries that are being transgressed: the boundaries of the characters' gender and of the fictional worlds which are separate entities but at certain moments become unified, their boundaries erased. Here textual markers play a decisive function in changing the gender evoked by an adjective (in Bellatin 2007), even as the contours of the characters as distinct identities are dissolved. These transgressions continue beyond the limits of the third autobiography. The voice of Bellatin / marionette-like girl / young man is indeterminate. It moves in the same phrase between these identities and in a recurrent self-consciousness or auto-reflexivity. The narrator's voice thus links his identity with the identity of the characters presented in the two preceding autobiographies, which the reader assumes to be separate and finished works. All the identities of every single main character in the novel are presented as alterities of the same author.

This is how the author associates with others, perceived as his own alterities – not only through metafiction, but also by means of self-consciousness. As a result, the real author and the fictional author with his otherness become only a single identity. The fictional characters and the real author come together through the work of Bellatin, while he disrupts the fiction-reality boundaries. Above all, the construction of his rhizomatic novel implies that, in the end, the rhizomatic parts tend to establish a link to actual reality as part of the rhizomatic ambit. In this way the novel incorporates the actual world to make it a part of what Doležel calls *heterocosmica* – that is, a compound of fictional worlds.

The author as transformer: paratext and hypertext

The title of Bellatin (2007; 2015) can be understood as an allusion to the eponymous artwork of Marcel Duchamp. However, the novel is no mere transposition of Duchamp's work. Rather, it establishes an aesthetic connection between the French artist and the two Latin American authors discussed in this chapter. The autofictions of Aira and Bellatin can be understood as transformative activities. The idea of the author as transformer has been formulated by Jean-François Lyotard (1990); it is linked to Duchamp as a definition of his aesthetic. Lyotard uses this term instead of performer, because

> [l]ike everyone else, I have problems with words performance, performer [...] Duchamp as a transformer seems to me comprehensible. I propose to replace *performer* by *transformer*.
> (Lyotard 1990, 31)

To me, Lyotard's use of the prefix *trans-* implies a metamorphosis of the self which is difficult to revert, like that of trans-sexual gender change. The artistic objects which Lyotard points out in Duchamp's œuvre in order to call him a transformer are *The Large Glass*, a work of paint, sculpture and drawing, *Given*, a work in which part of a body of a nude woman is visible through two peepholes, and the *Green Box*, the box that contains manuscripts, telegrams, drawings and instructions to build and rebuild *The Large Glass*.

Lyotard sees a correspondence between these works that forms a kind of rhizomatic web of significations, none of which are evident. The main signification of this rhizome is the identity of Marcel Duchamp. In other words, the identity of Duchamp is what is being disseminated through the others named Richard Mutt, Rrose Sélavy and finally Marcel Duchamp, and also in his works. As Lyotard and other critics see it, this is a system that allows Duchamp to expand his gender identity beyond the limits of the masculine. In the picture of Rrose Sélavy, there is a dedicatory: 'Lovingly Rrose Sélavy, alias Marcel Duchamp' (Lyotard 1990, 3). Duchamp's signature from/for himself/herself can be understood analogously to the phrase 'he has taken out a loan with himself' (Derrida 1985, 8), referring to Nietzsche's *Ecce Homo*.

> He [Nietzsche] has taken out a loan with himself *and has implicated us in this transaction through what, on the force of a signature, remains of his text*. [...] he does not live presently: 'I live on my own credit; it is perhaps a mere prejudice that I live [...].'
> (Derrida 1985, 8–9)

In Duchamp's case, taking 'out a loan with himself' amounts to selecting an object of the material world, which can be a urinal or a real person, in order to re-name it, re-place it and finally re-signify it as an autonomous entity. There may also be other ways to produce the so-called 'readymade', not only in art but also in literature. Following Derrida, its production can be explained as writing down the proper name as the first signature of an autobiography. In biography, Derrida points out, the proper name and the text cannot be separated (1985, 10). Therefore, he continues, Nietzsche's *Ecce Homo* represents a break with the limits of the logic of self-representation (Derrida 1985, 11). It is a work in which Nietzsche speaks about himself and fictionalises himself in a certain way. Of course, Derrida never uses the term autofiction. However, what is important about Nietzsche, Duchamp and the discussed Latin American authors is the way they use the text (the textual corpus) as a paratext of themselves, in order to fictionalise themselves.

This notion of paratext has been presented by Gérard Genette (1997b). Paratexts are textual or non-textual elements surrounding the main text, such as front covers, prefaces, etc. However, not only these attached elements are paratextual. There are other objects that Genette terms 'epitext' or 'any paratextual element not materially appended to the text within the same volume, but circulating, as it were, freely, in a virtually limitless physical and social space' (1997b, 344).

This means that there are elements separated from the text as well as attached to it; they are in continuous communication with the text, adding significance to it. This idea is central for understanding how the authors Aira and Bellatin, as well as Marcel Duchamp, construct, thanks to paratextuality, their artistic works and – fictional/factual – identities in a complex way.

The notion of paratext extends further than has been shown so far. In literary and artistic works, paratexts are linked to other texts and paratexts to disseminate the meaning and identity of the work and its author, no longer separable from one another. For example, the *Green Box* is a paratext of *The Large Glass*, expanding and interpreting the work. In Mario Bellatin's fictions many references are more than intertexts: they establish the chance to disseminate the text by continuing it. Following the theory of Genette, they can be called 'hypotexts' (originary texts) and 'hypertexts' (rewritings of the hypotext) (Genette 1997a, 5–30).

Moreover, paratexts in Bellatin are so important that they are used in back cover reviews, as images in covers and also as images in photographic dossiers, placed at the end of the text or within the text. Sometimes these serve to authenticate parts of the novel's plot. For example, in *'Biografía ilustrada de Mishima'* (Bellatin 2013, 511–84; illustrated biography of Mishima) the author appears in an image with the description: 'Couple of analysts who worked in the Mishima case' (Bellatin 2013, 580). These can also be used as a false clue to mislead the reader. This procedure is also well illustrated by the note on the back cover:

> The Large Glass is a party that takes place annually within the ruins of the destroyed buildings in Mexico City, where hundreds of families live. The act of living among the traces left behind by broken buildings represents an important symbol of social invisibility.
> (Bellatin 2007, back cover)

However, nothing mentioned here is referred to in the main text. The note has been added as a paratext, part of Bellatin's game. A similar feature can be observed in the front cover image, which portrays a destroyed building and a little shadow entering it. These paratexts indicate that anything in the book may be assumed to lead anywhere.

Moreover, the dissemination of fiction in Bellatin's novels serves to link other novels, short-fictions and paratexts. Other fictional ontological entities move from one fictional world to another, not only to that of Duchamp's *Large Glass*. For example, the marionette-woman (or Bellatin) says that s/he knows a man named Mr Dufó who has a Volkswagen Karmann Ghia and who is also the main character of the previously published short-fiction entitled *'El auto del señor Dufó'* (Bellatin 2014, 205–8; Mr Dufó's car). This is a fictional metalepsis, common to find, for instance, in Cervantes.

According to Bellatin's public talks, essays or other texts, another way to link different works is a performance (or an 'installation') included in characters' utterances; it resembles a set of instructions for creating a work of art. For instance, *The Hundred-thousand Books of Bellatin* (2014, 653–64), a text that appeared in Mexican newspapers and magazines, is more than an explanation how to write that quantity of books. The main issue here is the performance or the communication of instructions: it looks like Duchamp's *Green Box*. The text starts with the memories of Bellatin as a child without an arm (Bellatin 2014, 653). He writes his first book about dogs, illustrated with images of dogs drawn by him or represented using newspaper clippings. In the second autobiography, the marionette-woman remembers that her first book was about dogs. The images of dogs described by her are exactly like those used by Bellatin in the first book. This game becomes really complex when literary critics, academics and journalists start to quote this allusion as evidence of a fact about Bellatin's real life. In Genette's terms, this is the scope of the paratextual, namely 'the public authorial epitext' (1997b, 351–52).

This is an example of Bellatin choosing his own, real or fictional, feature – to be disseminated as his fictional identity and also as the identity of the marionette-woman, in order to move from fiction to real life. He is confident that he can modify his identity through this process, both the identity that others develop for him and that he fabricates for himself. These actions can be understood as a way to express and modify the real world. For this reason they can be viewed as aesthetic or performative acts. To sum up, Bellatin, Aira and Duchamp can be considered as performers of themselves. They construct and reconstruct their identities in a constant performance, using text and paratexts: they transform themselves at both factual and fictional levels.

Breaking with teleology and hermeneutics: rhizomatic identity disseminated

The crisis that may be seen here is no mere traditional confrontation between referential and fictional spaces of autofiction, as Gasparini (2004) puts it. What the writings of Aira and Bellatin set into action is another twist on the way of constructing autofiction.

First, the confrontation between reality and fiction is extended to the real author, reader, commentators and critics. Fiction and reality are linked into a rhizome; as a result, one is affected by another. The binary opposition fiction–reality, in which fiction is always inferior, is transformed into a relation of supplementarity. As Derrida puts it, the supplement may change from a complement into the main element. Both Bellatin and Aira, as well as Duchamp, bring this process to light – not only on the textual level, but also in the actual world.

Second, these fictions are more than self-conscious or auto-reflexive; they perform a self-deconstructive process. The critic and the deconstruction of teleology and hermeneutics are within the text. Textually, Aira's autofiction expresses a way in which the narrator-author gives a promise to talk about how he became a nun. However, the internal textual process is twofold: how to avoid speaking, as that would lead to 'a negative (apophatic) attribution', or 'return [...] to this rhetoric of negative determination' (Derrida 1992, 74). Although to avoid speaking implies the chance '[t]o keep something to oneself', one cannot avoid 'dissimulation, for which it is already necessary to be multiple and to differ from oneself – also presupposes the space of a promised speech, that is to say, a trace to which the affirmation is not symmetrical' (Derrida 1992, 87).

In Bellatin's case, this *differance* of the self implies an absence of the original and the origin, as well as the impossibility of a *telos*. For this reason his autofictions are anti-teleological. Moreover, the absence implies a resistance to the usual ways of reading an autofiction novel, tracing the links to the real author. In the third autobiography of Bellatin (2007), the character Bellatin observes:

> [There is] the necessity of erasing any trace of the past, to blur a determined identity as much as possible [...it is necessary to] changing tradition, name, history, nationality, religion has been constant in my life. [...Fiction is] a true time that truly does not exist, and which for that same reason I consider to be more real than real.
> (Bellatin 2007, 142–6)

This quote expresses not only a self-consciousness but also an aporetic way of dissolving the usual subordination of fiction to reality. At the same time, due to the absence of self in autofiction, the *telos* is unattainable.

This anti-teleology, closely linked with anti-hermeneutics, is a kind of anti-textual teleology. In the third autobiography Bellatin asks us:

> What is there of truth and what is there of lie in each of the three representations, in each of the three autobiographical moments [...] that I have presented here?
>
> (2007, 142)

The same thing happens with Duchamp, as Lyotard sees it:

> To interpret is futile. You might as well try to circumscribe the true effect of the *Large Glass* and hence its true content; the *Glass* is made precisely in order not to have a true effect, nor even several true effects, according to a mono- or polyvalent logic, but to have uncontrolled effects.
>
> (Lyotard 1990, 64)

This also happens when Bellatin (2007) is seen as an autobiographical, autofictional piece of art. In Duchamp's own words, the result needs to be expressed as an *aporia*: 'The *Glass* is not my autobiography, nor is it self-expression' (Tomkins 2014, 12). As a consequence, the reception of art does not lead to the understanding of its meaning, let alone the only and supreme meaning. Rather, art produces, as Lyotard says, a number of uncontrolled effects.

To sum up, Duchamp and Bellatin represent the performance of autofiction in several ways: changing the meaning of their previous artistic works and identities, linking possible worlds in a rhizomatic fashion and dissolving the hierarchical oppositions of fact/fiction, truth/lie, real identity/constructed identity. They reveal complex textual/paratextual relations, boundaries of fiction and the distance between representation and fiction. They perform themselves, and for that reason they are transformers.

This complex phenomenon is one of the hallmarks of contemporary Latin American literature. I do not agree with many scholars who label narratives like those by Bellatin and Aira as *anti-autofiction*, assuming the demise of autofiction as a genre. Evidently this kind of autofiction subverts many aspects of autobiographical fictional narratives, establishing self-reflective, critical perspectives. Lastly, the authors of Aira (1993; 2006) and Bellatin (2007; 2015) confront the so-called *reality* with fiction, in order to relocate and rearticulate the former.

Note

1 If not stated otherwise, all translations from Spanish are by the author.

References

Aira, César. 1993. *Cómo me hice monja*. Buenos Aires: Beatriz Viterbo Editora.
Aira, César. 2006. *How I Became a Nun* (1993). Translated by Chris Andrews. New York: New Directions.
Alberca, Manuel. 2007. *El pacto ambiguo. De la novela autobiográfica a la autoficción*. Madrid: Biblioteca Nueva.
Bellatin, Mario. 2007. *El gran vidrio. Tres autobiografías*. Barcelona: Anagrama.
Bellatin, Mario. 2014. 'El auto del señor Dufó'. In *Obra reunida* 2, 205-8. Madrid: Alfaguara.
Bellatin, Mario. 2015. *The Large Glass: Three autobiographies*. Translated by David Shook. London: Eyewear Publishing.
Bellatin, Mario. 2013. 'Biografía ilustrada de Mishima' (2009). In *Obra reunida*, 511–84. Madrid: Alfaguara.
Bellatin, Mario. 2014. 'Los cien mil libros de Bellatin'. In *Obra reunida 2*, 653–64. Madrid: Alfaguara.
Deleuze, Gilles and Félix Guattari. 1987. *A Thousand Plateaus: Capitalism and schizophrenia* (1980). Translated by Brian Massumi. Minneapolis: University of Minnesota Press.
Derrida, Jacques. 1973. 'Differance' (1968). In *Speech and Phenomena and Other Essays on Husserl's Theory of Signs*, translated by David B. Allison, 129–60. Evanston, IL: Northwestern University Press.
Derrida, Jacques. 1985. 'Otobiographies: The teaching of Nietzsche and the politics of the proper name' (1982). Translated by Avital Ronell. In *The Ear of the Other: Otobiography, transference, translation*, edited by Christie McDonald, translated by Peggy Kamuf, 1–38. New York: Schocken Books.
Derrida, Jacques. 1992. 'How to avoid speaking: Denials' (1987). Translated by Ken Frieden. In *Derrida and Negative Theology*, edited by Harold Coward and Toby Foshay, 73–142. Albany: State University of New York Press.
Doležel, Lubomír. 1998. *Heterocosmica: Fiction and possible worlds*. Baltimore, MD and London: The Johns Hopkins University Press.
Doubrovsky, Serge. 1977. *Fils*, Paris: Galilée.
García, Mariano. 2006. *Degeneraciones textuales. Los géneros en la obra de César Aira*. Rosario: Beatriz Viterbo Editora.
Gasparini, Philippe. 2004. *Est-il je? Roman autobiographique et autofiction*. Paris: Seuil.
Genette, Gérard. 1997a. *Palimpsests: Literature in the second degree* (1982). Translated by Chana Newman and Claude Doubinsky. Lincoln and London: University of Nebraska Press.
Genette, Gérard. 1997b. *Paratexts: Thresholds of interpretation* (1987). Translated by Jane E. Lewin. Cambridge: Cambridge University Press.
Genette, Gérard. 2004. *La Métalepse. De la figure à la fiction*. Paris: Seuil.
Lejeune, Philippe. 1975. *Le pacte autobiographique*. Paris: Seuil.
Lyotard, Jean-François. 1990. *Duchamp's TRANS/formers* (1977). Translated by Ian McLeod. Venice, CA: The Lapis Press.
Tomkins, Calvin. 2014. *Duchamp: A biography*. New York: The Museum of Modern Art.

10
The scene of invention: author at work in J. M. Coetzee's *The Master of Petersburg*
Laura Cernat

The reader's bias: the first page and the 'second self' fallacy

It has been thought for a long time that to write – and, particularly, to publish – means to provide a given idea with the most suitable formal realisation, in such a way that the form remains definitively tied to the notion it incarnates. The era of print has fuelled that illusion, not only consecrating a certain format of literary work (the book), but also dissociating the book from the world and the 'implied author' of a fictional universe (Booth 1983, 70–7) from the writer inhabiting the real universe. A few axioms specific to the age of print – the book as the unalterable form of a literary work, the reader's linear progression through it and the concrete author's withdrawal from it – account for a distorted view of the process of writing that focuses on the 'reader's bias': the notion that the production of a literary text takes the same linear course as the process of its reading, and that the result of creative work is somehow guaranteed.

Although experiments, from Joyce's circular and ramified structure in *Finnegans Wake* (1939) through Julio Cortázar's labyrinthine *Rayuela* (1963; Cortázar 1966) to Mark Z. Danielewski's telescopic *House of Leaves* (Danielewski 2000), have challenged this conception of linearity, the first sentence or the first page of a novel still tends to be surrounded with the aura of a threshold to another world, leading to a misrepresentation of creative work. This, among others, affects contemporary biofiction – that is, 'literature that names its protagonist after an actual biographical figure' (Lackey 2016, 3) – and biopics, short for 'biographical motion picture' (Minier and Pennacchia 2014, 2): genres that frequently use the trope of sudden inspiration to depict artistic innovations.

In this chapter, biofictional and cinematographic mythologies of writers at work are briefly discussed and compared to an exception: J. M. Coetzee's *The Master of Petersburg* (1994), my main case study. Contrasting this novel with other biofictions, as well as tracing the connections and discrepancies between Coetzee's novel and Dostoevsky's life and texts, can shed light on the old controversy around the implied author and reframe the relevance of the biographical. The intertwining of biography and autobiography, literary criticism, history and counterfactual elements in Coetzee's text suggests that literature performs a more complex task than the simple separation or the simple conjunction of a biographical self and an 'abstract author' (Lintvelt 1989, 17–22; Kindt and Müller 2006, 130–6). Furthermore, Coetzee's example points towards the unique affordances of the novel at a time when biographical and biofictional narratives are ubiquitous across media and accessible in popular genres that hold sway over larger audiences.

From 'second self' mythologies to the narrativisation of inspiration

Like many other enduring critical habits, proclaiming that the person who is engaged in a creative process is different from the one who goes about their daily life goes back to the Romantics. Long before Proust's distinction between the social self and the 'profound self' who creates art (Proust 1971, 224) started to circulate (following the posthumous publication of *Contre Sainte-Beuve* in 1954), Shelley was writing, as early as 1821, that 'the poet and the man are two different natures' (Shelley 1964, 310). Despite its anti-Romantic aim, literary theory has also adopted this false dichotomy ever since its foundations were laid by Russian formalists. New Criticism continued to entertain it through concepts such as the 'intentional fallacy' (Wimsatt and Beardsley 1946, 468–88), while poststructuralism, for all its iconoclasm, consolidated it. Seán Burke and Dominique Maingueneau converge in identifying the effort of exorcising the traces of biographism as a constant of theory, working across diverse schools of criticism. Be it through the 'reduction of the author in the interests of establishing a science of literature' (Burke 1998, 10) or by consolidating the Proustian split between an authentic self of the writer and a superficial one (Maingueneau 2006, 33–7), literary scholarship (with the arguable exception of genetic criticism) claimed to strip the text of accidental trivialities and to see it for what it really was. But since literary texts are necessarily, indeed trivially, always composed by human beings, this claim entails a typically unacknowledged Romantic legacy: the text is portrayed as a product of a medium of inspiration essentially unaffected by the vicissitudes of the quotidian.

Not surprisingly, the figure of the author as the privileged recipient of inspiration is also a staple of popular culture. When staging the biographies of creative minds in biopics, Hollywood depicts the writer's block as a completely dry interval, hinting that revolutionary ideas hide where you least expect them, then flash forth fully formed. This accords with the mystique of the first page, which frames the early moments of writing as liberation and fulfilment, disregarding the arduous journey ahead. This perspective validates in turn the idealised representation of the creator as a radically different entity from the subject of everyday experience – be it by depicting the artist as a clumsy social misfit in daily life or by divorcing, in good Proustian tradition, the social self from the 'profound self' (Proust 1971, 224).

From Agnieszka Holland's 1995 movie *Total Eclipse,* which casts Leonardo DiCaprio in the role of an irreverent Rimbaud, through *A Beautiful Mind* and *The Hours* in the early 2000s and on to *The Imitation Game* (2014), the eccentricity of men and women of genius has been insistently emphasised. Their aversion to practicalities and their lack of social skills presumably indicate the rupture between the 'world of ideas' and the 'real world'. Film scholars have already observed that 'biopics on authors (…) rely heavily on romantic concepts of authorship' (Müller 2014, 185) and that 'the act of literary creation, which is far less cinematically attractive than the visual or performing arts, has always posed a problem for screenwriters and directors' (Moine 2014, 57).

Bringing together these two insights, this section aims to show how the general romanticisation of the creator figure applies more precisely to the problematic scenes that depict the act of literary creation.

In his account of 'poetic inspiration', inherited by the Romantics from the Greek conception of the *aiodos,* M. H. Abrams lists four characteristics that distinguish it from 'normal ideation':

> a. the composition is sudden, effortless, and unanticipated; b. the composition is involuntary and automatic; c. in the course of composition, the poet feels intense excitement, usually described as a state of elation and rapture; d. the completed work is as unfamiliar to the poet as though it had been written by someone else.
>
> (Abrams 1958, 189)

It will be no surprise that most of these features of the creative process are present in contemporary Hollywood portrayals of inspiration, revealing an enduring idealisation of the creative process. In *The Hours*, we see Virginia Woolf jotting down sentences almost automatically, in a state of intense concentration but also surprise (2002, 00:09:50–00:10:50 and 00:26:31–00:27:01). As Hermione Lee pointedly remarks, Woolf is shown surrounded by dozens of pages after just a few hours, whereas the drafting of *Mrs Dalloway* actually took years.[1] Similarly, in *Total Eclipse*, Arthur Rimbaud is imagined writing through the night (1995, 01:27:00–01:28:35), after weeks of lying in bed to undergo a self-proclaimed inner transformation (1995, 01:09:25–01:10:05). In *A Beautiful Mind* John Nash is portrayed at his desk, frenetically working on his thesis, while the seasons pass by (2001, 00:21:46–00:22:40). Of course, much of this is necessary cinematic artifice, but its effect is undeniably the framing of inspiration as something sudden, enthralling and uncontrollable.

Apart from these features (misfit artist and miracle-like work), a slightly subtler mechanism is at work. Art and creative discovery are severed from the life story in the very process of depicting their emergence, through what I propose to call a narrativisation of inspiration. By this I mean that the story of how a discovery was made is infused with ulterior knowledge of the achieved work, retrospectively projected onto the moment of invention; this is then framed in the fictional universe as an awakening rather than a breakthrough.

The clearest examples of this procedure are the episodes in which Nash, as depicted in *A Beautiful Mind*, has the revelation of his governing dynamics theory by calculating his friends' chances of getting a date (2001, 00:19:50–00:21:00) and Alan Turing, in *The Imitation Game*, realises the solution to breaking the Nazi code by listening to a love anecdote (2014, 01:12:25–01:13:55). Especially in the first case, where the discovery of a complex mathematical theory is at stake, the implausibility is striking. The screenwriters try to explain governing dynamics in a simplified way and present this explanation (derived from Nash's theory) as the source of the theory itself. The circularity of this model echoes Belén Vidal's observation (2014, 6) that biopics are often structured both along a '*teleological* axis' (through the suggestion of the hero's predestination for the discovery or achievement) and along a '*theological* axis' (on which 'the moral justification for the predestined historical actor's immortality is already embedded in the figure's myth') (Vidal 2014, 6). Applying Vidal's observation at a micro-level, not to the narrative as a whole but specifically to the scene of invention, it can be said that its representation reverses teleology for the benefit of a lay theology or myth-making. The moment of discovery, which led to the theory, becomes an illustration for the theory – a *post hoc ergo propter hoc* move meant to establish the discovery as an iconic part of cultural heritage. As a consequence, *A Beautiful Mind* provides valuable insight into the artificiality of many Hollywood biofictional narratives. More than anywhere else, the fact that the outcome of the creative process is already known when recounting its stages becomes clear to the critical eye.

This notion of the narrativisation of inspiration can be considered an example of the more general tendency in biopics to 'boil down complex social processes to gestures of individual agency' (Vidal 2014, 3). Yet it goes one step further by simplifying even the way in which individual agency is represented, making it depend on fortuitous sudden discoveries rather than on sustained effort. The effect that Hollywood success stories have of staging 'a "natural" collapse of the future into the past' (Vidal 2014, 5) is also illustrated by these stories of inspiration, which make liberal use of chronology to generate the impression of serendipitous discoveries.

Films are thus governed by reader's bias even more than novels are, proving that the biopic tendency of 'muddying the distinction between life and works [...] by positing life as the most definitive wellspring for works' (Strong 2020, 238) does not fully go against the grain of the 'second self' myth, in as far as it continues to portray inspiration as sudden and miraculous. Admittedly, as Franssen (2014, 108–9) remarks, the interpretation of biopics such as John Madden's *Shakespeare in Love* can reveal a postmodern and intensely ironic 'layering'. This serves to highlight the artificiality of narrative conventions that require inspiration to come from life rather than books and to crystallise in sudden realisations. Whether they romanticise writers naïvely or in a tongue-in-cheek manner, however, none of these films are realistic in portraying the author *as author* rather than as the hero of a plot based on revelations and inspiration. Finally, the narrativisation of inspiration also reveals that the biopic, with its 'almost naïve illusion of a correspondence between author's life and work' (Müller 2014, 185), only seemingly goes against poststructuralist claims about the 'death of the author', but in fact partakes of the same broader gesture, constructing an aura of mystery or ineffability around creativity.

Perhaps a noteworthy exception among biopics is the German film *Werk ohne Autor* (2018), directed by Florian Henckel von Donnersmarck (*Never Look Away* in English translation). Based on the life of the painter Gerhard Richter, the film integrates experiments and failures into the trial and error process of artistic creation, thus suggesting that new discoveries do not always guarantee success or satisfaction. Even though a tendency of presenting one work as central and linking it to an artificial happy ending persists in this carefully crafted narrative, inspiration is not framed as drawing on contingent or external factors. Rather, it lies in a moment of condensed awareness of what is essential in one's own life story. The glimpse of unconscious truths (*Werk ohne Autor* 2018, 02:45:45–02:45:55) has more influence upon the artist's technique than anecdotes, coincidences or revelations. Moreover, viewers are led through the gradual discovery of a form linked to lived experience, which subverts the myth of sudden inspiration and may mark a shift in the evolution of the genre of biopic beyond the 'formulaic' character described by Minier and Pennacchia (2014, 5) – or at least indicate a shift within the most current formulas.

Reader's bias in biographical novels: taking the masterpiece for granted

Novels, unlike films, focus less on the artist as medium. Instead they restore more of the uncertainty experienced in the moment of creation, as this passage from Michael Cunningham's *The Hours* reveals:

> She may pick up her pen and find that she's merely herself, a woman in a housecoat holding a pen, afraid and uncertain, only mildly competent, with no idea about where to begin or what to write.
>
> (Cunningham 1999, 35)

However, in the attempt of acknowledging the risks of writing, Cunningham's text performs a different artifice, reaffirming the split between the subject of everyday life and the deep self who performs the creative act. The novel explicitly refers to 'an all but indescribable second self, or rather a parallel, purer self, [...] an inner faculty that recognises the animating mysteries of the world' (Cunningham 1999, 34–5).

The task of writing becomes a question of accessing this second self. Meanwhile the uncertainty of achievement is explained through the fleetingness of this mysterious capacity, and through the fear of remaining trapped in one's everyday self. The only way in which this kind of narrative demystifies the writer's creative process is through re-mystifying the writer's person as the carrier of this double self.

While this is a step away from Hollywood's narrativisation of inspiration, some degree of distortion endures. Although the risk involved in writing is captured in the description of the creative process, and although Cunningham departs from the text of *Mrs Dalloway* to rework it into the story of Clarissa Vaughan, *The Hours* never abandons the knowledge that we have, as readers, of *Mrs Dalloway*. The rewriting takes the book's success as its point of departure, as illustrated by the numerous quotes and paraphrases from Woolf's novel in Cunningham's book, proving the persistence of a reader's bias.

Similarly, in Alain Buisine's novel *Proust: Samedi 27 novembre 1909* (1991), the imaginative reconstruction of a day in Proust's life culminates with the scene in which, late at night, Proust sets to work on the early drafts of *À la recherche du temps perdu*. Despite Buisine's efforts to convey the distance between this work of drafting, 'de-writing' and 'rewriting' (Buisine 1991, 210), and the work that we now know, his novel fails to make us forget that the *Recherche* is ineluctably there all along. In *Rimbaud le fils* (1991), Pierre Michon takes a step away from this assumption, portraying the young Arthur Rimbaud writing with no certainty of the value of his work. He then reasserts the reader's knowledge of the young man's destiny, for instance by using the metaphor of a halo, invisible to the poet, that the imagined audience is invited to project around his head (Michon 1991, 36). Bracketing Rimbaud's future glory by casting him in the role of pupil is only a way of reasserting it, with increased strength, in the final pages. Michael Kumpfmüller, in his biofiction about Kafka, depicts the toil of the writing process more closely:

> He writes and writes every evening, as if with hammer and chisel [...] as if the paper were stone, something that did not obey him willingly.
>
> (2014, 110)

However, even he later speaks about 'a radiance' in Kafka's face after a night of ceaseless writing (2014, 119).

All these read first and foremost like the constructs of passionate readers, who know that the works of art were bound to endure. This knowledge, inaccessible to the writer in the moment of working on a text, separates the reader's perspective from that of the writer. In so doing, it risks relegating biofiction to the status of a secondary product of literary history, something we read only to extend the pleasure we get from canonical masterpieces.

Writing without 'eureka': J. M. Coetzee's take on inspiration

At first glance, the final chapter of *The Master of Petersburg* reveals the same features described by Abrams and encountered in other biofictions. Coetzee's Dostoevsky writes suddenly and seemingly without effort ('it takes him no more than ten minutes to write the scene, with not a word blotted', Coetzee 2004, 249), the process appears to be automatic ('the building, with its [...] blind corners, begins to write itself', 2004, 242) and the result seems unfamiliar to the writer ('he recognises nothing of himself', 2004, 250). Yet the writer's elation, essential to reader-centred biofictions, is completely missing: the written words 'are not words of salvation' (2004, 241).

Much like other biographical novels, Coetzee's text engages an abstract outside entity, somewhat like a second self, in the writing process:

> he is not himself any longer [...] he is not a god but he is no longer human either.
>
> (Coetzee 2004, 242)

However, there is a fundamental difference. The writer is neither passively receiving nor passionately seeking his abstract self: he is negotiating with it, looking to control whatever presence manifests itself in the act of creation. As a good craftsman 'he knows what he is doing' – even as he watches, from 'outside himself', the 'contest of cunning between himself and God' (Coetzee 2004, 249).

Dostoevsky is portrayed as having 'lost his place in his soul' (Coetzee 2004, 249), 'betrayed everyone' and even having 'given up his soul in return' for the money he received for his books (2004, 250). By advancing a different image of inspiration, devoid of bliss and hope, Coetzee performs a daring and difficult task: he is unveiling the mechanisms of a writer's motivation and the reality of creative anxiety, which the old tale of the second self and the rapture of writing conveniently eclipsed.

Dostoevsky and the economy of inspiration: the 'poet' and the 'artist'

Coetzee's choice of Dostoevsky as a prototype for his character is anything but accidental. Judging by his reflections, Dostoevsky apparently shared the belief in inspiration and the artist's second self. In a letter to Apollon

Maikov he wrote that 'the essence and even the scansion of the verse depend on the poet's soul and [appear] suddenly, ready-made in his heart, quite independently of himself' (Dostoevsky 1987, 307).

However, this mystical conception of inspiration is nuanced by what Dostoevsky calls

> the poet's *second* act, no longer so profound and mysterious, but only his artistic performance [...]. At this point the poet is not much more than a jeweller.
>
> (1987, 308)

Apparently similar to Proust's opposition between '*moi profond*' and '*moi social*', and to Shelley's discrimination between 'the poet and the man', Dostoevsky's distinction between the two stages of creation reveals a different division between art and life – not between the everyday and the creative self, but within the creator. He does not locate poetic inspiration in a higher realm nor equate artistry with prosaic craftsmanship:

> In order to write a novel, one must acquire [...] one or several strong impressions actually experienced by the author's heart. This is the poet's job. [From] this impression are developed a theme, a plan, a harmonious whole. This is already the artist's job, although artist and poet help each other [...].
>
> (Dostoevsky 1969, 31)

This contradicts several romantic clichés. If the 'poet's job' is to acquire 'strong impressions', inspiration does not visit him as a magic external phenomenon. Instead it condenses lived experiences into a meaningful pattern. Biographical material plays a key role in providing the poet's 'impressions', but it is also interwoven with the artist's work of refinement. Jacques Catteau hints at this in his discussion of Dostoevsky's interest in news items (2005, 180–6), while Robert Dion remarks that Dostoevsky's own parody of Turgenev as Karmazinov in *Demons* verges on biofictional appropriation (Dion 2021, 70). Dostoevsky himself knew that his approach revolutionised realism:

> The idea I have of reality and realism is quite different from that of our realists and critics. My idealism is more real than their realism.
>
> (Dostoevsky, quoted in Catteau 2005, 190)

Demons (1873),[2] the main Dostoevskyan hypotext of *The Master of Petersburg*, inspired by the murder of student Ivanov at the hands of revolutionary anarchist Sergey Nechaev and his acolytes, reveals the role of real-life stories in artistic inspiration. Dostoevsky was working on what he considered to be the most important project of his career, initially called 'Atheism' and later 'The Life of a Great Sinner'. This hagiography in reverse was meant to reflect the complete human experience, from innocence and saintliness to depravity, and thus to address the question of 'the existence of God' (Dostoevsky 1987, 331–2). He set this project aside around the time he came across the Nechaev affair, and eventually gave it up.

However, instead of a sudden switch from one project to another, it is more accurate to speak of their osmosis. Dostoevsky's biographer Joseph Frank remarks that *Demons* 'did not spring full grown' from discussions of Ivanov's assassination, but resulted 'from the gradual infiltration of this horrendous event […] into various plans' (1995a, 397). Catteau similarly describes 'a haemorrhage which left the original project ["The Life of a Great Sinner"] bloodless' (2005, 250).

Nonetheless, the work done on the 'Great Sinner' project was not completely lost. Of all the heroes who inherit features of the Great Sinner, Stavrogin, a prominent character in *Demons*, comes closest to the protagonist of the abandoned novel. Yet Stavrogin was one of the characters over whom Dostoevsky hesitated the most. He assigned this figure contradictory features such as a lack of 'firmness of character' (Dostoevsky 1968, 111), a dislike for everything 'sham' and shallow and a wish to live in poverty (1968, 154), the pride of a 'haughty aristocrat' (1968, 173) and a complete lack of moderation (1968, 266). This hesitancy indicates that the Great Sinner was not simply transplanted into *Demons*. He was rediscovered piece by piece: little in the notes prefigures the Stavrogin of the final text. Two intertwined narratives can thus be discerned: the artist's failure to keep up with the poet (hence the abandonment of the 'Great Sinner' project) and the poet's correction of the artist's toilsome attempts (resulting in the hesitant creation of Stavrogin).

Imperfect symmetries: three interlinked layers of interpretation

In *The Master of Petersburg* Coetzee imagines Dostoevsky returning to Russia to mourn the death of his stepson Pavel Isaev, who in reality lived longer than Dostoevsky. Furthermore, Coetzee has the fictional Dostoevsky meet the fictional version of Nechaev. Since the publication of Coetzee's novel, many alterations to the historical record have been discussed. David Attwell remarks that Petersburg has no shot tower (2016, 163), suggesting that Coetzee (whose plot relies on a fictional shot tower) is signposting the unreality of his narrative by playing with geography. What has been less discussed is that the meeting between Dostoevsky and Nechaev is flagged as fictional from the start: quite apart from Dostoevsky being abroad, Nechaev was not in Petersburg but in Moscow, where Ivanov was murdered on 21 November 1869 (Avrich 1988, 41). He only fled to St Petersburg in late November, whereas Coetzee has him meet Dostoevsky there on 18 November (Coetzee 2004, 203). The writer also changes the character of Ivanov radically, turning him into a beggar whom Dostoevsky tries to help.

Frank was among the first to point out some of the deliberate inaccuracies. If his reproach about Coetzee's potential deception of his readers (Frank 1995b, 53) can be taken lightly today, when an internet search can identify the counterfactual elements, Frank's other critical comment, regarding the lack of 'realistic psychological motivation' (1995b, 54), requires more serious consideration. Some aspects of Dostoevsky's relationship with his stepson resonate with the grief and guilt that the imagined Dostoevsky feels after learning about Pavel's imagined death; Dostoevsky's concern for Pavel (1987, 180), his worries about the boy's ingratitude (1987, 281, 282, 313) and his fear that his love for the stepson was not reciprocated (1987, 258) are all attested in the writer's correspondence. But does this explain the sense of utter spiritual crisis experienced by Coetzee's character? Something remains amiss, especially in the father's repeated fantasy about reviving the son's seed (Coetzee 2004, 76, 241), which strongly hints at a blood relation. Frank is thus right, but only partly.

It could still be that the plausibility of the fictional Dostoevsky does not lie in his continuity with the person we know from the letters. Attwell, for instance, admits that

> Coetzee's treatment of the relationship between Dostoevsky and Pavel is burdened to an extent that is never fully explained ... The inconsolable Dostoevsky of Coetzee's creation is not in a world of credible motivations. He arrives [...] from another world altogether.
> (Attwell 2016, 166–7)

Here Attwell inserts the tragic story of the death of Nicolas Coetzee, J. M. Coetzee's son, around the time he started work on this novel. A fragment from Coetzee's early notes suggests a connection, speaking of 'the vow he had made: that he would write his son into immortality' (quoted in Attwell 2016, 167).

Just like the link with the biography of Dostoevsky, the autobiographical reading is partly supported by the text. One of the purposes of the fictional shot tower could be to create a situation in which Pavel falls to his death from a height, which is what happened to Nicolas Coetzee (Kannemeyer 2012, 455–6). Kannemeyer notes that the writer often struggled to wake his son up for school in the mornings (2012, 453), a detail that appears in *The Master of Petersburg* (2004, 15). He also observes (Kannemeyer 2012, 458–9) that the ages of Dostoevsky and Pavel in the novel coincide with those of Coetzee and Nicolas at the time of the latter's death. If this suggests an autofictional reading with the character Dostoevsky as a projection of Coetzee, some aspects of the author's biography (Coetzee's financial help for Nicolas and the son's ingratitude; Kannemeyer 2012, 454) coincide not only with the fictional but also with the real relationship between Dostoevsky and Pavel, as the Russian writer's letters show. However, Kannemeyer warns against political speculations about Nicolas (2012, 452), which should dissuade the reader from bringing autobiography and fiction too close together.

Attwell's response to the imperfection of the autobiographical analogy is to speak of the fictional mourner as 'an amalgam' of Coetzee and the fictional Dostoevsky: 'Coetzee is writing about the fictional Dostoevsky in himself' (Attwell 2016, 168). Labelling the genre of the text as 'autobiographical historical fiction' (2016, 174), Attwell claims that Coetzee is 'imagining his own grief as Dostoevsky's' (2016, 170). Yet more recent interventions have deemed Coetzee's novel 'auto/biographical fiction' (Herbillon 2020, 393) or 'exofiction' (Dion 2021, 59). However, these approaches do not take into account that in Coetzee's novel there are two Dostoevskys (real and fictional). Making the fictional Dostoevsky feel Coetzee's grief (Attwell 2016, 170) is complemented and complicated by the link between the fictional Dostoevsky's moral struggle and Dostoevsky's efforts to write *Demons*.

Interpreting Coetzee's narrative as a reconstruction of Dostoevsky's creative process despite the counterfactual elements has been quite frequent in responses to the novel (see for example Attridge 2004, 117, 129; Adelman 2000, 357; Popescu 2007, 3–4; Scanlan 1997, 475; Attwell 2016, 170). Another typically made claim is that Coetzee is recovering Stavrogin not as he appears in *Demons,* but as he was meant to be, had the chapter called 'At Tikhon's' not been censored (Attridge 2004, 127; Adelman 2000, 356). Nonetheless, as Anthony Uhlmann points out, the actual texts that Coetzee presents as Dostoevsky's in the last chapter (Coetzee 2004, 242–9) do not pertain to any of the notes for *Demons*, nor to the surviving version of 'At Tikhon's' (Uhlmann 2014, 56). The assumption that Dostoevsky in *The Master of Petersburg* is starting to write *Demons* rests on another imperfect symmetry, namely between the fragments in the last chapter and specific episodes from *Demons* (the seduction of a child, for example, echoes the suppressed 'At Tikhon's' chapter, while the story of Maria 'Lebyatkin'[3] compresses a plotline from the published version).

Tracing Dostoevsky's creative process from his notes and letters allows for the delineation of yet another imperfect symmetry: that between Coetzee as creator and the historical Dostoevsky. Some analogies have been signalled: Popescu (2007, 4) refers to the 'homologies, metonymies and structural equivalences' between the political contexts of 1860s Russia and 1980s South Africa, also mentioned by Attridge (2004, 133), Scanlan (1997, 463) and Attwell (2016, 183–6). Uhlmann (2014, 59–66) traces parallels between Coetzee's discussion of censorship in *Giving Offense* (Coetzee 1996) and Dostoevsky's 'offensive' parable about the destruction of innocence in 'At Tikhon's'. Censorship is also briefly discussed by Adelman (2000, 351–2). Central to what brings Coetzee and Dostoevsky together is the process of creating a character who seems to exceed all moral dichotomies. This is suggested by Uhlmann, who sees Coetzee's novel as 'an excoriation of what it means to write' (2014, 57), and by Attwell, who describes Coetzee's own work on the drafts for *The Master of Petersburg* as 'extremely peripatetic' (2016, 175), resembling Dostoevsky's own quest. Attwell qualifies Coetzee's pouring of 'his own anguish in the vessel of Dostoevsky's writing' (2016, 174–5) in terms of overcoming an 'anxiety of influence' (as theorised by Harold Bloom). Scanlan similarly speaks of Coetzee 'challenging Dostoevsky' (Scanlan 1997, 467). These remarks reveal that Coetzee is using the fictional Dostoevsky not just as a self-projection, but also to address the historical writer.

Instead of Attwell's 'amalgam' of Coetzee and the fictional Dostoevsky, *The Master of Petersburg* can be understood on the basis of a tripartite structure. The autobiographical layer, the fictional narrative and the historical record, though autonomous, are inextricably interlinked. Each brings the other two together: first, Coetzee and his grief are the missing link between Dostoevsky and Dostoevsky's fictional double; second, the writing of fiction draws the two real authors closer;

and third, the allusions to the historical Dostoevsky's work give substance to an otherwise transparent parable of loss. This interlacing, where no two elements are directly connected, but the triad is indivisible, can be visualised as the Borromean rings diagram, used by Lacan in his seminars on Joyce (Lacan 2016, 11). Without addressing Lacan's system here, I would like to borrow the diagram as a potential expression of this intricate link between reality and fiction established by the novel.

The three layers of interpretation connected in a Borromean knot cannot all be perfect circles. At least one has to be slightly elliptical – and the imperfect symmetries allow for just that. The structure is anticipated by Uhlmann's description of 'processes of refraction', in which 'primary materials [...] are deliberately distorted and composed to generate new meaning' (Uhlmann 2014, 57). On how these processes combine, Uhlmann writes:

> Coetzee [...] develops a compositional method that works through refraction of source material [...]: he distorts events related to the Nechaev affair [...]; he further draws in and distorts the tragedy of his own son Nicholas's death from a fall which is echoed by Pavel's fall [...]. Finally, in the last chapter, 'Stavrogin', Coetzee distorts Dostoevsky's process of composition in re-imagining his relations to the young girl Matryosha.
>
> (Uhlmann 2014, 59)

An example of distortion is provided by Attridge's hesitation about whether to interpret Pavel's death in the novel as a parallel for Shatov's murder in *Demons* – and implicitly for the historical murder of Ivan Ivanov. Attridge remarks that this analogy is 'clouded' by the character Ivanov, the beggar who is killed in Coetzee's novel around the date of the student Ivanov's murder, 'as if the actual death has been displaced onto two separate fictional deaths' (Attridge 2004, 118). This displacement is further clouded by the real death of Nicolas Coetzee, which Attridge mentions only briefly (2004, 136). The autobiographical detail complicates the chain of analogies so that no perfect correspondence can be found (the two real deaths and the two fictional ones resonate only obliquely).

Another example of distortion is the role of 'migrant images' (Catteau 2005, 198) that breach the boundary between reality and text(s). One such image is the journey of the Mother of God (Coetzee 2004, 200–1), taken from *The Brothers Karamazov* (Frank 1995b, 55). Another, as yet undiscussed migrant symbol is the printing press

(Coetzee 2004, 197–203). The handing over of a printing press is used by Verkhovensky's group to lure Shatov in *Demons* (2006, 549, 551, 554, 573, 596, 599); Nechaev and his acolytes relied on the same pretext in reality to kill Ivanov (Avrich 1988, 42). The fact that the fictional Dostoevsky is shown a printing press (at a time close to the historical date of Ivanov's murder) eerily puts Dostoevsky in the position of the victim. While for readers familiar both with *Demons* and with Nechaev's crime, the effect of introducing a printing press in *The Master of Petersburg* is a play with both history and intertextuality, for a less informed audience it is just a reflection upon the writer's role, a *mise-en-abyme* like the printing press episode in *Don Quixote*, which thematises literary production within the literary work. The effect of this image correlates with an apparent displacement of the hierarchy between reality and fiction which, upon closer scrutiny, can be noticed in other techniques, particularly in the use of names, place-names and pronouns to distort the relationship between what the novel presents as fiction and what it presents as reality. This artifice will be analysed in the following section.

Indirect metalepsis and displaced heterobiography

The writings of Coetzee's fictional Dostoevsky (Coetzee 2004, 242–5, 247–9) have, perhaps wrongly, been decoded as early notes for *Demons*. Most critics (Scanlan 1997, 475; Adelman 2000, 356; Attwell 2016, 180) have treated the character in the sketches as a version of Stavrogin. Attridge (2004, 126) does note that 'Stavrogin' is just the name of the chapter and does not appear in the text, but he does not discuss the implications of this observation. If the character in the two fragments is unnamed, despite the allusion in the chapter title, why should this character be (an early version of) Stavrogin? Is it even the same character in both fragments? The only names in the passages are 'Svidrigailov' in the first fragment (Coetzee 2004, 244) and 'Maria Lebyatkin' in the second (2004, 247). The only place-names are 'Petersburg' (in both fragments – 2004, 244, 248), 'Switzerland' (first fragment – 2004, 245), and 'Tver' (second fragment – 2004, 247). What does this say about the fictional universe that Dostoevsky is creating in Coetzee's alternative world?

Svidrigailov is not a character in *Demons*, but in *Crime and Punishment*. He has often been considered a precursor of Stavrogin because of his extreme cynicism. In a scene that foreshadows Stavrogin's passive complicity in Marya Lebyadkina's murder (Dostoevsky 2006, 532), Svidrigailov contortedly confesses to having caused his wife's death (Dostoevsky 2007, 282–3). Like Stavrogin (Dostoevsky 2006, 678), Svidrigailov ends up killing himself (Dostoevsky 2007, 511). More importantly, in a vivid dream leading up to his suicide, he lusts for a sleeping five-year old girl sick with a fever (Dostoevsky 2007, 509)[4] – perhaps the earliest foreshadowing of Stavrogin's confession (Dostoevsky 2006, 691–701). Both Svidrigailov (Dostoevsky 2007, 286–8) and Stavrogin (Dostoevsky 2006, 703–4) are haunted by the ghosts of their victims. Both admit that they suffer from idleness and commit crimes out of boredom (Dostoevsky 2007, 291; 2006, 701), a theme taken up in *The Master of Petersburg*.

Who is 'he'?

In Coetzee's version, the fictional Dostoevsky writes: 'He remembers Svidrigailov: "Women like to be humiliated"' (Coetzee 2004, 244). This is an allusion to something that Svidrigailov tells Raskolnikov privately: 'there are occasions when women find it extremely agreeable to be insulted' (Dostoevsky 2007, 283). Who then is Coetzee's 'he' who 'remembers Svidrigailov'? The simplest answer is that 'he' is Raskolnikov, the only witness of Svidrigailov's monologue. However, this would be anachronistic (*Crime and Punishment* was published in 1866 and *The Master of Petersburg* is set in 1869) and it would mean that the two fragments belong to different stories, since the second one mentions Lebyadkina from *Demons*.

Another hypothesis is that 'he' refers to Stavrogin in both fragments, as the references to Switzerland (visited by Stavrogin in Dostoevsky 2006, 54–5, 64, 704) and to Marya Lebyadkina suggest. In this case, if Stavrogin remembers Svidrigailov, we are dealing with a 'horizontal metalepsis of enunciation' (Pier and Schaeffer 2005, 136, 145–6, 154–5) – a transgression between two storylines that are co-ordinated within another narrative.

A third path is to look at the mysterious 'he' as a composite character, combining features of different antiheroes. This is a more productive interpretation because, in *The Notebooks for 'A Raw Youth'*, Dostoevsky used the masculine pronoun to designate one of his characters without giving him a name. We can find notations such as: '*He* is an idle person' (Dostoevsky 1969, 31); '*He* is a preacher of the Christian religion [...]. And then [...] he smashes an icon' (1969, 34); 'The Youth is amazed at how He, with all his charm, is so cold and spiteful' (Dostoevsky 1969, 84). Following Catteau, one could relate this 'he' character to a version of Stavrogin not truncated by censorship: 'The Stavrogin of the "Confession" came back to life in [...] the still unnamed and universal HE' (Catteau 2005, 266). The italicized *'He'* appears in early notes for the 'Great Sinner' (Dostoevsky 1968, 64); Coetzee may be offering a condensation of Dostoevsky's notes for various characters or even reconstructing the Great Sinner.

This last possibility still leaves room for doubt because of a place-name mentioned in the second fragment, Tver. While the real Dostoevsky spent some time in Tver in 1859 after his imprisonment, and *Demons* is set in a town modelled upon Tver, the town's name is never mentioned in the novel. The naming of Tver in the fragment might point to the fact that 'He' refers not to a purely fictional character but to a version of Dostoevsky himself, so the fiction within the fiction is partly autobiographical. In this case 'He remembers Svidrigailov' would mean that the author remembers the words of his character.

Before starting to write the two fragments, the fictional Dostoevsky sketches something which is only reported, not given word by word:

> High summer in Petersburg [...] In the room a child [...] lying naked beside a man [...] her face pressed against the curve of his shoulder, where she snuggles and roots like a baby.
> (Coetzee 2004, 241)

'Who is the man?' the next paragraph asks, giving no names, no personal pronouns either (the child is 'in its grasp', the body's, not 'his grasp'). Then the following paragraph starts: 'He sits with the pen in his hand' (Coetzee 2004, 241).

The assumption is that 'he' in this instance is Dostoevsky, because this is what the whole novel has been training the readers to think: Dostoevsky is rarely named by his surname, or even referred to as 'Fyodor Mikhailovich'. Usually the name appears when other characters address him directly. But the narrator hardly ever calls his protagonist 'Dostoevsky'. Because Dostoevsky is the focaliser not naming him seems natural, although in reality avoiding ambiguities takes great skill, as this passage shows:

> At any moment he could grasp him about the waist and tip him over the edge into the void. But who is *he* on this platform, who is *him*?
> (Coetzee 2004, 119)

In the last chapter, this reflex of perceiving an unnamed 'he' as the character Dostoevsky has already been established. This allows Coetzee to build his text in such a way that the reader is ready to follow the collision between 'he' (the writer) and 'the figure', which is referred to as 'it' ('he must know its name', Coetzee 2004, 237). Just before the writing of the two fragments begins, the two entities, personal and impersonal, merge:

> In his writing he is in the same room […]. But […] he is not himself any longer, not a man in the forty-ninth year of his life. Instead he is young again […] He is, to a degree, Pavel Isaev, though Pavel Isaev is not the name he is going to give himself. […] Through this young man the building […] begins to write itself […].
>
> (Coetzee 2004, 242)

If the description above is taken at face value, the 'he' in the fragments is (partly) a version of Dostoevsky, re-imagined as a young man. At the same time this younger version of the fictional Dostoevsky is a composite character; he bears some of the traits of Stavrogin and some of Coetzee's fictional Pavel and fictional Nechaev. Because these characters belong to different levels of reality (some are based on history, some borrowed from fiction), the technique is a form of metalepsis.

Indirect metalepsis

Gérard Genette discusses metalepsis not only as a narrative artifice, but also as a stylistic device (Genette 2004, 16–17) – one that hints, sometimes very subtly, at a breach in the order of diegetic frames. Understood in this sense, the disruption indicated by metalepsis – 'any intrusion by the extradiegetic narrator or narratee into the diegetic universe (or by diegetic characters into a metadiegetic universe)' (Genette 1980, 234) – is made explicit by the fact that the author-figure is projected into the world of his characters. Of course, the character could be said to be only based on Dostoevsky, in which case the fragment can be considered a *mise-en-abyme* (Popescu 2007, 4).[5] Still, the fact that the novel moves Marya Lebyadkina, a fictional character, to Tver, a location in the real world, should still count as a form of metalepsis (Pier and Schaeffer 2005, 136, 157–8) – more particularly a 'vertical metalepsis of the enunciated' (Pier and Schaeffer 2005, 146–8, 156–7), because a character is seemingly brought *in corpore* to the ontological level of her creator.

This metalepsis as 'figure' (Genette 2004, 17–18) draws awareness to the broader metalepsis as fictional mode, which governs the logic of the novel. Dostoevsky is constantly confronted with the world of his characters. Maximov resembles Porfiry Petrovich from *Crime and Punishment*, Matryona is obviously a transposition of Matryosha, Stavrogin's victim from 'At Tikhon's', and the story of the seduction of the feeble-minded Marya Lebyadkina by Stavrogin from *Demons* is attributed to Pavel, who is as real as Dostoevsky (Coetzee 2004, 72–4) but who is said to have stayed with 'his aunt in Tver' (2004, 72) – another counterfactual element. The entire universe of the novel is eerily familiar to readers of Dostoevsky, an eeriness often associated with effects of metalepsis and *mise-en-abyme* (Cohn 2012, 110; Pier and Schaeffer 2005, 162).

If the category of biofiction is premised on the onomastic coincidence between an actual historical figure and a fictional character (Lackey 2016, 3), and if Maria is as 'real' as Pavel and Dostoevsky in the universe created by Coetzee, then her story, written by Coetzee's Dostoevsky, is that of a biographical figure from this universe bearing the same name as its prototype – thus seemingly an intradiegetic biofiction. However, the counterfactual reading and the metalepsis hypothesis compete. If we refuse to believe that a real Maria Lebyadkina existed, then there is no real prototype and no biofiction in this fragment. The metaleptic device becomes obvious: a character is mingled with the world of historical persons.

The knowledge of Dostoevsky's work and his biography must be combined in order to discern the elements of biofiction, counterfactual narrative or metalepsis. This is why the artifice Coetzee uses may be called 'indirect metalepsis': to a reader with zero knowledge of *Demons* and of Dostoevsky's biography, the transgression would go unnoticed. The complexity of Coetzee's use of metalepsis should be no surprise; this technique is central to his style, as Alexandra Effe shows in her 2017 book on the topic. However, Effe, who focuses on overt metalepsis, touches only briefly on *The Master of Petersburg* (Effe 2017, xiv, 15).

Double 'he': heterobiography in the third person?

As discussed, Coetzee's elusive use of the third person pronoun combined with a minimum of naming creates a reading reflex of assuming that any undetermined 'he' in this novel is Dostoevsky. Many chapters begin in the third person without mentioning who 'he' is, expecting the reader to fill in the gaps. As an effect, any undetermined 'he' becomes linked to the person through whom the narration is focalised. Yet precisely because the reader has access to this person's thoughts – something possible in the third person only in literature, as

Käte Hamburger famously showed[6] – and because the reader no longer needs a previous reference to situate this pronoun, this particular 'he' almost works like an 'I'.

According to Émile Benveniste, the third person should be considered a 'non-person', differing radically from the first and the second persons because it relies on a previous reference (1971, 221). Forms such as 'he' only serve to 'replace or relay one or another of the material elements of the utterance' (Benveniste 1971, 221). However, in Coetzee's use, 'he' stops being this grammatical non-person; it rather becomes a reference to the consciousness that the reader is accessing, without a close reference to a previous noun. Coetzee's 'he' thus becomes the impersonal correlative of an 'I' that conceals itself. In an article on 'Autobiography in the third person', building on Benveniste's theory, Philippe Lejeune discusses the scarce situations in which the third person becomes a substitute for the first person in autobiographical writing. According to Lejeune (1977, 34), the use of 'he' with 'no explicit reference' is one of the ways of producing identification between 'he' and 'I'.

A possibility to explain the ambiguous third person pronoun as a slanted reference to the author is suggested in Lucia Boldrini's theory of heterobiography. Focusing on biofictions written in the first person, Boldrini stresses that these biofictions emphasise 'the displacement involved in speaking as another'; they lay bare 'the gap of the "double I" of heterobiography' (Boldrini 2012, 4), as they challenge our assumptions about the nature of subjectivity. The question relevant for my analysis is whether this double discourse, the overlap of historical reinvention and autobiographical reflection, can also occur in third person biofictions, particularly in ones with internal focalisation. Boldrini does hint at this (2012, 13, 15), so the hypothesis is worth considering.

If the grammatical regime of the elusive third person used by Coetzee works very much like the first person, this 'he' might function according to the complex and paradoxical reading pact of a 'double he', analogous to the 'double I' (Boldrini 2012, 4). Coetzee is known for using the third person in autofictional accounts (1997, 2002) or when talking overtly about autobiography (1992, 394). In some of the notes for *The Master of Petersburg* (quoted in Attwell 2016, 175), the pronoun 'he' transparently refers to Coetzee, not to Dostoevsky. In the novel, therefore, a connection between the 'he' that refers to the protagonist and the 'he' that obliquely disguises the author can be established. In the last chapter, for instance, the identity hidden behind the fictional Dostoevsky takes contour and the 'I' behind the 'he' emerges:

He recognises nothing of himself. If he were to look in a mirror now, he would not be surprised if another face were to loom up.

(Coetzee 2004, 250)

In almost Borgesian fashion, the fiction draws to a close by revealing its author behind the disguise of Dostoevsky. 'He', presumably Dostoevsky, does not recognise anything of himself because the writing, described as 'betrayal' (Coetzee 2004, 250), has betrayed him too, exposing his voice as just a fiction that envelops another subjectivity. The reader is not told whose face the mirror might reveal, but one begins to guess Coetzee's presence. This is still an incomplete metalepsis, however, as the author sketches the gesture of emerging from the page without completing it.

If Dostoevsky's creation staged, in Bakhtin's famous words, a *'plurality of consciousnesses, with equal rights and each with its own world'* (Bakhtin 1984, 6), by lending an 'I' voice to several characters, each of whom reveals a centre of subjectivity, Coetzee's reconstruction of this creation goes in the opposite direction; it blends everything into the impersonal paste of the third person. As both the universe in the novel and the one sketched in the fragments within it slide along the flight lines of metalepsis and *mise-en-abyme*, the writing hollows itself out like a Klein bottle.[7] Neither pure illusion nor pure realistic transposition, *The Master of Petersburg* emphasises the paradoxes of representation.

Forms of truth in counterfactual biofiction

Writing has become for the fictional Dostoevsky a form of '[p]erversion: everything and everyone to be turned to another use' (Coetzee 2004, 235). And it seems to be the same for Coetzee. If it is so, writing counterfactual biofiction is no longer a reconstruction of the truth of the other person (Schabert 1990, 1–4, 21–3), but a relentless usage of historical figures to advance a different worldview (Lackey 2018, 14; 2020, 42). And yet, when readers of Dostoevsky open *The Master of Petersburg* without pedantic intentions, they recognise the themes that obsessed him. If a link survives between Coetzee's character and the common perception about the Russian writer, then some kind of referentiality survives. Though perverting, in the same gesture, autobiography and literary history, cultural memory and even our grammatical reflexes, Coetzee's narrative has still not completely done away with representation in favour of usage.

Coetzee's own observations suggest that this novel aims at telling a form of truth about the historical Dostoevsky, just as Dostoevsky's fiction told some truth about his time:

> In *The Possessed* the names of personages are not historical names and the identities are not historical identities. Yet no one is going to say that *The Possessed* is not about the Russia of 1870. It's not as though Dostoevsky himself does not imagine or reimagine history.
>
> (Coetzee quoted in Scott 2020, 24)

Interestingly, Dostoevsky himself reflected on this rapport between reality and fiction. In *A Writer's Diary,* responding to accusations of making the Nechaev case seem too generic, Dostoevsky acknowledged that

> *My* Nechaev character is [...] unlike the actual Nechaev. I wanted to pose the question [...] how is it possible in our [...] society [...] to have not a Nechaev but *Nechaevs,* and how does it happen that these *Nechaevs* eventually acquire their own Nechaevists?
>
> (Dostoevsky 1994, 279).

This idea of personalising a historical figure ('*my* Nechaev') surprisingly foreshadows recent attitudes towards biofiction, such as Joanna Scott's reference to the protagonist of her novel *Arrogance* (1990) as 'my Schiele' (Scott 2016, 32).

Just as Dostoevsky's Verkhovensky was not Nechaev but 'the type that really corresponds to this crime' (Dostoevsky 1987, 340), so Coetzee's Dostoevsky can be considered the 'type' that corresponds to the creation of *Demons*. Because a literary work is at stake, this 'type' may be described by Wayne Booth's term 'the implied author':

> Our sense of the implied author includes not only the extractable meanings but also the moral and emotional content of [...] action and suffering of all of the characters. It includes [...] the intuitive apprehension of a completed artistic whole.
>
> (Booth 1983, 73)

Coetzee's artifice involves a thought experiment: what would an author look like if he were identical with the implied author of his works? Through all the counterfactual elements, readers are shown that the author they imagine on the basis of their readings could never have written the book they know. Coetzee's *reductio ad absurdum* thus challenges our inherited ideas about the implied author.

When Booth calls the implied author a 'second self' (1983, 71), he means something radically different from Proust's distinction between the social self and the profound self of the artist. As Booth further clarifies, the implied author is 'created' by the real-life writer, along with everything else in the fictional universe (1983, 75). Coetzee's novel reasserts this crafted nature of the implied author, removing the mysterious 'second self' aura. Although Coetzee is, in Lackey's terms, 'using' and not 'representing' Dostoevsky (Lackey 2018, 14), he does so to revive some issues that genuinely concerned Dostoevsky. Even at its wildest, fiction does serve a form of truth, albeit just the truth of its own creation.

An epilogue: back to the scene of invention

When Coetzee's Dostoevsky finally sits down at his desk, 'he writes […] in a clear, careful script, crossing out not a word' (Coetzee 2004, 245). We know that the actual Dostoevsky hardly ever wrote without crossing out anything (Dostoevsky 1987, 230, 232). Why does Coetzee introduce yet another distortion?

Building on A. S. Dolinin's remarks, Konstantin Barsht identifies three stages in Dostoevsky's creative practice: devising the 'word-sign' (the drafting of various plot outlines around the same idea), crafting a structure which converged around a focal point (or 'translating' the envisaged idea from its non-verbal form into literary methods) and finally dictating and correcting proofs (Barsht 2016, 101). This corresponds roughly to Dostoevsky's reflections about the roles of the poet and the artist. However, the artist's role, according to Barsht, is not simply to render the poet's vision intelligible; it is also to create a written equivalent of the vision encoded in the symbols produced in the first stage: 'the synchronous and atemporal visually motivated ideographic sign was converted into a linear, temporalised intelligible sign that forms the syntagmatic axis of the work' (Barsht 2016, 24).

The 'artist' (called also the 'jeweller' by Dostoevsky) painstakingly polishes and perfects his art precisely so that it looks spontaneous, so that it can resemble the synthesis of experience accessed by the poet.

Instead of receiving some external inspiration and starting to transcribe the magic formula directly, the writer jots down just an approximation, a symbolic representation of the vision in his mind. He then transforms it, with the help of artifice, into something that resembles a spontaneous creation more than the initial draft would have. The reader is tricked into believing that what they read as the first sentence really came first and that everything was written cursively and neatly. But creating a coherent vision takes both time and toil. Coetzee touches on this in an interview with Wim Kayzer:

> Writing in itself as an activity is neither beautiful nor consoling. […] It's industry […] productiveness […]. Beauty and consolation belong not to the activity, but to the results […]. The book you write may or may not […] have beautiful prose. Having written a book […] may or may not be consoling. But writing a book is different […] it's work.
>
> (Coetzee 2000)

As remarked above, the fictional Dostoevsky feels no joy when his writing is done, no sense of promise. Differing from most biofictional depictions of creative processes, the result of writing is, in this novel, a supreme sense of separation from the world of beauty, truth and loyalty. Nonetheless, writing is portrayed as an utmost necessity. It is not done for money or fame, nor for a specific audience:

> If he writes so clearly today, it is because he is no longer writing for her eyes. He is writing for himself. He is writing for eternity. He is writing for the dead.
>
> (Coetzee 2004, 245)

The historical Dostoevsky wrote in spite of everything: imprisonment, poverty, the death of his first wife and his brother in 1864, then of his infant daughter Sonya in 1868. Had Pavel died too, *The Master of Petersburg* insinuates, and had Pavel been closer to Dostoevsky, writing would have still had to happen. Not out of resilience, not out of genius; simply out of necessity. The philosophy of creativity offered by Coetzee in the 'Stavrogin' chapter is not about hope or endurance. It has the same neutrality as that impersonal 'he'. Incomprehensible from the routine retro-perspective of the anticipated masterpiece and free from reader's bias, this demystified conception of writing offers the best insight into the survival of literature as a medium.

This chapter has sought to illuminate the perspective of a writer who is thinking through the creative process of another writer, and using this reflection to understand aspects of their own creative process. The intricate case of Coetzee's balancing between auto- and biofiction[8] and his complex use of metalepsis on different layers, depending on the reader's awareness of the historical record, are rare reminders of literature's enduring ability to challenge the myths around its own creation. As Ungureanu (2022) brilliantly proves, such metaleptic ingenuity is also possible in film, but it is premised on the filmmaker's deep familiarity with literary techniques and frames of mind.

Delving into Coetzee's sources and strategies in *The Master of Petersburg*, this chapter has traced the palimpsestic quality of Coetzee's writing: its layering, its fundamental instability as work in progress and its return upon itself as revision or re-invention. All these features confer upon the novel a plasticity that exceeds the common conception of print as a linear medium. Only the most subtle of cinematic and cybernetic tools can aspire to go so far into the labyrinth of discovering, within the author's self, other (apparently lost) facets and selves. However, Coetzee's novel also shows that this labyrinth extends into the dark recesses of the mind, where only the guiding thread of a predecessor's own despair can shine a feeble light. At the other end of this self-transformation – this 'perversion', as Coetzee calls it (2004, 235) – the author also encounters the insurmountable reality of loss, the sombre ectasis of limited resurrection, only on paper, or, with the last words of his novel, the 'gall' taste of self-betrayal (Coetzee 2004, 250). Writing has become a pyrrhic victory.

Notes

1 As Hermione Lee has observed, 'I wish that the idea of "creativity" didn't consist of an inspirational flash, of the first sentence leaping to the novelist's mind, shortly followed by a whole book. (Woolf took about three years, drafting and redrafting, to write *Mrs Dalloway*, and the first sentence she started with wasn't the first sentence she ended up with)' (2005, 55). For the order of fragments on which Woolf started working on *Mrs Dalloway* see Woolf (1980, 311). The opening sentence of *Mrs Dalloway* closely resembles the first sentence of 'Mrs Dalloway in Bond Street': 'Mrs Dalloway said she would buy the gloves herself' (Woolf 1985, 152). This sentence was written between April and October 1922 (Wussow 1996, ix). However, the first and second notebooks of Woolf's 'The Hours' manuscript (the future *Mrs Dalloway*), written from 27 June 1923 and respectively from 18 April 1924, begin with very different sentences (Woolf 1996, 3, 147), while the words 'Mrs Dalloway said she would buy the flowers herself' resurface in this final formulation towards the end of Notebook Two in a draft from 20 October 1924 (Woolf 1996, 252). For an interpretation of Daldry's choice to overlook this order as a metaphor rather than a mistake, see Ungureanu (2022, 134).
2 I am using the translation by Pevear and Volokhonsky (Dostoevsky 2006). The novel has also been translated as *The Devils* or *The Possessed*. Coetzee's biofiction often alludes to possession.
3 This is Coetzee's spelling for 'Lebyadkina'.
4 The connection between Svidrigailov's dream and Dostoevsky's lust for Matryona in Coetzee's novel has been discussed by Adelman (2000, 354).

5   For a comparison and a distinction between *mise-en-abyme* and metalepsis, see Cohn (2012, 108–11). For coincidences between metalepsis and *mise-en-abyme*, see Pier and Schaeffer (2005, 162).
6   'Epic fiction is the sole epistemological instance where the I-originarity (or subjectivity) of a third-person qua third-person can be portrayed' (Hamburger 1973, 83).
7   The Klein bottle, a mathematical construct referring to a non-orientable surface which connects back to its origin in an infinite loop, has often been used as a metaphor for literary metalepsis.
8   The term 'auto/bio/fiction' has recently become more current. It is the topic of a Research Seminar Series at Goldsmiths, University of London, organised by Lucia Boldrini, Natasha Bell and Lucia Claudia Fiorella, in which the author of this chapter also participated (https://sites.gold.ac.uk/comparative-literature/events-series-auto-bio-fiction/).

References

A Beautiful Mind. 2001. Directed by Ron Howard, performance by Russell Crowe. Universal Pictures, DreamWorks and Imagine Entertainment.
Abrams, Meyer Howard. 1958. *The Mirror and the Lamp: Romantic theory and the critical tradition* (1953). New York: Norton.
Adelman, Gary. 2000. 'Stalking Stavrogin: J. M. Coetzee's *The Master of Petersburg* and the writing of *The Possessed*', *Journal of Modern Literature* 23.2: 351–7.
Attridge, Derek. 2004. *J. M. Coetzee and the Ethics of Reading: Literature in the event*. Chicago, IL and London: University of Chicago Press.
Attwell, David. 2016. *J. M. Coetzee and the Life of Writing: Face to face with time*. New York: Penguin Random House.
Avrich, Paul. 1988. *Anarchist Portraits*. Princeton, NJ: Princeton University Press.
Bakhtin, Mikhail. 1984. *Problems of Dostoevsky's Poetics* (1929, 1963). Translated by Caryl Emerson. Minneapolis and London: University of Minnesota Press.
Barsht, Konstantin. 2016. *The Drawings and Calligraphy of Fyodor Dostoevsky: From image to word*. Translated by Stephen Charles Frauzel. Bergamo: Lemma Press.
Benveniste, Émile. 1971. *Problems in General Linguistics*. Translated by Mary Elizabeth Meek. Coral Gables, FL: University of Miami Press.
Boldrini, Lucia. 2012. *Autobiographies of Others: Historical subjects and literary fiction*. New York and London: Routledge.
Booth, Wayne C. 1983. *The Rhetoric of Fiction*. 2nd edition. Chicago, IL: University of Chicago Press.
Brown, Tom and Belén Vidal, eds. 2014. *The Biopic in Contemporary Film Culture*. New York and London: Routledge.
Buisine, Alain. 1991. *Proust: Samedi 27 novembre 1909*. Paris: Éditions Jean-Claude Lattès.
Burke, Seán. 1998. *The Death and Return of the Author: Criticism and subjectivity in Barthes, Foucault and Derrida*. 2nd edition. Edinburgh: Edinburgh University Press.
Cartmell, Deborah and Ashley D. Polasek, eds. 2020. *A Companion to the Biopic*. Hoboken, NJ: Wiley-Blackwell.
Catteau, Jacques. 2005. *Dostoyevsky and the Process of Literary Creation*. Translated by Audrey Littlewood. Cambridge: Cambridge University Press.
Coetzee, J. M. 1992. *Doubling the Point: Essays and interviews*. Edited by David Attwell. Cambridge, MA and London: Harvard University Press.
Coetzee, J. M. 2004. *The Master of Petersburg* (1994). London: Vintage.
Coetzee, J. M. 1996. *Giving Offense: Essays on censorship*. Chicago, IL: University of Chicago Press.
Coetzee, J. M. 1997. *Boyhood: Scenes from provincial life*. London: Secker and Warburg.
Coetzee, J. M. 2000. 'On beauty and consolation. Interview with Wim Kayzer'. YouTube. Accessed on 10 July 2020. https://www.youtube.com/watch?v=_zaUGK02yCk.
Coetzee, J. M. 2002. *Youth: Scenes from provincial life II*. London: Secker and Warburg.
Cohn, Dorrit. 2012. 'Metalepsis and mise en abyme'. Translated by Lewis S. Gleich. *Narrative* 20.1: 105–14.
Cortázar, Julio. 1966. *Hopscotch* (Rayuela, 1963). Translated by Gregory Rabassa. New York: Pantheon Books.
Cunningham, Michael. 1999. *The Hours* (1998). London: Fourth Estate.

Danielewski, Mark Z. 2000. *House of Leaves*. New York: Pantheon.
Dion, Robert. 2021. 'De quel savoir sur l'écriture la biofiction est-elle le lieu? Sur Le Maître de Pétersbourg de J. M. Coetzee', *Littérature* 203: 59–72.
Dostoevsky, Fyodor Mikhailovich. 1968. *The Notebooks for* The Possessed. Translated by Victor Terras, edited by Edward Wasiolek. Chicago, IL and London: University of Chicago Press.
Dostoevsky, Fyodor Mikhailovich. 1969. *The Notebooks for 'A Raw Youth'*. Translated by Victor Terras, edited by Edward Wasiolek. Chicago, IL and London: University of Chicago Press.
Dostoevsky, Fyodor Mikhailovich. 1987. *Selected Letters of Fyodor Dostoyevsky*. Translated by Andrew R. McAndrew, edited by Joseph Frank and David E. Goldstein. New Brunswick, NJ and London: Rutgers University Press.
Dostoevsky, Fyodor Mikhailovich. 1994. *A Writer's Diary. Vol. I, 1873–1876*. Translated by Kenneth Lantz. Evanston, IL: Northwestern University Press.
Dostoevsky, Fyodor Mikhailovich. 2007. *Crime and Punishment* (1866). Translated by Richard Pevear and Larissa Volokhonsky. London: Vintage.
Dostoevsky, Fyodor Mikhailovich. 2006. *Demons* (1873). Translated by Richard Pevear and Larissa Volokhonsky. London: Vintage.
Effe, Alexandra. 2017. *J. M. Coetzee and the Ethics of Narrative Transgression: A reconsideration of metalepsis*. London: Palgrave Macmillan.
Frank, Joseph. 1995a. *Dostoevsky: The miraculous years, 1865–1871*. Princeton, NJ: Princeton University Press.
Frank, Joseph. 1995b. 'The rebel: *The Master of Petersburg* by J. M. Coetzee', *The New Republic*, 16 October 1995, pp. 53–6.
Franssen, Paul J. C. M. 2014. 'Shakespeare's life on film and television: *Shakespeare in Love* and *A Waste of Shame*'. In *Adaptation, Intermediality and the British Celebrity Biopic*, edited by Márta Minier and Maddalena Pennacchia, 101–14. London and New York: Routledge.
Genette, Gérard. 1980. *Narrative Discourse: An essay in method*. Translated by Jane E. Lewin. Ithaca, NY: Cornell University Press.
Genette, Gérard. 2004. *Métalepse: De la figure à la fiction*. Paris: Seuil.
Hamburger, Käte. 1973. *The Logic of Literature*. 2nd edition. Translated by Marilynn J. Rose. Bloomington and London: Indiana University Press.
Herbillon, Marie. 2020. 'Rewriting Dostoevsky: J. M Coetzee's *The Master of Petersburg* and the perverted truths of biographical fiction', *The Journal of Commonwealth Literature* 55.3: 391–405.
Joyce, James. 2012. *Finnegans Wake* (1939). Edited by Robbert-Jan Henkes, Erik Bindervoet and Finn Fordham. Oxford: Oxford University Press.
Kannemeyer, J. C. 2012. *J. M. Coetzee: A life in writing*. Translated by Michiel Heyns. Melbourne: Scribe.
Kindt, Tom and Hans-Harald Müller. 2006. *The Implied Author: Concept and controversy*. Translated by Alastair Matthews. Berlin and New York: De Gruyter.
Kumpfmüller, Michael. 2014. *The Glory of Life* (2011). Translated by Anthea Bell. London: Haus Publishing.
Lacan, Jacques. 2016. *The Sinthome: The seminar of Jacques Lacan, Book XXIII*. Translated by A. R. Price, edited by Jacques-Alain Miller. Cambridge and Malden, MA: Polity Press.
Lackey, Michael. 2016. 'Locating and defining the bio in biofiction', *a/b: Auto/Biography Studies* 31.1: 3–10.
Lackey, Michael. 2018. 'Usages (not representations) of Virginia Woolf in contemporary biofiction', *Virginia Woolf Miscellany* 93: 12–14.
Lackey, Michael. 2020. 'The Bio-national symbolism of founding biofictions: Barbara Chase-Riboud's *Sally Hemmings* and Lin-Manuel Miranda's *Hamilton*', *a/b: Auto/Biography Studies* 35.3: 25–48.
Lee, Hermione. 2005. *Virginia Woolf's Nose: Essays on biography*. Princeton, NJ and Oxford: Princeton University Press.
Lejeune, Philippe. 1977. 'Autobiography in the third person'. Translated by Annette and Edward Tomarken. *New Literary History* 9.1: 27–50.
Lintvelt, Jaap. 1989. *Essai de typologie narrative: Le 'point de vue'. Théorie et analyse*. Paris: Corti.
Maingueneau, Dominique. 2006. *Contre Saint Proust ou la fin de la Littérature*. Paris: Belin.
Michon, Pierre. 1991. *Rimbaud le fils*. Paris: Gallimard.

Minier, Márta and Maddalena Pennacchia. 2014. 'Interdisciplinary perspectives on the biopic: An introduction'. In *Adaptation, Intermediality, and the British Celebrity Biopic*, edited by Márta Minier and Maddalena Pennacchia, 1–32. London and New York: Routledge.

Moine, Raphaëlle. 2014. 'The contemporary French biopic in national and international contexts'. In *The Biopic in Contemporary Film Culture*, edited by Tom Brown and Belén Vidal, 52–67. London and New York: Routledge.

Müller, Anja. 2014. '"The child is father of the man …" – and the author: Screening the lives of children's authors'. In *Adaptation, Intermediality and the British Celebrity Biopic*, edited by Márta Minier and Maddalena Pennacchia, 179–94. London and New York: Routledge.

Pier, John and Jean-Marie Schaeffer, eds. 2005. *Métalepses: Entorses au pacte de la représentation*. Paris: EHESS.

Popescu, Monica. 2007. 'Waiting for the Russians: Coetzee's *The Master of Petersburg* and the logic of late postcolonialism', *Current Writing: Text and reception in Southern Africa* 19.1: 1–20.

Proust, Marcel. 1971. *Contre Sainte-Beuve. Pastiches et mélanges. Essais et articles*. Edited by Pierre Clarac and Yves Sandre. Paris: Gallimard.

Scanlan, Margaret. 1997. 'Incriminating documents: Nechaev and Dostoevsky in J. M. Coetzee's *The Master of St. Petersburg*', *Philological Quarterly* 76.4: 463–77.

Schabert, Ina. 1990. *In Quest of the Other Person: Fiction as biography*. Tübingen: Francke.

Scott, Joanna. 2016. 'On hoaxes, humbugs and fictional portraiture', *a/b: Auto/Biography Studies* 31.1: 27–32.

Scott, Joanna. 2020. *Conversations with Joanna Scott*. Edited by Michael Lackey. Jackson, MI: University Press of Mississippi.

Shelley, Percy Bysshe. 1964. *The Letters of Percy Bysshe Shelley, vol. 2: Shelley in Italy*. Edited by Frederick L. Jones. Oxford: Clarendon Press.

Strong, Jeremy. 2020. '*Fleming*, adaptation, and the author's biopic'. In *A Companion to the Biopic*, edited by Deborah Cartmell and Ashley D. Polasek, 231–44. Hoboken, NJ: Wiley.

The Hours. 2002. Directed by Stephen Daldry, performed by Nicole Kidman, Meryl Streep, Julianne Moore, Stephen Dillane. Paramount Pictures, Miramax, Scott Rudin Productions.

The Imitation Game. 2014. Directed by Morten Tyldum, performed by Benedict Cumberbatch, Keira Knightley, Matthew Goode. Black Bear Pictures, Bristol Automotive.

Total Eclipse. 1995. Directed by Agnieszka Holland, performed by Leonardo DiCaprio. FIT Production, Portman Production, SFP Cinema, K2.

Uhlmann, Anthony. 2014. 'Excess as Ek-stasis: Coetzee's *The Master of Petersburg* and *Giving Offense*', *The Comparatist* 38.1: 54–69.

Ungureanu, Delia. 2022. *Time Regained: World literature and cinema*. London and New York: Bloomsbury Academic.

Vidal, Belén. 2014. 'Introduction: The biopic and its critical contexts'. In *The Biopic in Contemporary Film Culture*, edited by Tom Brown and Belén Vidal, 1–32. London and New York: Routledge.

Werk ohne Autor (*Never Look Away*). 2018. Directed by Florian Henckel von Donnersmarck, performed by Tom Schilling, Sebastian Koch, Paula Beer. Pergamon Film, Wiederman und Berg Filmproduktion.

Wimsatt, William K. and Monroe C. Beardsley. 1946. 'The intentional fallacy', *Sewanee Review* 54.3: 468–88.

Woolf, Virginia. 1980. *The Diary of Virginia Woolf. Volume II: 1920–1924*. Edited by Anne Olivier Bell and Andrew McNeillie. New York: Harcourt Brace Jovanovich.

Woolf, Virginia. 1985. *The Complete Shorter Fiction of Virginia Woolf*. Edited by Susan Dick. London: Hogarth Press.

Woolf, Virginia. 1996. 'The Hours', The British Museum Manuscript of *Mrs Dalloway*. Transcribed and edited by Helen M. Wussow. London: Pace University Press.

Wussow, Helen M. 1996. 'Introduction'. In 'The Hours', The British Museum Manuscript of *Mrs Dalloway*. Transcribed and edited by Helen M. Wussow, ix–xxvi. London: Pace University Press.

Index

Illustrations have *italic* page references and notes 'n'.

A Beautiful Mind (2002 film) 175, 176, 177
A Game at Chess (Middleton) 43, 47, 49, 52, 53
A Journey to the Western Islands of Scotland (Johnson) 56, 66
A Pair of Blue Eyes (Hardy) 103
'A triumph of Black life?' (Nabugodi) 121
A Writer's Diary (Dostoevsky) 194
Abrams, M. H. 175, 180
'Absent Editor', fiction of 81
Adelman, Gary 185
aesthetic autonomy 125
agency
    author as agent in the field 123–38
    authorship as 11–12
    and desire 14–16
Aira, César, *Cómo me hice monja* 13, 159–70
Akenside, Mark 29
Akuli (shaman/narrator) 73, 74, 77, 78
Alberca Serrano, Manuel 13, 160
alterity, emergence of 13–14
Andersson, Linda Burnett 60
Andrade, Mário de, *Macunaíma* 8–9, 73, 84–6
anonymity, transcendental 9–10, 92
anthropologists
    – author – translator 78–81
    German 73–83
anti-Catholicism 44, 45
Archaeology of Knowledge, The (Foucault) 1–2
Arecuná people 73–83, 88n14
arrêt de mort (death sentence) 118
'assemblages of enunciation' 5–6
Aston, Ben, *He Took His Skin Off For Me* 152
Athanasiadou, Angeliki 45
Attridge, Derek 185, 186
Attwell, David 183–4, 185
'*authemes*' 9, 77, 79
authority, control and 48–50
authors/authorship
    as agent in the field 123–38
    'author function' 5, 9, 41, 55, 68–9, 92, 93
    construction of in Lísias's works 149–54
    return of the 7, 41–53
    as a *trans*former 13–14, 159–70
    translation and 77–8
'auto/bio/fiction' 198n8
'autobiographical pact' 13
Autoficção (Sant'Anna) 144–5

autofiction
    as a 'performance of authorship' 12–13
    as (self-)criticism 141–55
autofiction authors as *trans*formers (Aira and Bellatin) 159–70
    paratext and hypertext 165–8
'autonomous pole' 131
'autonomy' 125, 129, 130–2
autonomy/ heteronomy distinction, pivotal axis of 125–6, 129, 130, 131, 147–8
autoreflexivity, of autofiction 14

Baguley, David 94, 95
Bakhtin, Mikhail 193
Barnes, Barnabe, *The Devil's Charter* 43, 51, 53
Barnes, John 35
Barsht, Konstantin 195
Barthes, Roland
    on the author 98
    on classical texts 22
    'The Death of the Author' essay 1, 2, 4, 41, 75, 91–2, 99, 149
    écriture 91, 97
    on language 52
Barzun, Jacques 93
Batailhey, Joseph 34
Baudelaire, Charles 128
Beardsley, Monroe C. 127
Beckett, Samuel, *Texts for Nothing* 1
Becoming Undone (Grosz) 104
Beer, Gillian, *Darwin's Plots* 96, 99
Bellatin, Mario 13, 14
    '*Biografía ilustrada de Mishima*' 167
    El gran vidrio. Tres autobiografías 159–70
Benjamin, Walter 118
Benveniste, Émile 192
Berensmeyer, Ingo 147, 156n3–4
bias, reader's
    in biographical novels 178–9
    first page and the 'second self' fallacy 173–4
biofiction 173, 191
'*Biografía ilustrada de Mishima*' (illustrated biography of Mishima) (Bellatin) 167
biographical novels, reader's bias in 178–9
biopics 173–8
births, multiple author 50–2
Black, Robert 67
Blair, Hugh 57, 58
Blake, William 67

Blanchot, Maurice, *Death Sentence* (*L'arrêt de mort*) 11, 118, 119
Bloom, Harold, *Shelley's Mythmaking* 110, 120
Boldrini, Lucia 192
Booth, Wayne 194, 195
bords (boundaries) 119
Borges, Jorge Luis 160
Borromean knot 15, 186
Boschetti, Anna 130
Bourdieu, Pierre 11–12, 30, 123–38, 139n12
Bourdieusian approaches to the author, (post-) 123–38
Boyd, Brian 106n3
Brazilian literature 73–87, 141–55
Brothers Karamazov, The (Dostoevsky) 186
Brunetière, Ferdinand, *L'évolution des genres dans l'histoire de la littérature* 96, 97
Bruster, Douglas 42, 49
Buelens, Gert 147, 156n3–4
Buisine, Alain, *Proust: Samedi 27 novembre 1909* 179
Burke, Seán 174
Burnett, Allan 60
Burns, Robert 67
Butler, Judith 4
Butler, Marilyn 109–10
Byron, Lord 109

Cabo Aseguinolaza, Fernando 148, 155
Campbell, John Francis (Iain Frangan Caimbeul) 67, 69n5
 Leabhar na Feinne 70n8
 Popular Tales of the West Highlands 62–3
capital, types of 98, 130
Carmichael, Alexander (Alasdair Gilleasbaig MacGilleMhìcheil), *Carmina Gadelica* 61
Carmina Gadelica (Carmichael) 61
Carroll, Joseph 97, 106n3
'Carta de los Kari-Oca' (declaration 2004) 86–7
Carvalho, Bernardo
 'Em defesa da obra' (In defence of the work) 144
 Nove noites (Nine nights) 144
Casanova, Pascale 130
Castro, Johanna Fernández 8–9, 73–90.
Catholicism 43, 44–5, 47, 51, 52
Catteau, Jacques 181, 182, 189
censorship 129, 185
Cernat, Laura 14–15, 173–97
Cervantes, Miguel de, *Don Quixote* 167, 187
Chandos painting 29
Chartier, Roger 25
Chatterton, Thomas 67
Cheape, Hugh 57, 67
Cheng, Li Feng 156n4
Chitnis, Rajendra 139n8
Church of Rome *see* Catholicism
Clarke, Eric O. 117
Cobbe, Charles 24
Cobley, Paul 86
Coetzee, J. M., *Master of Petersburg, The* 5, 14–16, 173–4, 180–97
 Giving Offense 185
 three interlinked layers of interpretation 182–7
Coetzee, Nicolas 184, 186

Coleridge, S. T. 67
collaborative authorship 73–83
 in the anthropological encounter 81–3
 'cultural networks' and 8–9
 individual and 74–7
 and the intertextual dialogue 84–6
Colonna, Vincent 142, 156n1
Cómo me hice monja (Aira) 159, 160–2
Concentração e outros contos (Lísias) 152–3, 156n6
Condell, Henry 31
confessional antagonism 42
Conflict of Conscience (Woodes) 43, 46, 48–9
Consilience: The unity of knowledge (Wilson) 97
consistency, plane of 6–14, 16–17
'continuums of intensity' 16–17
control, and authority 48–50
Cortázar, Julio, *Rayuela* 173
Cotton, Olivea 34
Crawford, Robert 67
'creative employer' 8, 66
Crime and Punishment (Dostoevsky) 15, 187–8, 191
criticism, literary 96
Cruz-Grunerth, Gerardo 13–14, 159–70
culture
 'cultural capital'
  Darwin as 16
  Shakespeare as 6–7, 21–38
  Shelley as 16
 'cultural difference' 86
 'cultural networks' 8–9
 'cultural performance' of authorship 147–9
 'cultural translation' 7–8
 'ordinary culture' 92, 105n1
Cunningham, Michael 178–9
Curley, Thomas M., *Samuel Johnson, the Ossian Fraud, and the Celtic Revival in Great Britain and Ireland* 56, 65–6
Cynthia's Revels (Jonson) 42
Czech literary field 12, 124, 128–9, 132–3, 138n4
Czechoslovakia 12

Dane, Joseph A. 113
Danielewski, Mark Z. (*House of Leaves*) 173
Dante Alighieri, *Divine Comedy* 156n1
Darwin, Charles
 'author function' 93
 'cultural capital' 16
 The Descent of Man 102–4
 Hardy and 102–5
 'Literary Darwinism' 91–105, 106n3
 The Origin of Species 96, 101
 scientific authority and literary assimilation 9–10, 91–105
 sexual selection 102–4
 Zola and 100–2
Darwin's Plots (Beer) 96, 99
Davies, Lydia 118
de Man, Paul, 'Shelley Disfigured' 10–11, 110, 112, 113–14
Dean of Lismore, Book of the 58
Deconstruction and Criticism (Bloom et al.) 11, 110, 120
deconstruction, pitfalls of 10–11

dedications, book 50–1, 53, 66
Dekker, Thomas
   The Double PP 45
   The Whore of Babylon 43–48, 50
Delegado Tobias 1–5 (Lísias) 145–9, 150, 154–5
Deleuze, Gilles
   'collective assemblage of enunciation' 5, 11
   Difference and Repetition 104
   on Lacan 15
   'the plane of consistency' 16
   Proust and 2
   rhizomatic structures 12, 162–3
Demons (Dostoevsky) 181, 182, 184–5, 186, 187, 189, 191, 194
Demoor, Marysa 147, 156n3–4
Derick Thomson (Ruaraidh MacThòmais) 59
Derrida, Jacques 161, 169
   Babel myth analysis 76
   Of Grammatology 37–8
   'Living On: Border Lines' 11, 110, 115, 117–19
   on Nietzsche 166
Descent of Man, The (Darwin) 102
desire, agency and 14–16
development, organisation and 16
Devil's Charter, The (Barnes) 43, 51, 53
differance 13, 161, 169
Digges, Leonard 34
Dion, Robert, *Demons* 181, 182
discordia concors (balance of opposites) 48
discursivity 2–3
Divine Comedy (Dante Alighieri) 156n1
Divórcio (Divorce) 148–9, 150, 151–2, 153–4, 156n9
Doležel, Lubomír, *Heterocosmica* 162, 163, 165
Dolinin, A. S. 195
Donnersmarck, Florian Henckel, von 177–8
Don Quixote (Cervantes) 187
Dostoevsky, Fyodor Mikhailovich
   The Brothers Karamazov 15, 186
   Coetzee and 5, 14–16, 173–4, 180–97
   Crime and Punishment 15, 187–8, 191
   Demons 15, 181, 182, 184–5, 186, 187, 191, 194
   'The Life of a Great Sinner' 182, 189
   The Notebooks for 'A Raw Youth' 188–9
   the 'poet' and the 'artist' 180–2
   A Writer's Diary 194
Doubrovsky, Serge, *Fils* 13, 142, 143, 153, 159, 160
dramatisation of literary theory 154–5
Droeshout, Martin the younger 6–7, 21, 24–30
Dryden, John, *Of Dramatik Poesie* 29–30, 38
Duchamp, Marcel 160, 165–6, 169
   Given 165
   Green Box 165, 167, 168
   The Large Glass 14, 165, 167, 170
Dudley, Kathryn Marie 76
Dunn, John 58, 67

écrivain (agent in the literary field) 134
Edmondson, Paul 24
Effe, Alexandra 191
El gran vidrio. Tres autobiografías (*The Large Glass. Three autobiographies*) (Bellatin) 159

'A character in modern appearance' 162, 163–4
'My skin, luminous' 162, 164
'The sheikha's true illness' 162–3, 164, 169–70
Elizabeth I 44, 45, 47
'empirical author' 6–7
Engels, Friedrich 99, 136
engravings 52, 53
   See also Droeshout, Martin
enunciation, collective 12–13
'enunciative analysis' 3, 5–6
epic fiction 198n6
Est-il je? (Gasparini) 159
ethos, literary 97, 133–6, 139n9
Every Man in His Humour (Jonson) 42
external–internal approaches (bridging the gap) 125, 127, 129

Favret, Mary 117
Ferguson, Adam 57, 69n1
Fernández Castro, Johanna 8, 73–83
fictional/factual identities 165–6
'fictionalisation of the self' 141–55
film studies 22, 174–8
Fils (Doubrovsky) 142, 159
Fingal (Macpherson) 58, 60
Finnegans Wake (Joyce) 173
first page and the 'second self' fallacy 173–4
'Fisiologia da dor' (Physiology of pain) (Lísias) 152–3, 156n8–9
'Fisiologia da solidão' (Physiology of solitude) (Lísias) 153, 156n8–9
Flaubert, Gustave 126, 128
Flight of the Skylark (Norman) 110
Fortleben (live *on*) 118
Foucault, Michel 1–4, 41–2
   Archaeology of Knowledge 1–2
   'author function' 5, 9, 41, 51, 55, 68, 76, 99
   Beckett as a springboard 1–3
   'The Discourse on Language' 3
   écriture 91–2, 97
   'enunciative analysis' 3, 4, 5–6
   'founders of discursivity' 93
   Freud and Marx 105
   on language 3
   'ordinary culture' 92, 105n1
   'Qu'est-ce qu'un auteur?' lecture 1
   'What is an author?' 69, 91–2, 99, 100
'founders of discursivity' 2, 93
Fragments of Ancient Poetry. Collected in the Highlands of Scotland and Translated from the Galic or Erse Language (Macpherson) 56, 57, 58
Fraistat, Neil 116
France, sociology of literature in 123–8, 130–2, 133–6
Frank, Joseph 182, 183
Franssen, Paul J. C. M. 177
French Revolution 111
Freud, Sigmund 2, 93, 100, 105
Fried, Michael 148
Fuks, Ladislav 12, 124, 128–9, 132–3, 138n7–8
   Of Mice and Mooshaber 136–7
   Mr Theodore Mundstock 128, 129

Gaelic scholars 55–69
Gamer, Michael 116
Gaskill, Howard, *Ossian Revisited* 59–60
Gasparini, Philippe, *Est-il je?* 159
Genette, Gérard 43, 50–3, 143, 163, 166, 190–1
German anthropologists 73–83
Germinal (Zola) 9, 100–2
Given (Duchamp) 165
Giving Offense (Coetzee) 185
Gladden, Samuel Lyndon 117
Glory of Life, The (Kumpfmüller) 179
Goncourt, Edmond and Jules de (brothers) 94
Goody, Jack 87n2
Gorky, Maxim 136
Green Box (Duchamp) 165, 167, 168
Grell, Isabelle 156n7
Grosz, Elizabeth, *Becoming Undone* 104
Guattari, Félix 5, 11, 12, 15, 16, 162–3
Gunpowder Plot (1605) 45

habitus and field 126–7
Hamburger, Käte 191–2
Hamlet (Shakespeare) 37
Hardy, Thomas 93, 95, 96, 102–5
  A Pair of Blue Eyes 103
  The Return of the Native 10, 103–4
Harrow, Susan 100
Hartman, Geoffrey H. 110, 118
Hawkins, Mike 98
Haywood, Ian 59, 67
'he', double 191–3
He Took His Skin Off For Me (2013 film) 152
'he'?, who is 188–90
Heinich, Nathalie 130, 134
Heminges, John 31
Henry VI Part I (Shakespeare) 43, 46, 53
Henry VIII 43, 45–6
Henry VIII (Shakespeare) 43
Herbert, William, 3rd Earl of Pembroke 51
hermeneutics, deconstruction of teleology and 168–70
heterobiography, displaced 187–93
Heterocosmica (Doležel) 163, 165
heterogeneity 4
heteronomy/autonomy distinction, pivotal axis of 125–6, 129, 130, 131, 147–8
'historical accident', author's dead body as a 10–11
Hogg, Thomas Jefferson 109
Holland, Agnieszka 175
Holland, Hugh 31
Holy Trinity Church, Stratford-upon-Avon 29
Home, John 57
Hours, The (2002 film) 175, 176, 178–9
House of Leaves (Danielewski) 173
Hume, David 96
Hummer, Maria 152
Hunt, Leigh 109, 113
Hutchinson, Capt Charles 25
Huxley, Aldous 96
'hybridity' 86
hypertext, paratext and (author as *transformer*) 165–8

'I' voice 44, 192–3, 193, 198n6
identity, author 3

identity, deferral of 13–14
Imitation Game, The (2014 film) 175, 176
imperfect symmetries 182–7
In Search of Lost Time (À la recherche du temps perdu) (Proust) 2, 179
indigenous oral narratives, translation of 8, 73–83
individual, and collaborative authorship 74–7
individuality, author 3
inscripteur (the role of the author in the text) 134
intensity, continuums of 16–17
'intentional fallacy' 127, 174
internal–external approaches (bridging the gap) 125, 127, 129
intertextual dialogue, collaborative authorship and the 84–6
invention, scene of 173–97
Irigaray, Luce 104
Isaev, Pavel 182, 183–4, 186, 196
Iser, Wolfgang 150
Ivanov, Ivan Ivanovich 182, 183, 186

Jakobson, Roman 143
Jew of Malta, The (Marlowe) 43, 49
Johnson, Samuel 56, 59–61, 66
Jolly, Thomas 53
Jones, Frederick L. 110
Jonson, Ben
  Cynthia's Revels 42
  Every Man in His Humour 42
  Poetaster 42
  'To the reader' epistle 24, 29, 30
  Volpone 42
Joyce, James, *Finnegans Wake* 173

Kafka, Franz 179
Kannemeyer, J. C. 184
Kari-Oca people 86–7
Kayzer, Wim 196
Klein bottle 193, 198n7
Klinger, Diana 156n11
Kneller, Sir Godfrey 29
Koch-Grünberg, Theodor, *Von Roroima zum Orinoco* 8, 73–84
Korthals Altes, Liesbeth 139n10
Kristmannsson, Gauti 68
Kropotkin, Peter 99–100
Kumpfmüller, Michael, *The Glory of Life* 179

Lacan, Jacques 15, 93, 186
Lagasnerie, Geoffroy de 138n2–3, 138n6
Lahire, Bernard 130, 138n2
Laing, Malcolm 62
languages, translating indigenous oral narratives 73–87
Lanoux, Armand 94–5
Large Glass, The (Duchamp) 14, 165, 167, 170
Latin American autofiction 159–70
Latour, Bruno 92–3
Lauder, William 67
L'Autobiographie en France (Lejeune) 143
Le Pacte autobiographique (Lejeune) 143
Le Roman expérimental (Baguley) 94, 95
Leabhar na Feinne (Campbell) 70n8
Lee, Hermione 176, 197n1

Lejeune, Philippe 13, 142–3, 159, 160, 192
Levine, George 96
L'évolution des genres dans l'histoire de la littérature (Brunetière) 96
Lísias, Ricardo 145–7
   Concentração e outros contos (Concentration and other stories) 156n6
   construction of authorship in works 149–54
   Delegado Tobias (Detective Tobias) 1–5 145–9, 150, 154–5
   Divórcio (Divorce) 148–9, 150, 151–2, 153–4, 156n9
   'Fisiologia da dor' (Physiology of pain) 152–3, 156n8–9
   'Fisiologia da solidão' (Physiology of solitude) 153, 156n8–9
   O céu dos suicidas (The Suicides' Heaven) 148
Lister, John 33, 34
literary assimilation, scientific authority and 91–105
literary criticism 96
'Literary Darwinism' 91–105, 106n3
'literary field', French theories of the 11–12, 123–8, 130–6, 137–8
'literary game' 138n2
'literary posture' 12, 133–6
literary theory, dramatisation of 154–5
'Little Book of Clanranald' 58
'Living On: Border Lines' (Derrida) 10
Lom, Iain (John MacDonald) 60
Love, Harold 79, 84, 87n4
Lowland Britain 8
Lyotard, Jean-François 14, 160, 165, 170

Macbeth (Shakespeare) 36, 37
McCall, Sophie 74, 87n3
McCulloch, Margery Palmer 67
MacDiarmid, Hugh 67
McHale, Brian 22
MacIntyre, Duncan Ban (Donnchadh Bàn Mac an t-Saoir) 69n7
MacKenzie, Niall 66
MacNicol, Rev. Donald (Dòmhnall MacNeacaill), *Remarks on Dr. Samuel Johnson's Journey to the Hebrides* 60–1, 69n7
Macpherson, James, *The Poems of Ossian* 8, 56–8, 60–8
   Fingal 58, 60
   Fragments of Ancient Poetry 56, 57
   Temora 58, 60, 69n5
Macunaíma (Andrade) 8–9, 73, 84–6
Macuxi people 85, 88n14
Madden, John 177
Maikov, Apollon 180–1
Maingueneau, Dominique 133, 174
Mallarmé, Stéphane 98, 99, 105n1
Marlowe, Christopher, *The Jew of Malta* 43, 49
Marshall, William 27
Marx, Karl 2, 93, 105, 125, 136
Master of Petersburg, The (Coetzee) 5, 173–4, 180–97
   three interlinked layers of interpretation 182–7

materiality of bodies 3–4
Mathieu, Jeanne 7, 41–53
Mayer, Jean-Christophe, *Shakespeare et la Postmodernité* 6–7, 21–38, 41, 50
Mayuluaipu (apprentice shaman/narrator/interpreter) 73, 74, 75, 77, 78, 88n7
mediation, processes of 12
Medwin, Thomas 109, 113
Meek, Donald E. (Dòmhnall Eachann Meek) 66
Meizoz, Jérôme 12, 30, 36, 124, 133–6, 137–8
Menezes de Souza, Lynn Mario T. 87
metafiction 14, 101, 162–4
metalepsis 163, 167, 197n5, 198n7
   indirect 187–93
Mhaighstir Alasdair, Alasdair mac (Alexander MacDonald), *Aiseirigh na Seann Chànain Albannaich* ('Resurrection of the Ancient Scottish Language') 60
Miceli, Sonia 12–13, 141–55
Michon, Pierre, *Rimbaud le fils* 179
Middleton, Thomas, *A Game at Chess* 43, 47, 49, 52, 53
'migrant images' (reality–texts) 186–7
Mill, John Stuart 96
Miller, J. Hillis, 'The Critic as Host' 11, 110, 119–20
Minier, Márta 178
mise-en-abyme 187, 191, 193, 197n5
monasteries, dissolution of the (1536–40) 51
Morganwg, Iolo 67
motivation, autonomy of 125
Moxon, Edward 114
Mr Theodore Mundstock (Fuks) 128, 129
Mrs Dalloway (Woolf) 176, 197n1
multiplicities of authors 3–4, 5

Nabugodi, Mathelinda 10–11, 109–21
Nachleben (afterlife) 118
narrativisation of inspiration 174–8
Nash, John 176
Naturalist novels 94–5, 100–1
Nechaev, Sergey 182, 183, 194
Nietzsche, Friedrich, *Ecce Homo* 93, 166
'nonscientific' writing 93
Norman, Sylvia, *Flight of the Skylark* 110
North, Julian 116
Notebooks for 'A Raw Youth', The (Dostoevsky) 188–9
Nove noites (Nine nights) (Carvalho) 144

Of Dramatik Poesie (Dryden) 38
Of Grammatology (Derrida) 37–8
Of Mice and Mooshaber (Fuks) 136–7
O'Neill, Michael 117
Ong, Walter, *Orality and Literacy* 87n2–3
oral tradition, transforming the 7–8, 73–83
Orality and Literacy (Ong) 87n2–3
'ordinary culture' 92, 105n1
'organization and development' 16
Origin of Species, The (Darwin) 96, 101
Ossian Controversy 7–8, 55–69
   eighteenth century 58–61
   nineteenth century 61–4
   twentieth and twenty-first centuries 64–9

Ossian Revisited (Gaskill) 59–60
Oxford Dictionary of National Biography, The 47, 52

'palimpsest' 78, 85
'paradigmatic author' 22
paratext
    early modern dramatic 41–53
    function of 7
    and hypertext (author as *trans*former) 165–8
Peacock, Thomas Love 109
Pemón peoples 73, 88n14
Pennacchia, Maddalena 178
'performance of authorship', autofiction as a 12–13, 79
performance of writing 147–9, 156n11
personne (the 'real person') 134
Piglia, Ricardo 146
plagiarism, accusations of 84
'the plane of consistency' 6–14, 16–17
'plateaus of intensity' 6–14
Plato 14
Poems of Ossian, The (Macpherson) 55–69
Poems (Shakespeare) 27
Poetaster (Jonson) 42
Poetical Works of Percy Bysshe Shelley, The (ed. M. Shelley) 10, 114, 116, 120
Poncarová, Petra Johana 55–69
Pope, Sir William 51
Popescu, Monica 185
Popular Tales of the West Highlands (Campbell) 62–3, 69n5
Posthumous Poems of Percy Bysshe Shelley (ed. M. Shelley) 114, 116
poststructuralism 174
posture, literary 12, 133–6, 139n9
printing presses 187
Procházka, Martin 1–17
prologues 42
Protestantism 43, 44–5, 51
Proust, Marcel, *In Search of Lost Time* 2, 179, 181
Proust: Samedi 27 novembre 1909 (Buisine) 179
psychoanalysis 156n7
publishing industry, rise of modern 7, 44
Pyle, Forest 112

rationalism, individualist market 98
Rayuela (Cortázar) 173
reader, and the reception 139n12
Reinelt, Janelle 156n5
religious conflict 7, 41–53
Remarks on Dr. Samuel Johnson's Journey to the Hebrides (MacNicol) 60–1
Renaissance, the 42–53
Responsibility of the Writer, The (Sapiro) 130
'Resurrection of the Ancient Scottish Language' (*Aiseirigh na Seann Chànain Albannaich*) (mac Mhaighstir Alasdair) 60
Return of the Native, The (Hardy) 10, 103–4
rhizomatic structures 4, 9, 14, 16, 162–3, 165
    rhizomatic identity disseminated 168–70
    rhizome of agency 12
    rhizome of modern authorship 5–6
Richter, Gerhard 177–8
Ricœur, Paul 100

Rimbaud, Arthur 175, 176, 179
Rimbaud le fils (Michon) 179
Romanticism 109–21, 174, 175
Romeo and Juliet (Shakespeare) 36
Roraima, Brazil 8, 73, 73–83, 85
Rossington, Michael 115
Rousseau, Jean-Jacques 111–12, 134
Rowley, Samuel, *When You See Me You Know Me* 43, 45–6
Russell Smith, Alfred 27
Russian formalists 143, 174

Samuel Johnson, the Ossian Fraud, and the Celtic Revival in Great Britain and Ireland (Curley) 56, 65–6
Sant'Anna, André, *Autoficção* 144–5
Sapiro, Gisèle 124, 130–2, 137–8
    The Responsibility of the Writer 130
    'The strategies of writing and the authorial responsibility' 12, 131
    The War of Writers, 1940–1953 130, 138n6
Sartre, Jean-Paul 126, 128
Scanlan, Margaret 185
scene of invention 173–97
Schlueter, June 24–5
Schoenbaum, Samuel 24
science, new (of the works of art) 124–8, 131–2, 133–6
scientific authority, and literary assimilation 91–105
scientificity, effects of 94–7
Scott, Joanna 194
Scottish Highlands 8
Šebek, Josef 11–12, 123–38, 139n11
'second self' fallacy, first page and the 173–4
'second self' mythologies 174–8
self-deconstructive process 169
(self-)criticism, autofiction as 12–13, 141–55
Shakespeare et la Postmodernité (Mayer) 41
Shakespeare in Love (1998 film) 177
Shakespeare, William
    Chandos painting 29
    Cobbe portrait 24
    collective quest for his image 24–30
    as 'cultural capital' 6–7, 21–38
    early readers of 30–7
    film studies 22
    graffiti 31, 35
    iconic Shakespeare 24–30
    Janssen portrait 25, 26
    merchandise 22
    origins of Shakespearean appropriation 30–7
    postmodern circulation of 21–4
    sales at Sotheby's 37
    visual impact of the Droeshout portrait 24–30
    Folios 5, 25, 35
    First Folio 22, 30–7
        Broadhead 26, 27
        Droeshout portrait 6–7, 24–30
        epitaphs to 31, 34
        Fo.1 no. 28 31, 32
        Fo.1 no. 32 31
        Fo.1 no. 45 35–6, 36
        Fo.1 no. 54 25, 34
        Fo.1 no. 70 33, 34

John Lister signatures *33*, 34
prelim epistles *32*
third flyleaf *35–6*, 36
title page *23*
Second Folio
flyleaves *28*, 29
Fo.2 no. 53 27, 29
Shakespeare's bust reproduction 29
Sherwen 27, *28*, 29
Third Folio
Fo.3 no. 8 27, 35, 36, *37*
Hamlet 37
Henry VI 43, 46, 53
Henry VIII 43
Macbeth 36, *37*
Poems 27
Romeo and Juliet 36
The Winter's Tale 34, 35
Sharp, William 63–4
Shaw, William 59
Shelley, Jane 109
Shelley Legend, The (Smith) 110
Shelley, Mary 10, 109, 114–17, 118
Shelley, Percy Bysshe
'cultural capital' 16
de Man on 10–11, 110, 112, 113–14
death of 5, 109–21
editing Shelley 114–17
living off 119–20
living on 117–19
poet 174, 181
The Poetical Works of Percy Bysshe Shelley 10, 114, 116, 120
Posthumous Poems of Percy Bysshe Shelley 10, 114, 116
'The Triumph of Life' 10, 11, 109–21
disfiguration in 111–14
Shelley, Sir Timothy 116
Shelley Society, The 109–10
Shelley's Mythmaking (Bloom) 110
Sher, Richard B. 60
Sherwen, John 27, *28*, 29
skeleton, of a novel 156n10
Smith, Helen 49
Smith, Robert M., *The Shelley Legend* 110
social and regional origins, of authors 130
Social Darwinian theorists 98, 100
'social strategy of an author' 131, 133
sociology of literature, French 123–8, 130–2
Spencer, Herbert 96, 98, 100
Sreenan, Niall 9, 91–105
Stack, D. A. 106n4
Stafford, Fiona 58, 68
Stiùbhart, Dòmhnall Uilleam (Donald William Stewart) 68, 69n6, 70n10
strategies, social and writing 12
'strategy of writing' 131
Stuart, John, third Earl of Bute 60
symmetries, imperfect 182–7
symmetry, lack of 15
Symonds, John Addington 96, 97

Taulipáng people 73–83, 88n14
'*teleological* axis' 176
teleology and hermeneutics, deconstruction of 168–70

Temora (Macpherson) 58, 60, 69n5
Texts for Nothing (Beckett) 1
The Winter's Tale, The (Shakespeare) *34*
'*theological* axis' 176
Thomson, Derick 64–5, 67, 68, 69n4
Tobias, Paulo 146
Total Eclipse (1995 film) 175, 176
'transcendental anonymity' 9–10, 92
transdiscursivity 91–105
'*trans*formance' 14
*trans*formers, autofiction authors as 13–14, 159–70
'transgression' 14, 78, 164, 188, 191
translation
anthropologist – author – translator 78–81
and authorship 77–8
Trelawny, Edward John 113
Trevor-Roper, Hugh 66
'The Triumph of Life' (Shelley) 10, 11, 109–21
Turgenev, Ivan 181
Turing, Alan 176

Überleben (living *on*) 118
Uhlmann, Anthony 185, 186

Velvet Revolution (1989) 133
Viala, Alain 130, 133, 138n5
Vidal, Belén 176
Viveiros de Castro, Eduardo 85, 86
Volpone (Jonson) 42

Waddell, Rev. Peter H. 61
Wang, Orrin N. C. 111
Wapichana people 85, 88n14
War of Writers, 1940–1953, The (Sapiro) 130
Weimann, Robert 42, 49
Weissmann, August 104
Wells, Stanley 24
Werk ohne Autor (*Never Look Away*) (2018 film) 177–8
Wheatley, Kim 113
When You See Me You Know Me (Rowley) 43, 45–6
White, Newman Ivey 110
Whore of Babylon, The (Dekker) 43, 44–5, 46–7, 48, 50
Wilson, Edward O., *Consilience: The unity of knowledge* 97
Wilson, Louise 49
Wilson, Ross 114
Wimsatt, William K. 127
Woodes, Nathaniel, *Conflict of Conscience, The* 41, 43, 46, 48–9
Woolf, Virginia, *Mrs Dalloway* 176, 197n1
works of art, new science of 124–8, 131–2, 133–6
'world literature' 130
writing, performance of 147–9, 156n11

Yale School (literary study) 110

Zola, Émile 93–6
Darwin and 95, 100–2
Germinal 9, 100–2
Le Roman expérimental 94, 95
Rougon-Macquart novel series 100